# SHROUD ENCOUNTER

*Explore the World's Greatest Unsolved Mystery*

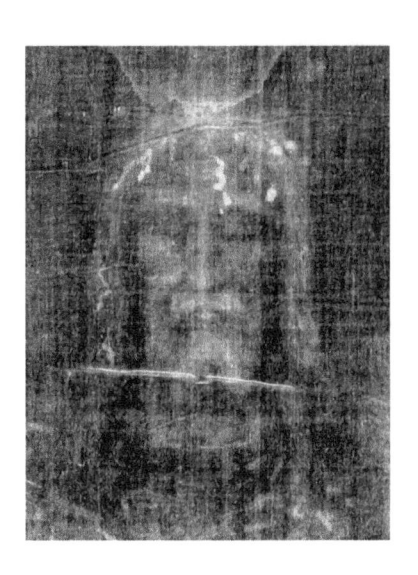

Russ Breault

Shroud of Turin Education Project Inc.

ISBN 979-8-88851-018-6 (Paperback)
ISBN 979-8-89309-805-1 (Hardcover)
ISBN 979-8-88851-019-3 (Digital)

Copyright © 2024 Russ Breault
All rights reserved
First Edition

All scripture verses used, unless specifically referenced, are from translations within the public domain, including the KJV (King James Version), ASV (American Standard Version), or WEB (World English Bible).

All rights reserved. No part of this publication may be reproduced, distributed, or transmitted in any form or by any means, including photocopying, recording, or other electronic or mechanical methods without the prior written permission of the publisher. For permission requests, solicit the publisher via the address below.

Cover design by Emily Breault, Bleu Lion Media

Covenant Books
11661 Hwy 707
Murrells Inlet, SC 29576
www.covenantbooks.com

# ENDORSEMENTS

Well-known and highly informed Shroud of Turin lecturer Russ Breault has treated his reading audience to a fact-filled lineup of historical, scientific, and biblical data regarding the most researched relic in human history. Beyond simply leaving disjointed facts in the wake, however, Russ weaves together many of these ideas regarding how these paths may converge, be intertwined, and be full of meaning. *Shroud Encounter* is highly recommended.

—Gary R. Habermas
Distinguished Research
Professor, Liberty University

*Shroud Encounter* is, *quite simply, a masterpiece*. Breault has been studying the Shroud for more than forty years, and the depth of his knowledge shines throughout. The author covers all the aspects of the Shroud with admirable conciseness and clarity. Breault imparts key data regarding science, theology, biblical exegesis, liturgy, and even prophecy. He includes a fascinating chapter on how Hitler tried to get his hands on the Shroud. Whether you don't know much about the Shroud or are well versed in it, you will learn much. *This book will be a prized possession in anyone's library.*

—Joseph Marino
Researcher and author of *The 1988
C-14 Dating of the Shroud of Turin*
and *Wrapped Up in the Shroud*

Russ Breault's knowledge about the Shroud of Turin and how it relates to the Bible is unparalleled. In this book, he has managed to discover intriguing new links between Scripture and the ancient cloth believed by many to have wrapped the body of Jesus. Even if you know nothing about the Shroud, *this book is invaluable* and contains all the basic information you need and much, much more!

—Joanna Emery
Author, *Journey of the Shroud*

Russ Breault's book, *Shroud Encounter*, is a tour de force encompassing every aspect of an ancient linen cloth revered worldwide by millions of believers to be the authentic burial cloth of Jesus Christ. No Shroud book has ever so comprehensively weaved together the history, mystery, scientific detail, biblical, and religious meaning with such precision, deep thought, and unique information. Whether a reader is first learning about the Shroud or already well versed, Breault's book is *remarkably suited to every level of knowledge.* Not only does he address the who, what, where, how, and why of the burial cloth with an image of a crucified man that modern science has yet to explain—but uniquely links aspects of history, culture, the Bible, Gospels, Judeo-Christian heritage and faith—unlike any previous Shroud author. Now and decades to come, Shroud Encounter will be considered *a breakthrough scholarly achievement.* Breault, who already ranks high among the world's most renowned Shroud experts and speakers, solidifies his legacy with this book.

—Myra Kahn Adams
Media producer, a political and religious writer with numerous national credits, and executive director of Sign from God, dedicated to educating people about the Shroud of Turin

Shroud scholar Russ Breault has *brilliantly brought together* the many various mysteries related to the most studied object known to exist and presents them all with comprehensive and engaging balance. The result is an exploration of the dimensions of human reason and faith in an encounter like no other. Breault's work is *a clarion call to a postmodern world* with the message that profound mystery yet exists and we cannot help but respond to its tug on the mind and heart.

—Cheryl H. White, PhD
Professor of History, Louisiana
State University at Shreveport

Having spent more than forty years in Shroud of Turin research, Russ Breault is one of the world's most open, honest, and reliable experts on this remarkable historical artifact. His extensive research and sober conclusions demand not only attention but also respect. Contemporary skeptics who persist in arguing that the Shroud has natural origins are as bereft of any plausible scientific or artistic explanations today as those in the past. To quote Sir Arthur Conan Doyle's alter ego, Sherlock Holmes, "Once you eliminate the impossible, whatever remains, no matter how improbable, must be the truth." As applied to Shroud of Turin research, the principle becomes this: once all the historical evidence is compiled and considered, all the forensic research and data are examined and all alternative interpretations are evaluated; only those who hold to an anti-supernatural bias can continue to adamantly disbelieve—in which case the burden of proof is on them to honestly confront the source of their doubt.

This is a remarkable and much-needed book that makes a valuable contribution to contemporary Christian apologetics. As such, it should be in the libraries of all churches and reputable Christian institutions as well as on the bookshelves of all Christians who take their faith seriously. Based on the evidence we currently have after many decades of critical evaluation, the conclusion has to be that in all probability, the Shroud of Turin is truly "the first gospel"—a startling testimonial to the reality of the physical bodily resurrection of Jesus Christ. As the early Christians proclaimed, "The Lord is risen!" to which we rightly respond, "He is risen indeed!"

—Jefrey D. Breshears, PhD
President, The Areopagus
Apologetics Forum, Atlanta

Russ Breault takes us on *an adventure of discovery* surrounding the greatest mystery in human history. Like a modern-day Indiana Jones, Breault delves into science, history, art, medicine, and theology for clues to unlock the treasure of the Shroud of Turin. He leaves no stone unturned. *I was captivated and couldn't put the book down.* As one of the world's best researchers on the Shroud, Breault knows the people, the places, and the events better than anyone. This is an intriguing book that leaves each of us with a decision: Is it an elaborate hoax, or is it authentic? Breault gives us what we need to tackle the mystery and perhaps make a life-changing discovery of our own.

—Dave Richardson
President, Assumptions Institute

One of the most respected and knowledgeable Shroud scholars and lecturers in the world, Russ has now put his expertise in writing in an important new book about the Shroud that *should be on every reader's shelf.*

—Barrie Schwortz
Documenting photographer for the
Shroud of Turin Research Project
and founder of the Shroud of Turin
Website (www.Shroud.com)

After the first scientific examination of the Shroud of Turin in 1978, tens of thousands of pages of scientific, historical, medical, and theological analyses have been published, followed by thousands of hours of audio and video documentaries explicating and illustrating this research and commentary. Over the past thirty-plus years, Russ Breault himself has made an enormous contribution to this still-growing Shroud library. In his new book, *Shroud Encounter,* Breault brings it all together in *a comprehensive compendium.*

Early on, Breault confesses that the wealth of evidence has convinced him of the probable authenticity of the Shroud as the burial cloth of Jesus. Then *he sets out to succinctly summarize all the key research on the Shroud and squarely addresses every controversy in compelling detail.* There are abundant photos essential to appreciating the unique properties of the Shroud. He refers to a plethora of books and articles written on the subject and to several video interviews of key experts. Breault brings the reader to the inescapable conclusion that no human artist and no known natural process can account for the mysterious image on this strip of ancient linen cloth. Unique for a book of such scientific detail, Breault goes beyond the issues of validation of the Shroud's authenticity to its impact on art, theology, liturgy, and the understanding of Scripture. *In the pantheon of Shroud literature, this is a book beyond compare.*

—Jim Cavnar
Founder and CEO, Cross
Catholic Outreach

It is with great appreciation that we recognize the awesome achievement of Russ Breault. In his recent book, he presents a vast amount of information on the Shroud, *much never published before.* We strongly recommend the book. The story of the Shroud needs to be told… Russ gives *an incredible and detailed account.* We have been blessed with his extensive research and outstanding presentations.

—Jim Fanning
Editor, *Shroud Sources*

In this sweeping work brought forth from years of dedicated study, Shroud of Turin, scholar Russ Breault casts a comprehensive light on the most studied artifact known to exist in the world. From the empirical to theological, from biblical to historical, Breault succeeds in striking an important balance for every inquiring mind who will read this work. With all that is known of the Shroud, dealt with here in stunning detail, we know its most important questions continue to elude definitive answers. Breault captures the essence of verifiable truth while leaving it open to all the greatest mysteries of mankind.

—Fr. Peter B. Mangum
JCL Rector of the Cathedral of St.
John Berchmans, Shreveport

I have long been fascinated with the Shroud of Turin, having gone to two official exhibitions, read several books on the subject, attended various lectures, and watched many informative videos; just about everything I have ever learned about the Shroud from all these sources is now contained in one well-organized and written book by Russ Breault! While his work is comprehensive in terms of information, Russ collects, analyzes, and synthesizes a vast amount of material and presents it in a manner that keeps the reader's interest while making even the more technical aspects of the Shroud research readily understandable. As a pastor who is at times asked why the Shroud is still worthy of our attention even after the results of the carbon dating tests of 1988, this book is "a keeper" in that it is one I can readily refer to respond to almost any question concerning it, which may be raised by my parishioners.

—Rev. Edward J. Healey
Pastor of Christ the King Catholic
Church, Mashpee, Massachusetts

# DEDICATION

This book is dedicated to my wife, Donna Hall, of Columbus, Georgia. We were married over forty years ago, and she has stood by me through thick and thin. She has never failed to support me in all my endeavors with the Shroud. I could not have written this book without her, much less taken part in the many conferences and the creation of websites, videos, and the hundreds of presentations I have given throughout the country. Along with my wife, I must include my three daughters (Melissa, Aimee, and Emily), who have all given their unflagging support to my work.

When my daughters were growing up, our basement was affectionately known as "Shroud Land." When the kids were in their teens, their friends would hang out in the basement. They could not help but gaze at all the Shroud exhibition and conference posters gracing the walls from around the globe. The inevitable question would arise—"What is your dad into?" The girls would do their best to explain. Every so often, I would come down, turn on a backlit transparency of the Shroud, and conduct a fifteen-minute course.

The kids would cry, "No, Dad! Not another Shroud lecture!"

Undeterred, I would say, "Calm down. Your friends will love it."

And they did, and they all remember it to this day.

# ACKNOWLEDGMENTS

Immeasurable thanks go to Mike Shotwell, a prominent architect who spent the last twenty-five years of his architectural career as a forensic expert witness in construction litigation cases preparing data for legal argumentation. He is also a published author and helped rework each chapter for clarity and readability. His wife, Gwyneth, also offered extraordinary assistance in the editing effort removing redundancies and creating smooth entrance and exit ramps for each chapter enhancing the flow of the book and providing levelheaded perspective and commentary. Together they make a terrific team, and I am humbled to have had their eager participation in this project. Both longtime Shroud enthusiasts, they hosted an important symposium in 1984, attracting experts from around the world. Thanks also are extended to theologian-philosopher Dave Richardson for his timely input on biblical and prophetic aspects of the Shroud. Together, Mike, Dave, Gwyneth, and I comprised a "brain trust"—a collaborative team for the fine-tuning of this work. It is a better book for our association.

Many thanks also go to Joanna Emery, who graciously helped edit an earlier version of the book. In addition, I want to offer my gratitude to my brothers in faith at the Loghouse Men's Group, who have given me much support over the years, with particular thanks to Jamie Bosworth, Bill Wiley, and Eric Stogner, who all helped with early drafts. Acknowledgments are also deserved by Joe Marino, Annette Cloutier, Terry Newman, Linda Barbour, and my graphic artist, Karen Jacks, who all offered commentary and helpful input.

I am grateful to Dr. Cheryl White and Kelly Kearse for specific input on chapters related to their expertise. In addition, I offer my gratitude to Robert Siefker for an important revelation regarding image formation. Special thanks are extended to all who contributed pictures for inclusion in the book and the many authors, scientists, and researchers with published books or papers that allowed me to draw upon their hard work.

An acknowledgement is certainly warranted for my brother, Bud Breault, and his wife, Marcia, as continual cheerleaders for getting this book published. He has arranged for me to speak at his church on Cape Cod multiple times over the years, and I am grateful for his support.

Lastly no acknowledgment regarding the Shroud would be complete without a tremendous thank-you to Barrie Schwortz, documenting photographer for the original Shroud Project and founder of STERA Inc. His tireless work to create and maintain the world's preeminent research site on the internet, the Shroud of Turin Website (www.shroud.com), is an invaluable resource for any Shroud researcher.

# CONTENTS

Acknowledgments .................................................................. xi
Foreword ............................................................................... xv
Essential Photographs ........................................................... xix
Preface .................................................................................. xxiii
Introduction ......................................................................... xxix

Part 1: Perspectives from Art and Science
Chapter 1:  The World of Art—Modern Attempts to
            Replicate the Shroud .................................................3
Chapter 2:  Science Tackles the World's Greatest
            Unsolved Mystery ....................................................18
Chapter 3:  Forensic Analysis of the Body ..................................26
Chapter 4:  Analysis of the Blood ................................................33
Chapter 5:  Understanding the Image .........................................38
Chapter 6:  Theories of Image Formation ...................................45
Chapter 7:  The Linen Cloth—First Century Textile? ................49
Chapter 8:  The Carbon-Dating Fiasco .......................................54

Part 2: The Long Winding Road: Following the Historical Trail
Chapter 9:  The Challenge of Art History ..................................77
Chapter 10: Clues from the Early Centuries: Piecing
            Together the Historical Trail ..................................92
Chapter 11: The Trail of Ancient Icons ...................................104
Chapter 12: The Intrigues of Medieval History .......................111
Chapter 13: The d'Arcis Memorandum ...................................134
Chapter 14: Confirming the Historical Trail through
            Pollens-Minerals-DNA .........................................143
Chapter 15: Hitler's Quest for the Shroud ...............................154

Part 3: Supporting Evidence Found in Scripture,
        Liturgy, Theology, and Prophecy

Introduction ................................................................................ 165
Chapter 16: Revelations on the Shroud's Early History
        through Scripture and Liturgy ............................... 167
Chapter 17: Prophecy Fulfilled: (Isaiah—Zechariah—David) ... 175
Chapter 18: Signs from the New Testament ............................... 181
Chapter 19: When Is a Scorch Not a Scorch? The
        Mystery of Holy Fire .............................................. 188

The Closing Argument ............................................................... 203
Notes .......................................................................................... 205

# FOREWORD

## Mike Shotwell

In 1984, after reading Ian Wilson's seminal work on the history of the Shroud of Turin and having been steeped in the reports from the 1978 Shroud of Turin Research Project (STURP), my wife and I organized what was the first international symposium on the Shroud, which featured the original STURP scientists. At that time, I was involved in my own faith journey, having liberated myself from a Marxist-atheist upbringing. Examining the evidence for and against the Shroud's authenticity was a compelling prospect.

The symposium was held in Los Angeles and attracted some 1,200 attendees. Among those were prominent Catholic leaders in the US, representatives from the Vatican, and important US ecumenical scholars from many Protestant denominations, as well as the general public. It was a day filled with multiple presentations from those with firsthand experience seeing and examining the Shroud—truly a day to be remembered, capped off with a reception at our home.

Some thirty years later, my wife and I relocated to the East Coast. Not long after, through a chance conversation, I discovered that a prominent Shroud researcher and presenter, Russ Breault, lived practically in my own backyard. It was with surprise and delight that we soon met and immediately found many commonalities, the largest being our mutual fascination with the Shroud of Turin. As I described the singular experience of the symposium from 1984, I learned that Russ had been, and still was, in close contact with most of the members of STURP, sharing ongoing research and discoveries. Our close friendship was firmly established.

Through the years, my admiration for Russ has continued to grow not only in respect to his qualities of discernment and integrity but also for his encyclopedic knowledge of all phases of Shroud and scriptural studies. His personality radiates with a wonderful humor and a joyfulness that emanates from his underlying faith. These traits have helped shape this important book.

The initial format that Russ proposed for sharing his knowledge was that of a novel. Knowing I had experience writing my own book and other published projects, along with my involvement with the Shroud, Russ was interested in discussing his ideas with me. From those conversations, we both came to the conclusion that he should change course and produce a factual work that would draw directly from his vast storehouse of knowledge accumulated over his forty years of study and analysis of the Shroud. It would allow for presenting not only the scientific and historical aspects of his topic but also the linkage of the scientific data with clues found in ancient scripture. His related insights and perspective have rarely been tackled in previous books on the Shroud. It has been my honor to take on the role of collaborator, working with Russ to make his vision come to life.

At the beginning of every one of Russ's Shroud presentations, of which he has given hundreds, he shares this profound statement from historian John Walsh:

> The Shroud of Turin is either the most awesome and instructive relic of Jesus Christ in existence…or it is one of the most ingenious, most unbelievably clever, products of the human mind and hand on record. It is one or the other; there is no middle ground.[1]

This encapsulates Russ's stance that the evidence for authenticity of the Shroud is indeed compelling; at the same time, he acknowledges the unrelenting resistance, found particularly in academia, which does not allow for a partnership between science and "religion." This bias was perfectly personified by the evolutionary biologist from Harvard, Richard Lewontin. As an atheist and Marxist, his scientific research could never "allow a divine foot in the door." This philosophy pervades much of current scientific endeavor.

Illuminating the relationship between science and faith is one of Russ's strengths, as seen in his Shroud presentations. He delights in revealing the multitude of remarkable scientific discoveries, and his ability to make it understandable to young and old is truly one of his gifts. Barrie Schwortz, the official photographer for STURP in 1978, is highly recognized for his own research and vast collection of Shroud scientific material and literature. Of his friend, he says simply:

> Russ is one of the most respected and knowledgeable Shroud scholars in the world.

I second that endorsement, having had the privilege of working with Russ on this valuable and timely project. Readers of all persuasions will find that there is much to be gleaned from taking this journey of exploration; it may even turn out to be a life-changing proposition.

*****

Mike Shotwell is author of *Immersed in Red, My Formative Years in a Marxist Household*.[2] In his profession as an architect, he most enjoyed his role as an expert witness in construction litigation, which required, first and foremost, the separation of fact from fiction. He has utilized those same analytical skills in his avid following of the research surrounding the Shroud of Turin.

# ESSENTIAL PHOTOGRAPHS

Shroud images courtesy of STERA Inc., Barrie M. Schwortz Collection.

Diagram: © Vernon Miller, 1978. No unauthorized reproduction of material on other websites is allowed without prior written permission from the Shroudphotos.com copyright holder. Original photos are available for free at www.Shroudphotos.com

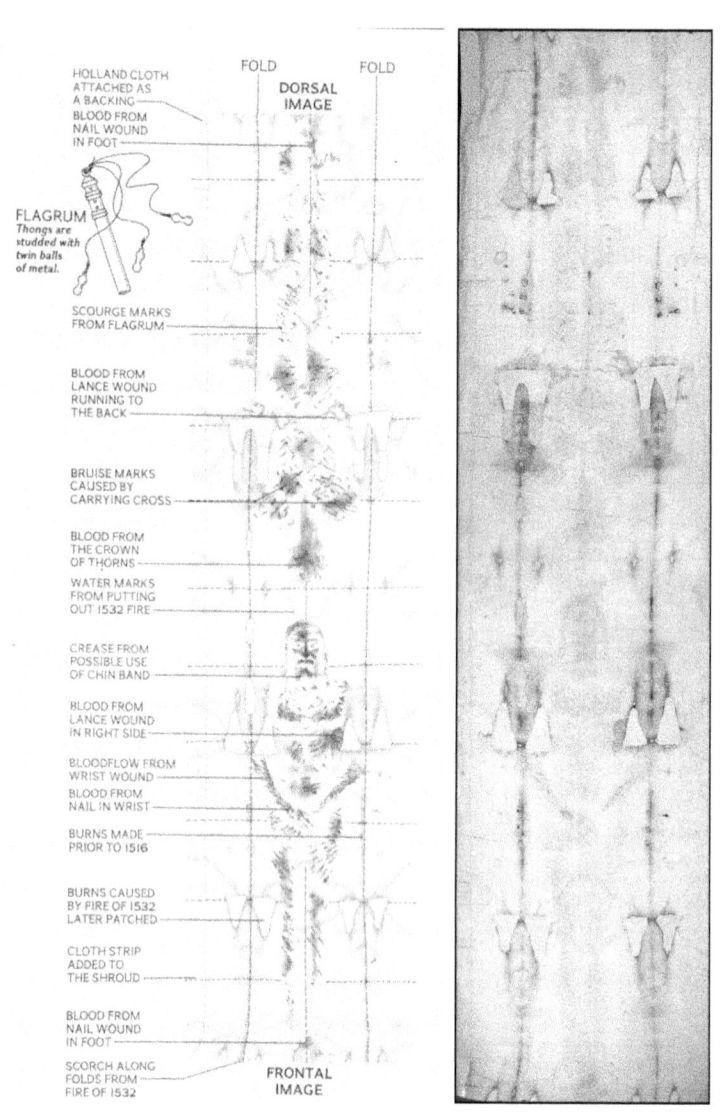

Full-length Shroud measuring 14 feet long and nearly 3.5 feet wide

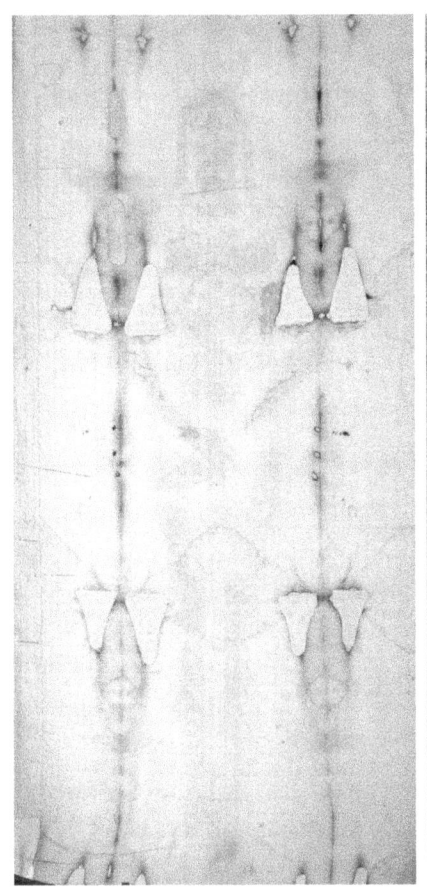

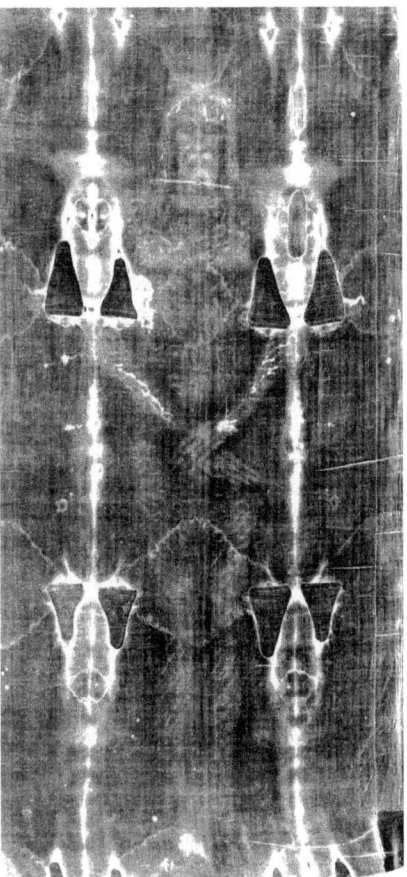

Frontal image (natural)   Frontal image (photo negative)

Image lies between two parallel lines, which are burns, patches, and scorch marks from a fire that occurred in 1532, when the top of the silver box (reliquary) it was kept in melted and burned a corner of the folded cloth, causing an origami burn pattern.

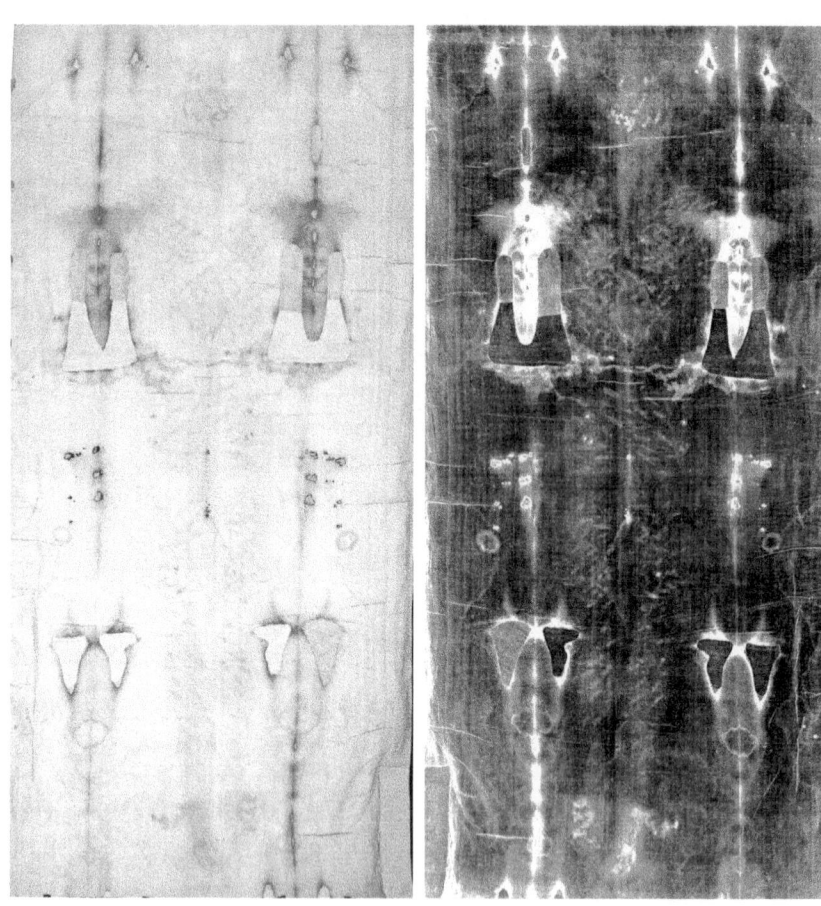

Dorsal image (natural)     Dorsal image (photo negative)

# PREFACE

There may be no greater mystery today than the Shroud of Turin. Also known as the Holy Shroud, Sacred Shroud, or Turin Shroud, this fascinating piece of fabric has been the hallmark of Turin, Italy, since 1578. Its fully documented history began in Western Europe in 1356, well before Christopher Columbus sailed away to discover another world yet with historical clues that trace back to first century.

The Shroud is a long linen cloth hand woven from flax measuring approximately fourteen feet long yet only three and a half feet wide. The cloth is etched with a faint front and back image of a crucified man with a pattern of bloodstains that match the wounds of Jesus described in the Bible. The overarching issue is whether it is the authentic burial garment of the historical Jesus or nothing more than an elaborate medieval hoax. After thousands of hours of scientific analysis, it remains an unsolved mystery.

My journey with the Shroud began in 1978, when I learned about a team of American scientists who gained permission to analyze the cloth following a rare six-week exhibition—the first in forty-five years. Over the next two years, articles about the team and what they discovered dribbled out to the press. Intrigued, I kept every article. In 1980, I was a graduate student in marketing and a writer for the college newspaper; and at that time, news of the Shroud was big. In fact, *National Geographic* ran a large feature story about it that June. I received approval to write an article on the topic for the school paper. After scouring multiple books and articles and calling the team scientists for quotes, the article was published as a two-part series.

Next, with the help of a campus organization, we sponsored a documentary film to run in the fine arts hall the same week the first article was released. It was the award-winning *Silent Witness*, produced by David Rolfe. Over six hundred people attended from the school and community, and it was gauged a wonderful success. I was thrilled and hooked at the same time.

Following these efforts, I quickly came to two basic conclusions: First, the Shroud was truly unique among any known artifacts, with profound implications; and second, few people knew anything about it. In no time, the focus of my life had unfolded in front of me within those few short weeks.

In December 1980, I made my first official presentation about the Shroud to an elite audience—the middle school youth at my church. That day, armed with a dozen slides from the Holy Shroud Guild, a gaggle of kids were wide-eyed as I explained the crucifixion and resurrection of Jesus using images of the Shroud projected on a blank wall. Word leaked out. With all the news about it, everyone wanted to know more. The next year, by word of mouth, I made presentations to over sixty churches across the Southeastern United States.

Every lecture spurred me on to learn more and do a better job presenting the material. I read everything available in the English language and made dozens of custom slides to illustrate every point. In October 1981, I attended the first United States scientific symposium on the Shroud held at Connecticut College in New London. I had the privilege of meeting all the scientists who were part of the Shroud Project along with historians, art experts, archaeologists, and others who came to attend this historic event.

After three years of digesting the data, the Shroud of Turin Research Project Inc. (STURP), organizers of the conference, issued a public release of their results that electrified the world. The Shroud image was not the work of an artist, and the blood is actual blood. The findings were exciting and confirmed my decision to learn all I could.

Doors began to open for me to introduce the Shroud to more and more people. Living in Columbus, Georgia, I became a regular speaker at Fort Benning. As the largest infantry training base in the country, I was able to present to countless soldiers as they rotated through the program. This led to more opportunities as military chaplains transferred to other bases.

Moving to Atlanta, I became acquainted with Father Albert "Kim" Dreisbach, an Episcopal priest and a dedicated Shroud scholar. We had first met in 1981 at the STURP conference and became fast friends and frequent collaborators as we attended conferences together in Paris, Rome, and Turin. Kim purchased the photographic exhibit developed by the Brooks Institute of Photography for the STURP conference and turned it into a beautiful permanent display on the ground floor of the Omni Hotel in Atlanta, which ran from 1983 to 1987. Thousands viewed the life-size images of the Shroud until Ted Turner bought the building and converted it to the CNN headquarters. Looking back, the timing of the exhibit closure seemed almost providential: the following year the atmosphere surrounding the Shroud would dramatically change as a result of carbon dating.

In October 1988, the final verdict of three carbon-dating labs would throw Shroud followers, including many of the scientists, into deep confusion. The three laboratories rendered a carbon date of 1260 to 1390. This was an inexplicable result and completely at odds with the massive scientific research that had been accomplished. In response, Father Kim sent out an essay to fellow Shroud researchers on the "preponderance of evidence" and why things did not seem to add up.

We regrouped at an international conference in Paris during September 1989, wishing to look more closely at the testing procedures. The chief question was why changes had been made to the elaborate protocols that had been established. Dr. Michael Tite of the British Museum, who oversaw the carbon-dating tests, was there to defend the laboratory reports. At that time, I was able to interview Dr. Tite on video as well as pioneering Shroud historian Ian Wilson. We later used both clips in a 1990 documentary, *Behold a Mystery—A Reexamination of the Shroud of Turin*.

It was the first documentary to challenge the carbon date and premiered at a Shroud conference held in 1991 at Columbia University. To my delight, Ian Wilson viewed it along with Father

Peter Rinaldi, president of the Holy Shroud Guild who was instrumental in getting the STURP team access to the cloth in 1978. It ran nationally on TBN (Trinity Broadcasting Network) and EWTN (Eternal Word Television Network).

The tide was shifting. In 1992, a major TV network show called *Unsolved Mysteries* hosted by Robert Stack tackled the subject of the Shroud and the carbon testing. In general, the public was unaware of all that had gone wrong with not only the sampling but also with the puzzling partial release of data. No one acknowledged the many early historical references to the Shroud. Also ignored were the obvious difficulties as to how it could have been created by a medieval artist without the use of artistic substances or any known artistic process, much less the application of blood from actual wounds, all of which were contrary to the carbon date. Things did not seem to add up.

I continued to increase my activities to add to the body of material concerning the Shroud. In 1999, Shroud experts from around the world gathered at a conference in Richmond, Virginia. We set up a TV studio and filmed half-hour interviews with these leading experts, producing twelve episodes of *The Shroud Report*, which are still available on YouTube today.

In 2008, I spoke at a conference in Columbus, Ohio, and also filmed every speaker over three days. The videos helped launch my ShroudUniversity.com website which today hosts hundreds of hours of Shroud conference videos as an archive for further research. That same year, I launched ShroudEncounter.com.

Along with my many national Shroud Encounter presentations, I participated in more projects. I took part in several documentaries, including as one of four primary experts on the award-winning two-hour History Channel program, *The Real Face of Jesus* which premiered in 2010 and aired in over twenty different countries. I also served as an expert on EWTN's documentary, *The Holy Winding Sheet*, as well as an advisor for CNN's episode on the Shroud in their *Finding Jesus* series. In 2023, I was interviewed for an episode of *History's Greatest Mysteries* on the History Channel.

I was also asked to be an advisor to the Museum of the Bible in Washington, DC, for the development of their high-tech exhibit on the Shroud of Turin. At a preview event on October 9, 2021, I took part in a panel discussion where I presented the scientific results of the STURP project. In uncanny serendipity, this was the same material released to the public at the very first conference I attended exactly forty years ago to the day, on October 9, 1981.

My long involvement with the Shroud of Turin, from my initial introduction more than forty years ago to my ongoing association with the scientists and researchers, as well as the exciting new discoveries currently being made, has all led me to write this book. It brings together puzzle pieces from different realms that form a captivating picture of an artifact that could very well be authentic. I hope you are intrigued and enriched by this exploration.

# INTRODUCTION

## Could the Shroud of Turin Be Authentic?

An affirmative answer to that question can never be proven "beyond a shadow of a doubt," since there is no record of fingerprints or DNA to provide an unquestionable match. But the proposition to be considered remains the same: either it is the authentic burial shroud of Jesus of Nazareth, or it is not. And if it is not, then what can it be? An unfathomable artistic fraud?

For me and many others around the world, the "preponderance of evidence" leans heavily in the direction of authenticity and continues to grow. In the pages ahead, compelling information related to history, science, and more, will combine to make the case for a positive verdict. As an opening statement, here is a brief look at the far-reaching investigations, positive and negative, that have set the stage for our Shroud Encounter.

*STURP and carbon dating*

Historians, coroners, archaeologists, chemists, physicists, botanists, medical doctors, image specialists, artists, textile authorities, and even atheists and anti-shroud adherents have spent decades attempting to solve the enigma of the Shroud of Turin, perhaps the greatest unsolved mystery to ever appear. Brought to Turin, Italy in 1578, it has been revered and cared for in the royal chapel of the Cathedral of St. John the Baptist. Under the auspices of the Catholic

Church, in 1978, the Shroud of Turin Research Project (STURP), was given hands-on access to the cloth for five days. Thirty-three scientists worked around the clock in shifts, to study, measure, and conduct tests; the first undertaking of its kind involving the Shroud. The goal was to discover how the mysterious image was formed. Then, in 1981, after three years of analyzing the collected data, they offered this summary statement:

> We can conclude for now that the Shroud image is that of a real human form of a scourged, crucified man. It is not the product of an artist. The blood stains are composed of hemoglobin and also give a positive test for serum albumin.[1]

Their findings were front-page news over the next seven years and spurred numerous books, articles, and documentaries. However, in 1988, the case for the Shroud was abruptly interrupted. Three carbon-dating laboratories determined the cloth could be no older than seven hundred years and pronounced the Shroud a medieval forgery. Confusion reigned, and the Shroud became a "cold case file." But… there is much more to the story.

Prior to the carbon testing, meetings were held to establish proper protocols. They involved the scientific advisor to the Cardinal of Turin, members of STURP and other scientists, and representatives of several carbon dating laboratories. Originally, seven labs, utilizing different processes, were designated, however, that number was inexplicably reduced to only three. The labs themselves lodged objections concerning potential credibility questions based on a smaller sample size but were overruled, and the testing ultimately proceeded.

Yet many other questions continued to be raised, from the location and number of cloth samples taken to the very handling of those samples, some of which happened behind closed doors. Combined with confusion over the choice of labs, the processes utilized in testing, and more, how could the results ever be deemed reliable or accurate? The whole undertaking had the earmarks of a fiasco.

*Case reopened*

In 2000, new evidence was presented by longtime Shroud researchers Joe Marino and Sue Benford at a worldwide conference in Orvieto, Italy, suggesting the sample area of the Shroud showed signs of repair. The study also indicated the presence of cotton in conjunction with the original flax. STURP chemist, Ray Rogers, built on these findings, and compared thread samples from the main body of the Shroud to samples taken from the area cut for carbon dating. He found they were not the same, providing hard evidence that the area tested was not chemically consistent with the rest of the cloth. With the 2005 publication of his findings in *Thermochimica Acta*, a respected peer reviewed journal, the cold case file of the Shroud suddenly reopened. The linen Shroud could once again be considered an archaeological artifact with more answers still to be discovered.

Coming forward, further counterarguments to the carbon testing results have been emerging, including new dating techniques that point to a first-century origin. Advances in blood analysis, forensics, and experiments related to image formation, all offer more insight into this mysterious cloth.

Recognizing this "either/or" challenge, my goal is to present the wide array of diverse evidence for authenticity as fairly as possible and let you, the reader, come to your own conclusions. With that objective in mind, the book is divided into three corresponding areas of research. The first is a synopsis of the evidence found in the realms of science and art. The second is an immersion into the twists and turns of the fascinating historical trail that directly challenges the arguments posed by skeptics. The third section explores territory not typically dealt with when considering the authenticity of the Shroud; significant areas of Scripture, ancient liturgy, prophecy, and theology provide rich details that align with, support, and confirm much of the research. If the Shroud is authentic, these will be important issues to consider.

# RUSS BREAULT

*The Shroud encounter begins*

As you learn about the Shroud throughout this book and perhaps through other references cited, you may feel like an archaeologist or a detective. As you begin to investigate, you will unearth one clue after another, discovering more and more about this profound mystery. Enjoy the dig!

# PART 1

Perspectives from
Art and Science

# CHAPTER 1

## The World of Art—Modern Attempts to Replicate the Shroud

We begin our investigation with the undeniable either-or proposition posed by the Shroud. It either is the authentic burial cloth of Christ, or it is not. It is one or the other. So if it is not a genuine relic of the crucifixion, then it must be the work of an artist or someone attempting to perpetrate a fraud, either of which would be the result of human effort. As such, investigators would expect to find corresponding evidence in support of this position. Such evidence has thus far eluded discovery. We, therefore, explore the mystery from the man-made artistic approach first.

What we know is that the Shroud image is astonishingly accurate in describing the imprint of a severely scourged man with the negative image offering far more intricate detail than what is seen with the naked eye, a reversal of anything rationally understood in the artistic realm. Skeptics are happy to dismiss the Shroud as the work of a medieval artist without knowing the identity of that person or how he/she accomplished such a masterpiece. Attempts to identify a specific medieval artist with the capability of creating such an image have devolved into the world of pseudohistory and lack desired credibility.

The Shroud of Turin Research Project (STURP) arrived in Italy with over seventy crates of scientific gear weighing almost ten tons, brought from a dozen different laboratories in the US, including

Sandia Labs and Los Alamos National Laboratory. As noted earlier, the scientific investigation was not designed to prove the Shroud as authentic but rather to discern the cause of the image and corresponding bloodstains. To recap the team's primary conclusions: there are no artistic substances on the cloth that can account for the image, and the blood tested positive for being actual blood. It is not paint.

The study did reveal that there are random particles of various substances on the cloth, including paint. However, these particles are not concentrated in the image areas and, therefore, do not account for the image. Over the centuries, the Shroud was exposed to the open air hundreds of times for various exhibitions, as well as being displayed inside the Cathedral of St. John the Baptist in Turin. The natural deterioration of the painted murals that grace the walls and ceiling would have allowed microscopic paint particles to drift onto the cloth.

In addition, there were over fifty known painted copies of the Shroud created over the course of three centuries beginning in the early 1500s. The bishop of Turin pressed these sanctioned copies to the original Shroud to elevate their relic status, greatly enhancing their value.[1] It has been demonstrated experimentally that pressing a typical oil-based painting to a clean white linen will cause particles of paint to transfer onto the cloth. This would account for the discovery of random particles of paint and other substances found during the team examination.[2]

Declaring the Shroud to be a medieval artwork supposes an artist or forger with an extraordinary amount of knowledge to "get it right." To begin, there are two distinct elements visible on the cloth. The first is the faint front and back image of a crucified man. The second, separate from the image of the man, is a complete pattern of bloodstains, including punctures around the head, a wound in the wrist, a gash in the side, piercings in the feet, and over 120 scourge marks impacting the body from the neck to the ankles.

The blood marks and body image have another marked dissimilarity. The blood soaks all the way through the cloth, whereas the image is purely superficial and does not penetrate beyond 1 to 2 percent of a single thread.

A further complication for an artist/forger is that there is no image found under the blood. This would require the application of all the blood spatters and other wounds *before* the image was created.

*Artistic styles.* One way of exploring the Shroud as a man-made artistic endeavor attributable to a specific artist would be to examine the artistic style. Every artist has a characteristic method that is unique and distinctive enough for an art expert to recognize and identify.

A good example known by almost anyone would be the *Mona Lisa*, painted by Leonardo da Vinci. A self-portrait of Picasso would be hard to miss. Others are also easily discernable, such as Claude Monet, Salvador Dali, or Vincent Van Gogh. The great Renaissance painters can also be identified, such as Michelangelo, Raphael, Donatello, and Botticelli. Every artist has a predictable style and technique, and the same holds true for lesser-known artists.

From this standpoint, the "style" of the Shroud is unequaled; there is nothing comparable. It stands alone throughout art history, making it exceedingly difficult to claim an artistic origin. Who was the artist? What technique did he use? What substances did he apply? All three questions remain unanswered.

*What is seen on the Shroud beyond the image and blood?* The closer one gets to the Shroud, the less detail one can see, which is the opposite of conventional art. In fact, if you get closer than six feet, the image seems to disappear. This phenomenon would pose a daunting challenge for any artist at any time.

The most prominent feature on the Shroud is a pattern of burns and patches from a fire in 1532. As the Shroud was locked away behind bars for security in a chapel in Chambéry, France, the structure caught fire and became an inferno. Many experts suspect arson. It was late at night, and the clerics could not find the keys needed to open the steel cage where the Shroud lay folded in a silver reliquary, the ornate container made specifically for the sacred linen. By the time the reliquary was retrieved, the top of the box had melted; and a glob of molten silver had fallen onto a corner of the cloth, burning all the way through the many folds, creating a distinctive repetitive pattern. Doused with water, the cloth was saved, but significant damage had occurred. (See "Essential Images.")

To look at the Shroud today, the first thing one notices is this pattern of burns and scorch marks that appear in parallel lines. Amazingly, or perhaps miraculously, the image itself was untouched except around the shoulders and elbows. A pattern of water stains is also clear. If the cloth is flipped over, one would see the burns penetrating the cloth along with the water and bloodstains that both soaked through the fabric. However, you would not see the image of the man.

The image on the Shroud, as touched on earlier, is purely a superficial phenomenon affecting only the top one to two microfibers of the linen—not threads, but microfibers. Each thread comprises about two hundred microfibers. Therefore, whatever caused the image only affects about 1 percent of a single thread, another enormous hurdle for our judicious medieval artist to negotiate. Not only did he have to paint the blood first and the image afterward, but he would also have to invent a new image process for this singular work that remains a mystery to modern science.

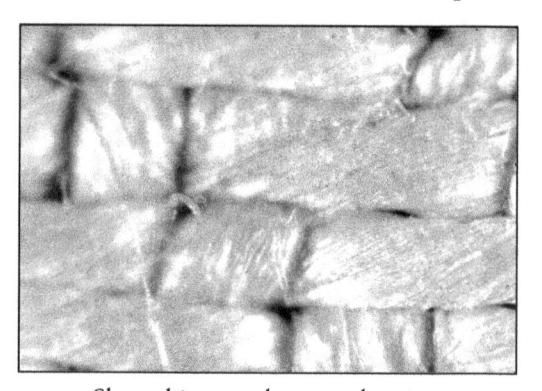

Shroud image close-up showing no artistic substances (Image courtesy of Barrie M. Schwortz collection, STERA Inc.)

Another important detail is that the intensity of the monochrome image is uniform over the entire cloth. There is no difference in color or density whether you are looking at the dorsal or frontal image. Normally we would expect any image derived from artistic substances to show variations where some paint or pigment penetrated deeper into the fibers of one area and less in another area. That is not what is observed on the Shroud.[3]

*Under the microscope.* There are no substances on the cloth to account for the image. Where the image appears darker, it is simply due to a greater number of microfibers affected by whatever caused the image. Where it is lighter, there are fewer microfibers affected. The microfibers act like pixels. One can view this effect by increasing or decreasing the image dpi on a computer.

Unlike the Shroud, the closer one gets to a painting, the more detail can be seen. If one were to view with 10X magnification on a typical artwork, the brushstrokes, the various colors, and different densities of the paint or any other artistic substance would be easily discernable. There would be no question that you were looking at a painting.

Portrait painting and facial close-up by artist Tai-Shan Schierenberg (Image courtesy of artist)

Yet if one examines a 40X close-up image area on the Shroud from the tip of the nose, one of the darkest parts of the image, there is little to see except a slight discoloration of the weave. It is as if nothing is on the cloth.

One would have to zoom in at several hundred times magnification to see the individually affected fibers. One can easily detect a painting of any kind with visual observation or, at most, a magnifying glass; yet it requires a microscope to see anything on the Shroud.

*No image deterioration.* Another interesting observation comes from analyzing old paintings that haven't been in pristine settings. Paint eventually flakes off the canvas over time, leaving a bare spot in the picture. Similarly, unattended murals in aging churches throughout Europe show this same effect. The image no longer exists where the paint has fallen away.

But this phenomenon has not happened with the Shroud. Keepers of the linen folded and rolled it hundreds of times over the centuries, yet there is no part over the entire image where anything has flaked off. This would be impossible if the image had been crafted with paint or pigment. Constant rolling and folding would have resulted in image disintegration. In addition, the superficial nature of the image shows no evidence of dye, ink, or stain. The image does not soak through the cloth, as does the blood, and there is no indication of capillary action from the application of liquids, further validating the absence of all known artistic substances.[4]

*The first photograph.* The Shroud was photographed for the first time in 1898. Secondo Pia, a lawyer and amateur photographer, with permission from the Turin authorities, photographed the cloth on the last day of a short nine-day exhibition held that same year. Using a large box camera, he made his first attempt, which failed to produce a satisfactory image. His second attempt, two days later, produced two images. The first used a fourteen-minute exposure and the second a twenty-minute exposure.

Back in his Turin apartment, he placed the photographic plate in a tray filled with developer solution. The plate was huge by today's standards, over twelve inches square. A few minutes passed as Pia waited for the chemicals to work their magic, and he then pulled the plate from the tray. What he saw in that moment stunned him so deeply he almost fell out the window of his apartment. For the first time, as he observed the now-famous photonegative image of the face, Secondo thought he was seeing the face of God.[5]

Sadly, members of academia, including the French Academy of Sciences, accused him of perpetrating a hoax. They assumed he had somehow manipulated the camera to create the effect. Few believed or accepted his discovery, and it was labeled photographic chicanery. It was not until 1931, at the end of a twenty-day exhibition, that a professional photographer named Giuseppe Enrie photographed the cloth again using far-better equipment and film, confirming Pia's discovery. Shroud images soon circulated the world through books, magazines, and newspapers.

*The photo negative.* Why does the Shroud image appear so much clearer and lifelike and with so much more detail in a negative? A typical photo negative shows very little detail. The only explanation appears to be that the image on the cloth itself must be a negative image to start with. Therefore, what one observes in the photonegative of the Shroud is really a positive image. In fact, it was the discovery of the negative image that captured the interest of the scientific community and launched the Shroud to worldwide prominence.

This observation touches on the bizarre because it is so contrary to human understanding, but it is difficult to refute. This one fact basically eliminates the Shroud as the deliberate work of a medieval artist or a forger attempting to perpetrate a hoax. The invention of photography occurred in 1830, almost five hundred years after the Shroud's documented arrival in Lirey, France.

Natural image and photonegative image of the face.
Note the unexpected detail of the negative image. (Image courtesy of Barrie M. Schwortz collection, STERA Inc.)

The photonegative image is so significant that in 2012, a prominent British art historian, Thomas de Wesselow, published an important book, *The Sign*, which stated unequivocally that the negative image prevents it from having come from the mind of a medieval master, no matter how skilled he may have been, because the concept would have never entered his imagination.[6]

Noted skeptics acknowledge the uniqueness of the positive/negative phenomenon with the Shroud image but skirt the issue or dismiss it as merely an accident. They suggest the ghostly image we see on the cloth in natural color was intentional while the superb photonegative image discovered in 1898 was an unintentional by-product. This skeptical response lacks any evidential credibility and, to be frank, given the massive scientific evidence to the contrary, seems flippant and insincere. No known negative of any painting or drawing has ever been produced that satisfies all the known attributes of the image and corresponding bloodstains. Imagine the scenario of a medieval artist painting blood on a linen canvas, and then overlaying it with a blurry monochrome image that is barely discernable from arm's length. Furthermore, this strange new process would not be revealed until five hundred years later after the invention of photography. One's mind must certainly stretch to fit around this story.

*Modern attempts to replicate an artistic process.* There have been several attempts at duplication over the past fifty years by various skeptics that range from paintings to rubbings and body imprints designed to show how an alleged medieval artist fabricated the image. Not one has yet been able to fully replicate the shroud image along with the corresponding bloodstains. By way of example, I've chosen a small but representative cross-section of theories and hands-on experiments undertaken over the years. The difficulties become apparent rather quickly; however, these efforts also show the strong desire to refute the Shroud as merely a fake. The final illustration even comes from a scientist.

*Charles Freeman.* One of the more recent theories popularized by British scholar Charles Freeman is that the Shroud was an "Easter prop" created in the 1300s. It allegedly began as a painted image; but after many centuries, all the paint flaked off, leaving only a "shadow," an astonishing photonegative image that was just an accidental by-product.

The theory proposes that the artist originally mounted the cloth to a wallboard and then covered it in gesso, a chalklike substance that would absorb the paint and prevent it from soaking through the cloth.[7] However, if the gesso would prevent the paint from soaking through, why did it not prevent the blood from soaking through?

Freeman's answer is that the artist must have added the blood later, after time had flaked off all the gesso.[8] How convenient. The problem with this simplistic answer is the blood was on the cloth first, not years later.

Freeman derives his gesso theory from the presence of calcium carbonate on the cloth, the primary ingredient of gesso; however, true Italian gesso is also composed of glue and white paint, neither of which are found on the cloth. Calcium carbonate is, however, an element of limestone, along with varying amounts of magnesium. This substance is found on the Shroud and is consistent with a cloth being laid down in a Jerusalem tomb carved out of limestone. Freeman discounts this explanation.[9]

*Luigi Garlaschelli.* Professor Garlaschelli, a prominent Italian skeptic, wrapped a long rectangular cloth over one of his students and painted the outside with red ochre pigment mixed with solid acid and salt. He captured only the prominent features such as the elbows, hands, knees, and upper parts of the legs and arms. He filled in the rest of the image freehand after removing the cloth from the student's body and used a bas-relief sculpture for the face to protect the student from chemicals. The experiment failed as the acids did not discolor the fibers without adding water.

Garlaschelli then tried a second experiment using 1.2 percent sulfuric acid mixed with a blue pigment to result in a semifluid paste and applied it to the sheet in the same way. It was then heated to 140 degrees centigrade (284 degrees Fahrenheit) for three hours to simulate aging. Next they washed it, removing all the blue pigment, revealing an image from the effect of diluted acid, not from the pigment. While this may be better than many attempts to replicate the image, it still falls short in many areas.

In their experiment, the pigment remained on the cloth while artificially aged in the oven. This does not simulate reality. If this process was the actual cause of the image, the pigment would have flaked off unevenly over the years as the cloth was rolled and folded hundreds of times for public or private exhibitions. Real aging, as opposed to simulated aging, would cause the image to appear uneven or blotchy as the paint gradually flaked off. It also assumes there would be no trace of the original pigment remaining on the cloth detectable today.

The Shroud image is nuanced in that it gently fades at the edges whereas Garlaschelli's image has sharper edges and clearer outlines. At points where the cloth copy was not in contact with the volunteer's body, there is no image. However, with the Shroud, there are image areas that appear lighter but would not have been in contact with the body. Areas closer to the body appear darker as more microfibers are affected by whatever caused the image. Garlaschelli's attempt is clearly a contact image.

Lastly he made the mistake every Shroud fabricator makes. He painted the "blood" on the cloth after the image was baked onto it. Not so with the Shroud. The bloodstains were on the cloth before the image was created. The blood is a contact process; the image is not.[10]

*Nicholas Allen.* Nicholas Allen made a splash in the late 1990s with the announcement of his "protophotography" theory that proposes a

> medieval photographer created a light sensitive emulsion, coated it onto linen cloth and "exposed" this medieval "film" using a room sized camera obscura and a dead body hanging in front of its crystal lens as the subject matter.[11]

As gruesome as this sounds, it gets worse. He proposed the alleged artist took this dead body and exposed one-half of the cloth at a time—four days for the frontal image and four more days for the dorsal image over eight days and a separate exposure for the face with a more focused lens. The body would also need to be in the bright sun over the course of eight days to project the image onto the cloth.[12]

A gas mask and a gallon of insecticide might have been useful here for Mr. Allen. Obviously, Allen was unaware of the rapid changes that occur as a body decomposes. The first stage is *autolysis* or self-digestion and occurs within hours of death as the body becomes completely rigid from rigor mortis. Stage two is *bloat*. The body can expand to almost twice its normal size from gases released as the body decays. An intense stench surrounds the body as insects and microorganisms move in. Stage three is *active decay*, when fluids release through orifices as organs, muscles, and skin become liquefied. All three phases of decay would occur within the first eight to ten days.[13] Amazingly, none of these stages of decay were "projected" onto the linen. The theory is simply preposterous.

*Leonardo da Vinci.* And then there is the most far-fetched artistic theory of them all—that the image was crafted by Leonardo da Vinci. The proponents of this theory start with the premise that the fake Shroud image could only have been crafted by someone with tremendous artistic skill, full knowledge of human anatomy, and an inventor, to boot. They credit da Vinci with devising a primitive form of photography and using a sculpture of his own face to project the image onto an ancient piece of linen. To account for the time lapse of over one hundred years after the Shroud's arrival in Lirey, France, it is said that "da Vinci's forgery was commissioned to replace an earlier version that was exposed as a poor fake, which had been bought by the powerful Savoy family in 1453 only to disappear for 50 years. When it returned to public view, it was hailed as a genuine relic, and experts say it was actually the artist's convincing replica."[14]

The problems with this are numerous, not least of which is that the complexity of photography was not yet invented, but there is also the well-known fact of da Vinci having kept meticulous notes on all his work, including experiments and inventions, but no citations exist that link him to the creation of the Shroud image.[15] While there seem to be no limits to the absurd, this notion periodically crops up in some books or documentaries, as shown above, hence its inclusion among these purported explanations.

Our final example is unique in that it was proposed by a scientist who associated with the STURP team, albeit somewhat briefly. Nevertheless, his direct access to Shroud samples and studies resulted in his theory enjoying quite a lot of notoriety.

*Walter McCrone.* The most prominent scientific skeptic was microscopist Walter McCrone, who proposed his own theory of how a medieval artist created the Shroud image. Founder of the McCrone Research Institute in Chicago, Dr. McCrone (d. 2002) was internationally known for his work in the field of microscopy, in particular as a particle expert. *The Particle Atlas* was his well-respected multivolume reference work. He also wrote his own book on the Shroud. His opinions continue to be referenced within the skeptical debate, so I offer his proposal for a painted shroud for the reader's consideration.

McCrone had known STURP lead chemist Ray Rogers for many years, and due to that relationship and his reputation, he was given samples from the Turin investigation for study. Rogers loaned him thirty-two Mylar sticky tape samples from the Shroud in late October 1978, which contained fibers, particles, and various other debris removed from multiple areas of the cloth. McCrone was confident that he could accurately identify any known particle, based on his extensive experience and what he called his "online computer," his brain.[16]

Using primarily polarized light microscopy, McCrone determined quite quickly that the red flakes found on multiple slides, including image areas, were iron oxide. Reporting the wide disbursement of these particles he alleged the image resulted from iron oxide suspended in a thin binder solution, creating the pigment red ochre, which he believed was undoubtedly used to paint the image. He contended that the darker "blood" areas were also red ochre with the addition of another pigment, vermilion.

To conduct his work, McCrone chose to place each of the tapes onto microscope slides and proceeded to examine them through the tape backing. To view the samples this way is somewhat ironic, as McCrone wrote in his book that Mylar tape was not such a good choice because it was optically inferior.[17] In any event, one property he observed from what he identified as iron oxide, was birefringence, a splitting of transmitted light due to the crystalline nature of the particle. It was also this finding of birefringence that told him the flakes were not blood, which does not respond in the same way.[18]

In contrast to this, Dr. John Heller, working later with the same tapes as McCrone, made the opposite finding. Heller was one of the blood experts working alongside Dr. Alan Adler as members of STURP. Recognizing that the nature of the Mylar tape would distort the visualization of some particles, the two painstakingly removed the tape and all adhesive, allowing full access to the fibers. The particles did not exhibit birefringence, and when they were removed using various solvents, the red flakes dissolved, verifying the presence of blood. Blood is soluble, but iron oxide is not. Same samples; different results.

McCrone understood that the binder solution needed as a medium for red ochre pigment would have contained some form of protein commonly available to the medieval artist. McCrone surmised this came from parchment scraps (animal hide). From a variety of tests, he identified the medium as a dilute gelatin-tempera solution that allowed for the even dispersal of the pigment throughout.[19]

With the pigment and the medium determined he initially declared that the image was a finger painting, but later decided that it was actually painted with a brush using the dilute pigment solution. He believed the yellow-straw color of the fibers in image areas was simply the result of the aging tempera.[20]

To verify his artistic conclusions McCrone asked an artist friend, Walter Sanford, to paint some shrouds using the dilute solution he devised of 0.01 percent red ochre in 0.01 percent gelatin solution which he proposed was employed by the unknown medieval artist. Sanford painted only the head portion and also made some using diluted blood. McCrone described how most were painted with a brush and took about thirty minutes to complete.[21]

Shroud expert Dr. Gilbert Lavoie was able to purchase one of the red ochre versions from Sanford for examination. It was quickly relegated to the long list of failed attempts. It was smudgy and clearly made with a liquid, as the paint binder solution soaked all the way through the cloth, staining both sides.[22] Nowhere in McCrone's book does he address this common fatal problem, of the pigment soaking through the cloth, as experienced by many a would-be Shroud copyist.

McCrone's claims were scrutinized and evaluated by many of the STURP scientists, whose own investigations produced very different findings. The scientists analyzed the Shroud, both image and non-image areas, with visible and ultraviolet spectrometry, infrared spectrometry, x-ray fluorescence spectrometry, and thermography. Chemist Ray Rogers made more observations with pyrolysis mass spectrometry, laser-microprobe Raman analyses, and microchemical testing. Each chemical compound absorbs wavelengths that are characteristic of its chemical structure. No evidence for pigments was found, nor protein that would indicate a paint medium.[23] Rogers stated:

> No positive tests for proteins were obtained with the reliable reagents applied to Shroud fibers from either background or pure image areas. *No proteins had been added to image areas.* The tests proved the image was not painted with an egg-tempera system, as claimed by McCrone.[24] (Emphasis added)

Surprisingly, with the tape samples in his possession for more than a year, McCrone himself never tested the straw-yellow fibers that make up the image for the presence of protein. A positive test would have cemented his theory. It indicates a clear lack of confidence in his own hypothesis. Instead, he lamented,

> Obviously, I could not have conducted staining tests for collagen tempera (protein) on the body-image fibers after STURP had taken my tapes away from me in January 1980.[25]

Rather than acknowledging and discussing the differing results with his colleagues, McCrone chose to go his own way, distancing himself from STURP. After two of his papers on his Shroud findings were reviewed and subsequently rejected by the group, he published them in his own journal, *The Microscope*, for which he was the editor.

The following quote is McCrone's personal assessment of the Shroud:

> My position at this point was that the "Shroud" had been painted by an artist using a common medieval collagen tempera (watercolor) paint with red ochre pigment...I believe the "Shroud" was painted by an artist shortly before it first appeared in history in 1356, say 1355 to allow a year 'for the paint to dry.' There is no blood on the "Shroud." That was my position by January 1, 1980 and I have maintained that position at every opportunity since.[26]

The theory put forth by McCrone has never been validated by his fellow scientists. In fact, the evidence continues to weigh against it. The main contribution he has made is to further clarify the vast difficulties encountered by those who have attempted to explain the image of the Shroud as a painting.

Beyond these examples lie many more, with all sharing the dubious distinction of failing the test. I would say the odds of finding a process or an artist capable of this creation are not looking good. Consequently, the time has come to see what the field of science has discovered.

# CHAPTER 2

## Science Tackles the World's Greatest Unsolved Mystery

In order to make the most of their allotted time, the Shroud of Turin Research Project spent two years leading up to the expedition planning and preparing various experiments, measurements, and tests designed to elicit specific information for further analysis. Several tons of equipment and scientific instruments were shipped to Turin from various laboratories in the USA. The team's examination would commence the day after the conclusion of a six-week exhibition of the Shroud in the Cathedral of St. John the Baptist, commemorating the four hundredth anniversary of its arrival in Turin. As the Shroud was a royal possession from 1453 until 1983, the cathedral connects to the royal palace. A large room in the palace was set up as an examination area with another room designated for rest and sleep. The team worked around the clock with the twenty-four hours broken down into shifts allowing work to continue as others grabbed a few hours of sleep.

*The scientists.* Four years before the 1978 testing, fellow scientists John Jackson and Eric Jumper, both original founders of STURP, observed through analysis of photographs that the intensity of the image varied in proportion to the distance the cloth was from the body. This discovery suggested the cloth had three-dimensional properties. The two were able to validate their observation by using a VP-8 Image Analyzer, which converts image intensity to vertical relief. When they scanned a picture of the Shroud, it produced an accurate three-dimensional image of a man with almost no distortion, unlike any known artwork or photograph.

It was the revelation of the VP-8 that became the catalyst for the Shroud Project and piqued the curiosities of so many qualified researchers. In 1977, these scientists met in Albuquerque, New Mexico, to discuss the investigative project that would take place in Turin the following year. The Shroud had not been on public exhibit since 1933, forty-five years prior. The mission was not to "prove" anything but to assess the nature of the image and the corresponding bloodstains. Ultimately, they hoped to determine how the image was formed and arrive at an explanation that might solve the centuries old mystery.[1]

*The examination.* On Sunday night, October 8, 1978, the public exhibition, seen by over three million people over six weeks, finally ended. Authorities removed the Shroud from where it was on display in the cathedral and marched as in a procession on a flat panel covered with red silk to a room in the royal palace set up for examination. The scientists awaited their prize with excitement and anticipation. The historic nature of what they were about to embark upon was not lost on any of them. For some, it was a journey that continues to this day.

A long steel table built in the United States designed to swivel 360 degrees was waiting to receive the sacred linen that would be attached with magnets. As the cloth was placed on the table, they noticed how well preserved it appeared to be though clearly yellowed from age with multiple creases from constant rolling and folding over the centuries.

The scientists bombarded the relic with ultraviolet radiation and x-rays and watched for fluorescence. They measured variations in the way the image, the "blood," and the background emitted or reflected energy across a wide range of the electromagnetic spectrum. In infrared, visible light, ultraviolet, and x-ray, they searched for "fingerprints" of the Shroud's chemical makeup.[2]

Other researchers took hundreds of close-up images using high-magnification photography at different levels of illumination.

Sticky tape was applied to remove various particles and debris—including fibers, dust, and pollen—to be examined later. They loosened the backing cloth and took pictures of the back side of the cloth opposite the image. At the end of the five days, after they worked in shifts around the clock with little sleep, catching naps on cots in an adjacent room, the examination came to an end. It could be clearly said that no other artistic or archaeological artifact had been subjected to more scrutiny. The Shroud was reverently wrapped in silk and returned to its place in the cathedral, where it would not be exhibited again for another twenty years, until 1998.[3]

The methods used by STURP to collect data included the following:

- Direct microscopy
- Infrared spectrometry
- X-ray fluorescence spectrometry
- X-ray radiography
- Thermography
- Ultraviolet fluorescence spectrometry

In addition, they collected a wide range of photographic data, including the following:

- Ultraviolet fluorescence photographs
- Raking-light photographs
- Normal front-lit photographs
- Backlit photographs of the entire Shroud
- Dozens of microphotographs of strategically selected areas of the cloth

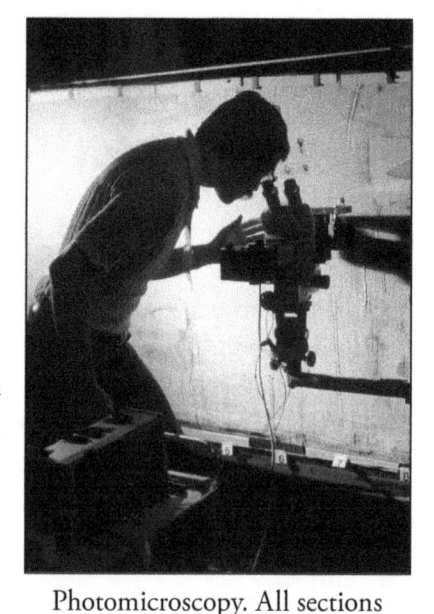

Photomicroscopy. All sections of the Shroud photographed at different levels of magnification. (Image courtesy of Barrie M. Schwortz collection, STERA Inc.)

From thread samples and sticky-tape samples taken from the surface of the cloth kept for further study, they conducted subsequent analysis using the following:

- Microscopy
- Pyrolysis-mass spectrometry
- Laser-microbe Raman analysis
- Various methods of microchemical testing

Following the team's conclusion of work in Turin, over the next four years, the scientists involved published the results of their research in twenty-four peer-reviewed scientific journal articles.

*Personal impact of the project.* Despite the dramatic results of the initial VP-8 analysis, all but one or two of the scientists expected the cloth to be a medieval fake created to trick the faithful. John Heller, one of the blood chemists from the New England Institute, said:

> I started out very arrogant. Nobody could have convinced me that there was any way the Shroud could have eluded a scientific answer. Scientists do one thing: measure. We're remarkably good at it, and the instruments we have are incredible.[4]

The eclectic team spanned a range of beliefs, including six agnostics, two Mormons, three Jews, and four Catholics. The rest were Protestants and not inclined to have much faith in relics. Including those who did not make the trek to Turin but were engaged in analyzing particles, fibers, or data brought back from Italy, the team grew to about forty scientists. Heller pointed out that including all the other specialists who collaborated on various offshoots of the investigation, over four hundred had added their input. Yet on the key question of how the image came to be, he said, "Every suggestion had been invalidated by the data."[5]

In 1983, Heller published *Report on the Shroud of Turin*, documenting the Shroud Project, and began by saying:

> By profession, I am a scientist; specifically, a biophysicist. By genesis, I am a New Englander, with all the skepticism...of the breed. All this being the case, I have always felt that relics are nothing but flummery from the Dark Ages.[6]

Heller's book documents how the STURP project came together, the tests performed, and all the intrigue that occurred along the way. Regarding why he wrote it, Heller said:

> I figure the faithful don't need it, the faithless won't read it, but there may be a lot of people in between who would like to have some more evidence. It seems to be working out that way. The Shroud has the ability to make people sit up and take notice.[7]

Although most scientists who were part of the team refuse to make any claim of authenticity, nearly all the members of the team came away convinced the Shroud is not a fraud. Could it be Jesus? That is not a question science can answer.

Sam Pellicori, a spectroscopist at the Santa Barbara Research Center, said it this way:

> Was it the actual burial cloth of Christ? Our research has not been able to prove that weighty conclusion, nor will science ever be able to say. But at the same time, some of the most exhaustive research ever conducted on any relic, object of art, or archaeological artifact in no way has eliminated that possibility.[8]

Heller concludes his book documenting the STURP investigation with the following words:

> There are some remarkable aspects to this voyage of discovery. The team itself—its formation, cohesion, diversity, collaboration, as well as its sacrifice of time, talent, and treasure—is unique in the scientific annals. The role of "coincidence" is awesome. Science undertook its specialty, which is measurement. We were supremely confident that answers would—indeed, must—be forthcoming. And we failed. Many team members were ordered or threatened to desist from the project, yet they persevered. Though it was believed that there would be a confrontation between science and religion, none occurred. Rather, the relationship was harmonious and synergistic.[9]

*My tribute to STURP.* As so many others involved in this historic project over forty years ago, John passed away in December 1995. The project was like a cosmic singularity that came about when space-age science was emerging, at the same time, antipathy toward religion was only simmering.

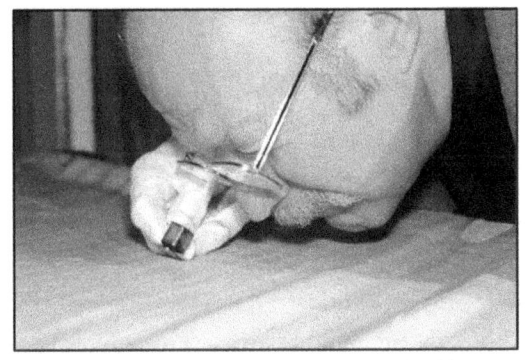

Chemist Ray Rogers analyzing the fibers with a high-powered magnifying glass (Image courtesy of Barrie M. Schwortz collection, STERA Inc.)

In our current culture, that simmering has moved closer to a boil, where the gathering of so many scientists to study a religious artifact would never get off the ground. This makes the magnitude and impact of the STURP project beyond our ability to measure. Nonetheless, the effects of that powerful fusion are still impacting the world today.

Recalling the historic STURP conference in 1981, which also launched my own lifetime of involvement, I include here the full official statement from the team:

> No pigments, paints, dyes, or stains have been found on the fibrils. X-ray, fluorescence, and microchemistry on the fibrils preclude the possibility of paint being used as a method for creating the image. Ultraviolet and infrared evaluation confirm these studies. Computer image enhancement and analysis by a device known as a VP-8 image analyzer show that the image has unique, three-dimensional information encoded in it. Micro-chemical evaluation has indicated no evidence of any spices, oils, or any bio-chemicals known to be produced by the body in life or in death. It is clear, there has been a direct contact of the Shroud with a body, which explains certain features such as scourge marks, as well as the blood. However, while this type of contact might explain some of the features of the torso, it is totally incapable of explaining the image of the face with the high resolution that has been amply demonstrated by photography.
>
> The basic problem from a scientific point of view is that some explanations which might be tenable from a chemical point of view, are precluded by physics. It can be also stated, that contrariwise, certain physical explanations which may be attractive are completely precluded by the chemistry. For an adequate explanation for the image of the Shroud, one must have an explanation which is scientifically sound, from a physical, chemical, biological, and medical viewpoint. At the present, this type of solution does not

appear to be obtainable by the best efforts of the members of the Shroud Team.

Furthermore, experiments in physics and chemistry with old linen have failed to reproduce adequately the phenomenon presented by the Shroud of Turin. The scientific consensus is that the image was produced by something which resulted in oxidation, dehydration, and conjugation of the polysaccharide structure of the micro-fibrils of the linen itself. Such changes can be duplicated in the laboratory by certain chemical and physical processes. A similar type of change in linen can be obtained by sulfuric acid or heat. However, there are no chemical or physical methods known which can account for the totality of the image, nor can any combination of physical, chemical, biological, or medical circumstances explain the image adequately.

Thus, the answer to the question of how the image was produced or what produced the image remains, now, as it has in the past…a mystery.

*We can conclude for now that the Shroud image is that of a real human form of a scourged, crucified man. It is not the product of an artist.* The blood stains are composed of hemoglobin and give a positive test for serum albumin. The image is an ongoing mystery and until further chemical studies are made, perhaps by this group of scientists, or perhaps by some scientists in the future, the problem remains unsolved.[10] (Emphasis added)

*The next four chapters will explore medical forensics and other avenues of scientific investigation employed by the STURP team to examine the body, analyze what appears to be bloodstains, investigate the nature of the image, and explore possible causes.*

# CHAPTER 3

## Forensic Analysis of the Body

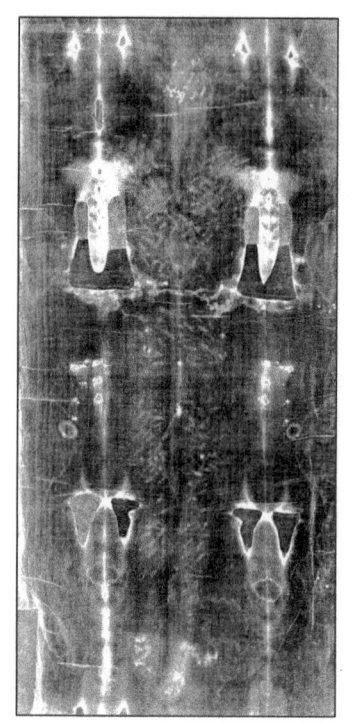

Photo negative of dorsal (backside) image (Courtesy of Barrie M. Schwortz collection, STERA Inc.)

The forensic pathologist often functions as both a coroner and a medical examiner, who scrutinizes bodies by autopsy to determine the cause of death. Several noted pathologists have analyzed the Shroud. The late Dr. Robert Bucklin, former coroner and medical examiner for Los Angeles, Houston, and Las Vegas, became part of the STURP team in 1978 to offer a medical perspective in that regard. Having conducted over twenty-five thousand autopsies, Dr. Bucklin was known as a national expert in the field. The following forensic analysis builds on a coroner-style report initially developed by him, with the inclusion of other sources to provide a comprehensive picture.

The full front and back body imprints, along with the unique characteristics of bloodstains on the cloth, make it possible to examine the image as if an autopsy were being performed on a person who died from similar circumstances.

The Shroud image appears to be an adult male measuring approximately five feet, ten inches tall (177.8 cm) and weighing about 175 pounds. The height is only an estimate because of possible stretching or shrinking of the cloth. The body appears to be "anatomically normal" and seems to be in a state of rigor mortis. This overall stiffness is apparent in the position of the legs, with the left leg elevated above the right, and also with the feet, which remain crossed, one over the other, as if placed that way. Something secured them in that position, presumably a nail or nails. Consistent with that, there appear to be two exit wounds on the bottom of one foot. Blood from one of the wounds is clearly trailing away from it. Again, we can only presume the wounds resulted from the nails used to secure the feet to the "stipe"—the upright portion of the cross.

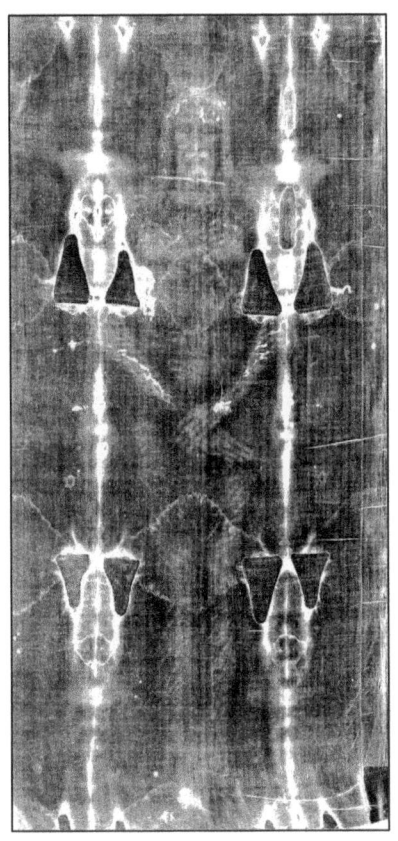

Photo negative of frontal image (Courtesy of Barrie M. Schwortz collection, STERA Inc.)

In 1968 there was a rare archeological find outside Jerusalem. In the tombs of Giv'at ha-Mivtar, archeologist Vassilo Tzaferis discovered an ossuary containing the bones of a crucifixion victim. An inscription on the outside read "Jehonathan the potter." The heel of the crucified man showed a nail penetrating the side of the foot. This confirms that crucifixion used nails, although it does not preclude the use of rope, as referenced in some accounts. The placement of the nail in this instance differs from what we observe on the

Shroud, but rather than being a contradiction, it merely shows there was more than one way to secure the feet to the cross depending on who was wielding the hammer.[1]

The man had shoulder-length hair and a medium-length beard forked in the middle under the chin. The back image indicates his hair may have been pulled back in an unbraided ponytail typical of first-century Jewish men.[2]

The startling evidence of an apparent "crown of thorns" is seen as a ring of puncture wounds around the scalp. Blood oozed from these punctures into the hair and onto the forehead. The dorsal view shows the puncture wounds extend all around the head. Dr. Fred Zugibe explains that because of the intricate array of nerves that lie between the skin and the cranial bone, the cap of thorns may have been the most painful part of the ordeal.[3] It was certainly a humiliating and cruel addition, a singular correlation with the account of Jesus being "crowned" as a mockery.

The direction of all the blood flows, for both front and back images, is downward. This is consistent with the evidence of gravity—that the man must have been in an upright position when these wounds occurred. There is an abrasion at the tip of the nose along with a swollen right cheek as compared with the left cheek, also consistent with injuries Jesus received.

A prominent bloodstain is visible along the left side of the body at the level of the ribcage, corresponding with a side wound. The upper portion of the stain shows an oval wound, which is characteristic of penetration produced by a sharp puncturing instrument consistent with a Roman lance. The variation within the stain reveals two types of fluid: blood and serum. This is consistent with a wound that occurred after death, as blood flowing from the chest cavity would have begun the natural separation into the two elements. In the first century, without the modern understanding of blood chemistry, the sight of serum coming out of the wound would appear like water, as related in John's gospel.

The pectoral muscles are prominent and show an expanded chest, yet the area under the chest above the navel appears drawn in. As a means of studying this effect, Shroud researcher and artist/physicist Isabel Piczek worked with volunteers who agreed to hang from a cross, tied with rope, allowing her to observe this phenomenon. She found that their chests would swell and their lower abdominal muscles would tightly contract in the same way depicted on the Shroud. This characterization of the torso is therefore consistent with someone who was crucified.[4]

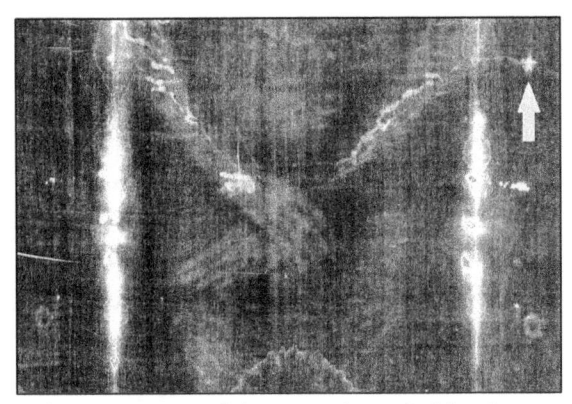

Photo negative of the arms showing bloodstain off the elbow noted by the arrow (Courtesy of Barrie M. Schwortz collection, STERA Inc.)

The arms are crossed over the mid and lower abdomen and were most likely dislocated from the shoulders, causing them to appear elongated. The right hand overlies the left wrist when looking at the photonegative Shroud image. The right wrist has a prominent puncture-type injury, believed to be from a crucifixion nail, which shows two blood rivulets derived from a single wound and separated by about a ten-degree angle. Since this direction of blood flow could not have happened with the arms in the prone position as we see them on the cloth, it is another indication the arms were originally above the head, as in crucifixion. Gravity, while in the upright position, clearly explains the direction of the blood flows that extend from the wrists to the elbows on the right and left forearms.

In addition, there is a bloodstain off the left elbow (see arrow) several inches away from the body. Dr. Gilbert Lavoie provided an insightful explanation for this apparent anomaly. He described how the blood that flowed down the forearms from the nail wounds would have pooled at the elbows. Subsequently, when the body was placed on the Shroud, the linen was likely tucked around the sides, absorbing the blood from underneath the elbow. When the unwrapped cloth is laid flat, the bloodstain from the underside then appears to be away from the body. This is also a strong validation of the cloth having surrounded a three-dimensional human being, rather than just a painted image on a flat surface, as some skeptics claim.[5]

Both hands on the Shroud show only four fingers and no thumbs. The nail wounds appear to be on the wrist. This nail placement is in distinct opposition to virtually every known artistic depiction of the crucifixion during the Middle Ages, where the wound is shown in the palm of the hand. Dr. Pierre Barbet, experimenting with cadavers, proved that a nail through the palm of the hand cannot hold the weight of a body; it would rip through the fleshy tissue between the fingers. The nail had to be in the wrist to be effective—precisely where we see it on the Shroud. This also explains the thumbs not being visible, as damage to a nerve and/or tendon would cause the flexing of the thumb into the palm.[6] Referring again to the 1968 excavation near Jerusalem, scratch marks seen on the bones of the arm show evidence that a nail was driven between the two bones of the forearm just above the wrist.[7]

After a presentation I gave in the Chicago area several years ago, I saw a real-world example of this anatomical phenomenon. An older man came up to me and explained how he had been in an industrial accident that sent a rod through his wrist, with the consequence of his thumb being permanently folded into his palm. He showed me his hand and invited me to move his thumb. I could not do it! It was a remarkable moment.

Examination of the back image shows multiple injuries. On the shoulder blade area on the right and left sides, there is a clear abrasion of the skin surfaces, consistent with the weight of a heavy object. It would suggest a beam rested over the shoulder blades

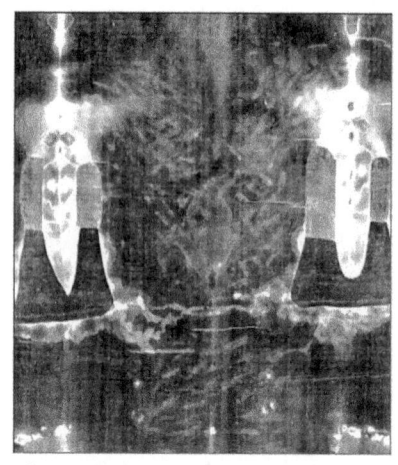

Photo negative of the dorsal image showing scourge marks and the blood flow across the lower back (Courtesy of Barrie M. Schwortz collection, STERA Inc.)

that produced a rubbing effect on the skin. The *patibulum*, or the crossbeam of a cross, could easily cause such an abrasion, and we know that the condemned would sometimes be forced to carry such a burden to their execution.

The historical record of known crucifixions shows it as a method of both torture and execution. The Romans wanted those crucified to remain alive as long as possible to maximize suffering and enhance the public spectacle. The first step in this brutal practice was the scourging of the victim, which sometimes weakened them close to the point of death, however, the number of lashes was not proscribed.

This practice is dramatically depicted on the Shroud, with many traumatic injuries seen, which extend from the shoulders to the ankles. Some type of flogging instrument, like a whip, left dumbbell-shaped imprints in the skin, causing blood to ooze from each wound. The direction of the injuries suggests two men were involved in the whipping. Forensic analysis shows one was taller than the other, based on the different angles of the whip marks. Over 120 scourge wounds are visible and the imprints would be consistent with the Roman use of a *flagrum*, a leather whip tipped with either metal or with bone, usually from sheep knuckles. Since we find no whip marks on the upper arms, the man would have been upright with his arms tied above his head at the time the whipping occurred.

The gospel accounts describe Pontius Pilate having Jesus horribly scourged, with hopes it would be enough to satisfy the angry mob and therefore prevent his execution, yet the crowd prevailed. The man of the Shroud exhibits these same graphic wounds.

Those who were crucified would sometimes linger for three or four days, largely depending on the severity of the scourging. To hasten death or end the suffering, soldiers would break the legs of the victim, causing the weight of the body to completely impede the ability to breathe. However, the man on the Shroud did not have his legs broken, indicating that he was already dead when the time came to remove him from the cross; another consistency with the account of Jesus' crucifixion, as the Sabbath was approaching and the Jewish high priest did not want bodies left on the cross during Passover.

Not surprisingly, forensic analysis indicates the cause of death for the man on the Shroud was most likely asphyxia, along with hypovolemic shock from severe dehydration and extreme loss of blood.

Dr. Bucklin's pathologist report, detailing his extensive findings, concluded with this simple yet profound statement:

> From this data it is not an unreasonable conclusion for the forensic pathologist to determine that only one person in history has undergone this sequence of events.[8]

# CHAPTER 4

## Analysis of the Blood

In concert with the forensic analysis of the body and corresponding blood flows is the analysis of the blood itself. This was performed by noted blood chemists Dr. Alan Adler and Dr. John Heller, with the addition of scientific work by other blood specialists. These findings add weight to the argument for authenticity, as well as posing quite a challenge for our medieval artist or forger to duplicate.

*Analysis of the blood chemistry*

The blood stains on the Shroud have all the characteristics of exudates from clotted wounds that were transferred to the cloth by direct contact with a severely wounded man. These markings represent, quite literally, the ooze that would have emanated from injuries on the body. Among the tests performed on samples removed, chemists identified several blood components including bile, bilirubin, hemoglobin, and serum albumin. The reddish color of the blood likely resulted from a high content of bilirubin, adding its distinct yellow-orange color. Bilirubin is released from the liver under conditions of severe physical stress.[1] Additional serological techniques revealed the blood serum proteins albumin and immunoglobulin which identified the blood as primate. However, as the samples were highly degraded, some chemists were cautious about going further in their conclusions. Still, other tests using fluorescence-labeled antibody techniques on albumin by surgeons and forensic experts Baima Bollone et al. were summed up by eminent immunologist Dr. Kelly Kearse:

> Bloodstained fibers were positive for expression of M, N, and most importantly, S antigens, ruling out a contribution of (nonhuman) primate blood. Moreover, since the S antigen has no counterpart in primates or other animals, these results support the conclusion that the blood on the Shroud is of human origin.[2]

Regarding studies of primate versus human blood, the chemistry is very complex, and more sophisticated methods continue to evolve. As for testing on the Shroud for blood typing, much has been revealed in this area and offers more intriguing possibilities in the future. The use of cross-checking and tests with greater sensitivities, including DNA, will likely give more clarity. Kearse offers a perspective on the overall blood typing of the Shroud by stating:

> In summary, the preponderance of current scientific evidence indicates that: (i) there is blood on the Shroud of Turin; (ii) the blood is of primate, i.e. human origin; and (iii) the blood type is most likely AB as determined by forward typing methods, specifically mixed agglutination and immunohistochemistry techniques.[3]

Examining the blood characteristics further, ultraviolet photographs of the wounds show a distinct serum clot retraction ring that appears as a clear halo around each wound. The thickest part of the ring is at the bottom of the wound, consistent with the effect of gravity on a bloodied man hanging in an upright position. It is important to note that fresh blood dripped or painted onto a cloth will not produce this effect. We can only replicate it with the exudate of coagulated blood consistent with actual wounds.[4]

*The blood stains, the image, and timing*

There has been a general consensus among scientists that the bloodstains resulted from direct contact with a body. An interesting aspect of this process is the question of timing. Dr. Gilbert Lavoie conducted experiments using human blood to show how blood-transfer images on a linen cloth appear remarkably like those seen on the Shroud. However, he could only replicate the effect when contact between the linen and a moist clot took place within 1.5 hours after the bleeding stopped. But if the wound were combined with sweat on the skin, the clot could remain wet for another thirty minutes. This is consistent with the time estimated for removing Jesus from the cross, placing him in Joseph's tomb, and hastily wrapping his body in a burial sheet in compliance with the Jewish Sabbath that began at sunset.[5]

Removal of the blood from a stained fiber shows no discoloration or degradation underneath. In contrast, fibers where the image is visible are marked by dehydration and oxidation. This discovery is important in showing that the blood from the wounds must have seeped onto the cloth prior to the emergence of the image. In other words, the blood-coated fibers appear to have been shielded from the image-forming process.

While the cause of the image remains unknown, it has been shown to be independent of direct contact, a conclusion consistent with computer imaging evidence. Computer imaging also reveals that the body image is slightly out of alignment with the blood images.[6] This intriguing fact further indicates that there was a difference in time from when the blood appeared on the cloth versus the image. In handling and preparation, the body or the linen could have been shifted. Alternately, knowing the body would have experienced rigor mortis, it is reasonable to assume that the easing of that condition could also cause the linen to shift slightly as the body relaxed. The process of rigor mortis begins one to two hours after death, reaches maximum rigidity over twelve to twenty-four hours, and eases after thirty-six hours.[7] This is also consistent with the time frame of Jesus being in the tomb, as described by many biblical scholars.[8]

*Skeptics question blood flow*

In 2018, Luigi Garlaschelli (whose attempts at duplicating the Shroud image were outlined in Chapter 1), published a paper with fellow skeptic, Matteo Borrini, debunking the Shroud based on blood-flow analysis, claiming they could not duplicate the flow of blood on the man's hands, arms, or torso. For their first experiment, they used fresh blood infused with anticoagulants, resulting in the blood flowing like water. When it was applied to one of the author's wrists, held vertically, it dripped straight down.

Contrary to their findings, the blood on the Shroud that seeped from the nail wound in the wrist was that of a severely traumatized and dehydrated man. Far from flowing like water, it would have oozed slowly down the arms of a victim who was dirty, sweaty, and sticky from the horrific ordeal. The flow also conforms to the arms having been raised at an angle, not strictly vertical.

In their attempt to duplicate the side "lance" wound, they used synthetic blood, again mixed with anticoagulants. With a mannequin in a standing position, using a blood-soaked sponge attached to a flat stick, they simulated a thrust to the side. But this was done horizontally, rather than at an upward angle as described in the forensic analysis. This failed as well.

These poorly constructed experiments did not remotely come close to duplicating the medical or environmental conditions of a real crucifixion. As a result, they carry little weight against renowned blood chemists and forensic pathologists with their many years of examining the Shroud.[9]

*Challenges to an artistic explanation*

The specificity and detail of the chemical and physical aspects of the blood found on the Shroud present obvious challenges to an artistic explanation. For instance, man-made paint compositions such as iron oxide suspended in a "jewelers' rouge" or vermilion are not able to simulate the chemical and physical characteristics of the bloodstains found under ultraviolet light. With respect to applying actual blood all over the body corresponding with wounds prior to creating the image, would have been an unnecessary and taxing complication. Similarly, producing a credible representation of Christ's burial cloth would not require this degree of realism; after all, relics, fraudulent or authentic, abounded. As for painting with real blood, Dr. Alan Adler described a challenging scenario that summed up the complexities:

> Blood...must have been taken from the exudate of a clot at a certain point in the clotting process. An artist would therefore have needed the exudate from the wounds of a severely tortured man, or baboon, and he would need to take the substance within a 20-minute period after the clotting had begun...[10] One would need a constant supply of fresh clot exudates from a traumatically wounded human to paint all the forensically correct images in the proper nonstereo register and then finally paint a serum contraction ring about every wound. Logic suggests that this is something a forger or artisan before the present century would not only not know how to do but even know that it was required.[11]

The presence of blood on the Shroud provides a trove of information that is remarkable in its scope. In conjunction with the extensive forensic research previously conducted, Dr. Adler made the following comment regarding the contribution of the blood evidence:

> No one would have ever dreamed, when we first started doing the analysis that the chemistry would provide corroborating evidence to what the pathologists concluded long ago about the Shroud figure.[12]

# CHAPTER 5

## Understanding the Image

So far, we have looked at the Shroud from many angles, including the possibility of the image being a creation of a medieval artist, the extensive hands-on scientific examination, analysis of the bloodstains, and a wide-ranging forensic evaluation of the man depicted on the linen.

We know that the STURP scientists employed chemistry and physics with the goal of trying to determine what the source could be that produced the remarkable image. Their conclusions outlining the lack of any artistic substances are very clear, along with the acknowledgment that the image-making process remains unknown. However, the fibers that make up the image itself have unique characteristics not seen on the rest of the cloth, and a review focusing on those facets will nevertheless add to our understanding of the Shroud image.

During the five days of testing in Turin, samples from the surface of the cloth were collected by the systematic application of Mylar sticky tape to carefully designated areas of the Shroud, with many covering the image. Twenty-one different reagents and solvents were used for testing the image fibers. The chemical reactions allowed researchers to deduce that there were no existing substances that might have caused the image, as they would have dissolved in the process. Conversely, the image itself was unaffected, confirming its permanence.

Further chemical studies, along with data from the vast array of visual examinations, produced distinctive findings regarding the image fibers.

*Dehydration and oxidation.* The image fibers all show evidence of dehydration and oxidation, which accounts for the discoloration of the cloth. We do not know the cause of this phenomenon. While the bloodstains appear to be from a contact process with the body, the image does not conform to the same explanation. This dichotomy between the bloodstains and the body image has led many to consider the resurrection as a cause. From a scientific standpoint, of course, we can only speculate about this untestable hypothesis.[1]

*Microscopy—the image depth.* From a microscopic perspective, the image only goes one to two fibers deep, resting on the crowns of the affected thread. Each thread is composed of one- to two-hundred microfibers; therefore, the image affects approximately 1 to 2 percent of each thread where the image is visible. The image does not penetrate through the fabric. The blood and water stains, however, completely soak through and are clearly seen on the reverse side, whereas the image cannot be seen.[2]

However, in 2002, the entire back side of the Shroud was scanned, revealing something never observed before. Shroud researchers Giulio Fanti and Roberto Maggiolo conducted in-depth image analysis from the scans and determined that faint images of the face and hands can be detected. The rest of the body remains indiscernible. Analyzing fibers from these areas shows the image did not penetrate the cloth but is purely superficial just as it is on the front side. No one has an explanation, but it makes an artistic origin even more unlikely.[3] A possible clue to the cause of this phenomenon will be explored later in the book.

Image close-up from the tip of the nose, one of the darkest parts of the Shroud image (Courtesy of Barrie M. Schwortz collection, STERA Inc.)

In the image areas, there is no cementing of the fibers together as with paint or other substances, which confirms the absence of any binding agent. The image area shows no evidence of capillarity, meaning the image does not appear under any crisscrossing fibers. This shows that no liquids were applied to create the image. Any liquid would have soaked through and affected all the threads and fibers. The image fibers are brittle and show "corroded" surfaces, as expected for dehydrated and oxidized material.[4]

The image process affects the fibers uniformly with the same depth and coloration throughout the cloth. In fact, it is a monochrome image as there is no variation in color. Affected fibers are adjacent to unaffected fibers, which confirms the image is not derived from paint, pigment, ink, dye, or stain as they would affect all the fibers where an artist might apply the substance. This phenomenon would not be possible using any of these materials unless they had been applied one fiber at a time, a far-fetched supposition that would require the use of a nonexistent medieval microscope. Additionally, the loosening of these fibers with a teasing needle does not reveal any powders as with a dust rubbing, nor can we see any pigments even with high-magnification microscopy.[5]

The shading of the image (where it appears either lighter or darker) is not the result of variations of color but by varying the number of affected fibers in each area, like pixels. It is therefore an areal density image based on the density of the image per square centimeter.[6]

*Three-dimensional attribute.* Perhaps the most intriguing characteristic of the image is revealed by computer imaging analysis, first discovered using a VP-8 Image Analyzer. This analog computer converts lights and darks into vertical relief, much like a topographical map.

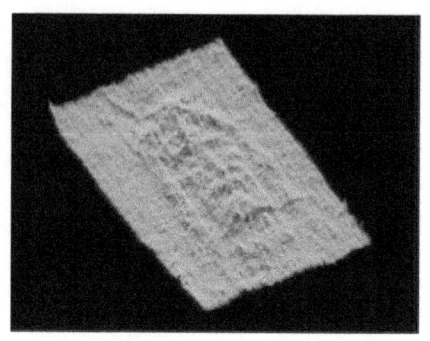

View screen from the VP-8 Image Analyzer revealing three-dimensional face image (Courtesy of Barrie M. Schwortz collection, STERA Inc.)

A standard reflected light photograph or a painting viewed in this way would look distorted. The Shroud image, however, when seen in a VP-8, appears to be in correct three-dimensional contour. The VP-8 simply assigns higher elevation to darks and lower elevation to lights on a gradient scale. Therefore, areas where the image appears darker, such as the nose or cheeks, have the highest elevation whereas the neck would have the lowest elevation. The Shroud appears to contain correct distance information for a cloth that draped a real human form.[7]

The image process was vertically collimated, meaning the source of the image was vertical and perpendicular to the body. The absence of side images and the top of the head (between frontal and dorsal images) shows it was not a radial phenomenon. The image source must also be able to act at a distance of up to four centimeters from the body, as determined by the drape of the cloth and the foreshortened position of the body.[8]

All attempts at replication have failed to duplicate the image as seen in a VP-8 Image Analyzer. The Shroud shows a gradual decrease of image intensity whereas even the best efforts to duplicate the image employing different techniques, allegedly used by a medieval artist, reveal sharp edges where the image abruptly ends. The Shroud image is a gradual fade with no sharp drop-offs.

New digital imaging technology has allowed for further examination of the cloth's mysterious 3D attributes. French researcher Thierry Castex is a geophysicist engineer and a specialist in seismic processing. Castex created a remarkable image in 2011 using software designed for creating seismic pictures to assist off-

New digital imaging technology used for seismic exploration reveals more of the Shroud's mysterious attributes and its 3D image. (Courtesy of Thierry Castex)

shore energy exploration. The result is nothing short of spectacular. Thierry describes how the

> software converts pixel intensity into height. The 3D viewer program generates a grayscale height map which is combined with the texture of the color image.[9]

*Bloodstains on hair or face? A clue to image timing.* The bloodstains in the hair are not in the hair. They are on the cheeks. They appear to be in the hair because the blood transferred from the face to the cloth by a contact process, but the image followed later. When we see the cloth flat, it gives the optical illusion of the blood being in the hair. Similar to what was described with the offset elbow stain.

Dr. Gilbert Lavoie conducted an intriguing experiment by using a life-size cloth replica of the Shroud. He cut holes in the cloth everywhere on the face and hair where blood was evident. He then wrapped the cloth over the face of a volunteer and proceeded to apply red paint through the holes onto the face of the volunteer. As with Jesus, the volunteer had long hair and a beard. Lavoie then took pictures of the man with the paint marks on his face and converted it to a negative, and just like the Shroud, the blood appeared to be in the hair but was clearly on the face. This was another proof the cloth covered a real body and was not simply an artistic rendering.[10]

| Volunteer lying his back as with the Shroud image | Cutout of all blood images seen on the face and hair of the Shroud | Cutout wrapped around volunteer with paint applied through the holes |

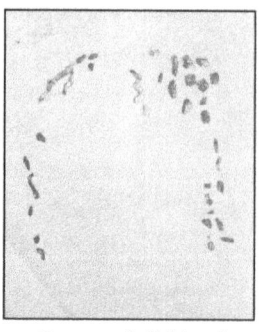

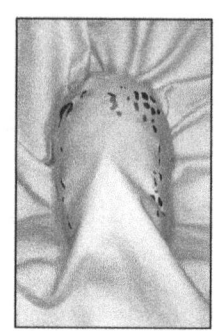

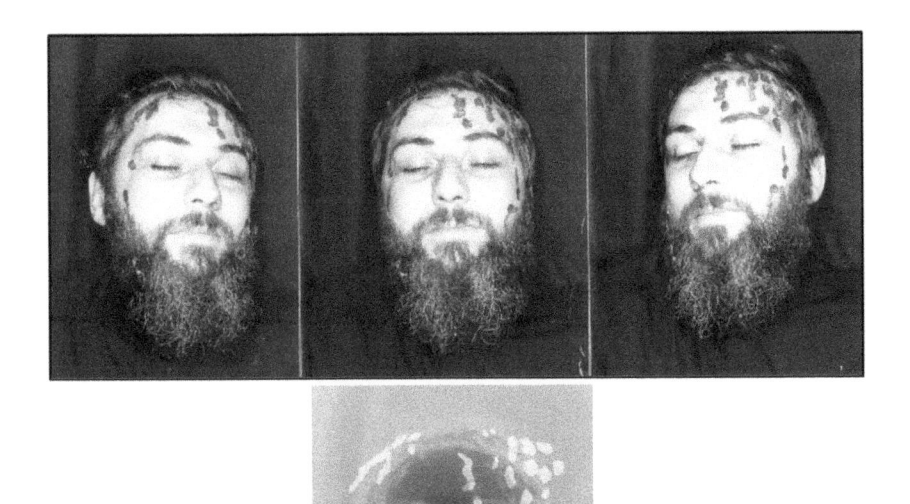

Paint on volunteer demonstrates the blood
was on the face and not in the hair.
Converting the image to a negative, bloodstains appear
to be in the hair but are actually on the face.
(All images courtesy of Gilbert R. Lavoie, MD,
from *Unlocking the Secrets of the Shroud*)

*A summary of image characteristics*

- The image is completely superficial, affecting only the top one to two microfibers. It does not penetrate the cloth as does the blood. A typical thread contains approximately two hundred microfibers. The image, therefore, rests on about 1 percent of a thread diameter.
- There is no outline to the image. Most artists start with an outline of what they are painting and then fill in.

- The image reveals identical intensity from top to bottom and front to back. Almost everything in the realm of art includes varying intensities because of different colors or densities of the artistic substance used. It would require a piece of modern technology to achieve this result.
- It is a monochrome image, meaning there is only one color with no variation. Where the image appears either lighter or darker, it is because of a numerical increase or decrease of the individual microfibers affected by whatever caused the image.
- There are no brushstrokes—no evidence of anything applied with a brush.
- There is no evidence of any liquids applied to create the image.
- There are no particles in between the threads, such as a dust rubbing.
- Other than random particles, researchers have found no artistic substances in a concentration that could account for the image.
- No paint binder was found to bind any pigments to the cloth.
- The image is a negative that converts to a positive image when light values are reversed in a photo negative.
- It contains distance information that allows for a 3D rendering of the image from the cloth having draped a real human form.
- There is no image under the blood; therefore, the bloodstains occurred first from a contact process, whereas the image happened later as a separate process.

The combination of these attributes serves to emphasize the improbable nature of the image on the Shroud. Physical aspects of the image fibers, the inherent 3D properties, and the independent nature of the bloodstains describe the totality of the image up to a point. Beyond that, we naturally reach the logical question of how the image came to be in the first place. In the next chapter, we will explore some of those possibilities.

# CHAPTER 6

## Theories of Image Formation

The past one hundred plus years of Shroud research and analysis has focused on answering one primary question: How was the image formed? There is no definite answer yet or possibly ever will be. But theories abound. Each theory may explain one attribute of the image but not another; hence, it remains a unique and baffling mystery. The Greek word for mystery is *musterion*, meaning "that which cannot be known by the natural mind." Yet human nature still strives to explain the unexplainable.

Beyond physics and chemistry, the other element incorporated in some of these theories is the question of what happened to the body that was wrapped in the Shroud. We know the biblical account, the central tenet of Christianity that describes the physical resurrection of Jesus. Understanding that this is singularly dismissed by many as beyond the realm of possibility, I would like to touch on this question from a slightly different perspective, related to the image itself.

The image on the Shroud shows a body at one moment in time; shortly after death. Had the body remained wrapped for any significant amount of time, decomposition would have begun and continued unabated. That in itself would have resulted in a whole host of physical emanations being deposited on the linen by simple contact. If that were the case, we would be seeing a much different image, that of a dead body having gone through the natural process of decay and putrefaction. In this regard, it is not unreasonable to examine a unique relationship between the body and the image.

Therefore, I have included some theories that link the image to the body within the Shroud. With that understanding, let's take a look at some possibilities that have been put forth.

*Contact process.* Early Shroud researcher Paul Vignon postulated that the image formed naturally from the interaction of sweat, oils, and aloes acting on the linen in a contact-only process. Yet his experiments showed that such a process would produce a blotchy and distorted result. In addition, such substances would penetrate the fibers in varying amounts or, in some areas, not at all. This is not what is observed with the Shroud image, which we know shows a uniform density across the whole of the cloth, and only on the top one to two microfibers. Contact alone does not explain the Shroud image.[1]

*Maillard reaction gas diffusion.* Chemist Ray Rogers proposed a gas diffusion process called a Maillard reaction to explain the cause of the image. Ammonia-based gases emanating from a decaying body (putrescine and cadaverine) could have interacted with a thin carbohydrate layer resting on the top layer of the linen. He hypothesized that this "impurity layer" occurred naturally when the cloth, during its initial manufacture, was soaked in a preservative Saponaria (soapwort) solution, leaving a thin carbohydrate film over the entire cloth.[2]

Chemists Alan Adler and John Heller, on the other hand, contended that the image resulted from dehydration and oxidation of the cellulose, not an impurity layer reaction. At the microscopic level, it is hard to distinguish between the two. Is there an impurity layer resting on the threads of the linen, or are we observing the outer cell wall of the cellulose? This question has still not been resolved.

In any event, there is no observational evidence that a Maillard reaction can produce highly resolved images. From other examples of this natural process, no images have emerged that appear to be anything more than a smudge. In addition, gases from decomposition concentrate around the body's natural orifices such as the mouth, eyes, and nostrils; but there is no sign of this seen on the Shroud. Lastly, we would not expect hair to be a source of the ammonia gases required to produce an image, yet the hair is clearly seen on the cloth.[3]

*Collapse theory.* There are characteristics of the Shroud image that suggest some form of radiation was involved in the image formation process. There are many theories that incorporate this possibility. Theoretical physicist Dr. John Jackson expands on this idea when he proposes his so-called fall-through hypothesis, also known as the collapse theory. It attempts to explain the disappearance of the body and the uniqueness of the image features from the resulting image formation. It postulates that the physical body was converted to a volume of light, emitting light radiation, and became "mechanically transparent," allowing the cloth to fall through the body to a depth of about eight millimeters, at which point the body vanished. Dr. Jackson understands that this theory goes beyond known scientific mechanisms, and requires more studies and data, but believes it is well-founded. Interestingly, it could explain the distinctive features of the image that show skeletal structure as well as fleshy tissue. For example, we can see contusions on the cheek, large orbits of the eyes, and almost x-ray-type depictions of the elongated fingers showing bones up into the palms. These body features would get incorporated into the image if the cloth were falling through the body, unlike a projection of the image as other theories suggest.[4]

*Neutron absorption.* A variation of this theory proposes that neutron radiation as the source of the image could have caused the aberrant carbon date, citing experiments where a sample of linen exposed to a microburst of neutron radiation can skew the amount of carbon 14 present in the linen. Carbon age of an object is determined by measuring the ratio of carbon 12, which remains stable, to carbon 14, which decays at a set rate where half the carbon 14 depletes after 5,700 years. This is called the half-life of a tested sample. Therefore, the presumed age of any carbon-based artifact such as bone, wood, or cloth is a ratio of how much carbon 14 remains. Hence, 25 percent depletes at 2,850 years; 12.5 percent depletes at 1,425 years; and 6.25 percent depletes at 712 years, which is the estimated age of the Shroud, as determined by the 1988 testing.

But what if the cloth were exposed to a neutron event that increased the amount of carbon 14, causing a first-century linen to appear 1,300 years younger? No one knows if this happened, but neutron absorption is a theory that explains both the disappearing body and a faulty carbon date.[5]

*Coronal discharge.* Another theory, developed by Giulio Fanti, looks at coronal discharge (CD) as a cause of the image. CD occurs when an electric charge surrounds the surface of a charged conductor. It supposes an electronic discharge occurred from an energy source that originated from within the body and formed a negatively charged plasma field, causing a discoloration of the linen fibers.[6]

*Burst of ultraviolet light.* Italian physicist Paolo Di Lazzaro proposes that a burst of electromagnetic energy could account for many of the Shroud image characteristics. According to him, ultraviolet (UV) radiation may be the best candidate for duplicating two key attributes of the image: (1) coloration that only penetrates a few microfibers and (2) a process that is low in temperature as the image is not the result of heat. Di Lazzaro and his team subjected their hypothesis to experiment by using a high-energy excimer UV laser. By applying a microsecond burst (forty nanoseconds) from the laser against a control sample of linen, they achieved the same color and image depth as seen on the linen. This was the first time anyone has experimentally correlated light with the Shroud image.[7]

*Conclusion.* How the image of a crucified man came to be on this ancient linen cloth is without a doubt the most crucial question when considering the Shroud's authenticity. This assortment of theories reveals some of the many scientific avenues that have been explored, and they all involve some type of interaction with the body that was wrapped within the Shroud. Naturally, as research has continued, new and intriguing possibilities and hypotheses of image formation have been developed. We will delve further into some of these in the course of part 3.

CHAPTER 7

---

The Linen Cloth—First Century Textile?

Within the world of ancient textiles, deciphering the past can be a challenge. One of those challenges in regard to the Shroud of Turin is the limited number of Jewish burial shrouds in existence. The common burial practice was to place the body in a tomb and let it decay naturally. After a year or more, family members would reenter the tomb and place the bones in an ossuary with the name of the deceased etched on the outside. After the bones were deposited into the ossuary, what remained of the burial cloth was burned or buried. This allowed for an entire family to occupy the same tomb for burial. However, researchers can still examine ancient burial practices from the time frame in question, in the same geographical area, and compare similar textiles. Early manufacturing techniques, and the materials used, offer further clues to determine probable age. We can then use textile analysis to ascertain if the Shroud could be an authentic first-century Jewish burial cloth. Let's consider the most common questions that arise.

1) Was flax utilized for cloth in the first century?
    The Egyptians had developed flax farming with fiber quality to equal what is grown today. Archaeological evidence and examples of existing linens from the period show they grew and harvested flax in the Middle East during the first century.[1]

2) Could a large cloth the size and dimensions of the Shroud be created using first-century loom technology?

In fact, Egyptian funeral linens that served as an outer wrapping to surround the mummified body were comparable in size. Egyptian looms pre-dating the first century could manufacture cloth with widths far exceeding the Shroud.[2]

3) Did the weavers have the technology to manufacture a 3/1 herringbone twill weave?

It is called herringbone because it looks like the rib structure of a herring—a distinctive V-shaped broken zigzag pattern clearly distinguishable from plain weave. The Chinese developed looms with the capability of producing complex twill weaves. Traders traveling the Silk Road to and from the Far East would have certainly brought knowledge of this advancement in fabric manufacture.[3]

Several examples have also been found refuting claims that twill patterns were not associated with Middle East cultures.

- *Egypt*—Twill-based textile dated to AD 100 was found near the Red Sea.[4]
- *Dura-Europos, Greece*—Workers excavated twill weave textiles dating to 300 BC.[5]
- *Murabba'atnear, the Judean desert, early first century*—Archaeologists excavated seven textile pieces made with a twill weave.[6]
- *Masada, Israel, early first century*—Researchers found fourteen twill-based textiles and several with a diamond twill weave, even more complex than the weave of the Shroud.[7]
- *China*—Twill pattern weave was found dating back to the ninth century BC and sold by merchant traders along the Silk Road.[8]

4) Would the preparers of the body have used a single flax linen as a burial cloth? Some people believe Jesus was wound in strips or that multiple pieces of linen were used.

Based on excavations in Jerusalem circa the first century, the Jews, as opposed to their Egyptian neighbors, would inter their dead in a single shroud made from wool, animal skins, or linen based on what the family could afford. Strips of cloth would be used to bind the body on the outside of the shroud to secure extremities such as the wrists, knees, and feet.[9]

Also, there were different rules for people who died by violent death with significant loss of blood. In such a case, they would not wash the body, nor would they remove the clothes. Those attending to the burial would wrap the body in a single linen cloth called a *sovev*, which means "to surround" or "go around" and perfectly corresponds with the Shroud. In the case of Jesus, he was naked as the Romans had cast lots for his clothes. This is also what is observed on the Shroud.[10]

5) Could ancient textiles survive two thousand years without serious decay?

There are many examples of linen fabrics still in existence, including Tutankhamun's curtains from 1323 BC, over 3,300 years old. Flax fibers are impervious to moths, and after bleaching, the flax becomes resistant to bacteria and preserves well over long periods of time if kept dry. In addition, the complex weave of the Shroud has added to its strength and durability.[11]

6) What unique characteristics indicate the Shroud linen is first century?

Textile experts detected weaving mistakes on the Shroud, which could indicate the use of a more primitive loom. When weaving the herringbone pattern, the healds, or spools, of thread could occasionally miss crossing the warp (vertical) as the weft (horizontal) threads were pulled through, which was not uncommon.

The variegated appearance of the linen resulted from the bleaching process. The yarn on each heald would have been bleached separately, and at different times, creating variations that would account for slightly different hues. By the Middle Ages, they would have bleached the entire cloth, eliminating fluctuations.[12]

There is also the absence of wool fibers in the Shroud linen, an important finding that adds further validation to authenticity. It shows the Shroud was manufactured under the Jewish requirement not to mix plant and animal fibers, a custom not found in other cultures. Weavers were careful to produce wool and flax fabrics on separate looms to ensure they were "clean" in conformance with Jewish law.[13]

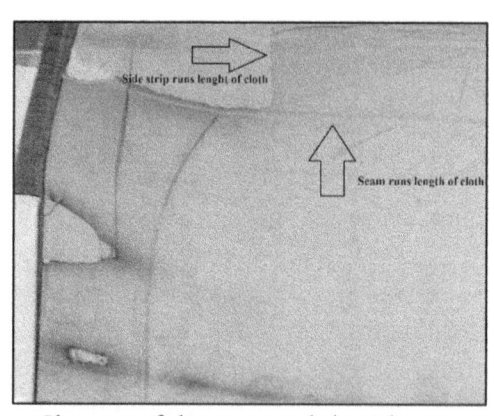

Close-up of the seam and the side strip across the upper edge of the Shroud (Image courtesy of Barrie M. Schwortz collection, STERA Inc.)

*The question of the side strip.* A side strip runs the entire length of the Shroud and is 8 centimeters wide and matches the rest of the cloth. Why was the strip added? Some researchers believe they joined it with the larger cloth to measure 2 × 8 Syrian cubits (21.7 inches) as a standard unit for purchasing bulk cloth. Without the side strip, the width would be about 3 inches short of 2 cubits.[14] Whether this indicates the Shroud was part of a larger cloth remains a question, but the joining of the two pieces of linen offers an intriguing clue to dating.

The seam used to attach both sections is a complex construction that made the seam minimally visible on the face of the cloth. Workers did all the stitching from the reverse side of the fabric. They constructed the seam with an interlocking design for maximum strength. Excavations have unearthed textile fragments with this exact seam construction from Masada, Israel, circa first century AD, which further supports an ancient manufacture for the Shroud.[15]

*Putting it all together*

- Egyptian flax was grown in the first century.
- Fabrics the size of the Shroud and larger were manufactured on looms in both Egypt and Syria.
- The technology and skill to make complex twill weaves were available.
- Many examples of complex weaves have been excavated from multiple locations.
- Flax is durable and could easily survive two thousand years, especially if kept dry. Examples go back to 1300 BC.
- Excavations support the use of a single Shroud as opposed to strips of fabric like the early Egyptians.

*In summary.* Based on textile analysis, the linen used for the Shroud of Turin exhibits attributes that can reasonably place it within the first century. The answers to the common questions posed above do nothing to negate the possibility that the Shroud could, in fact, be a genuine Jewish burial garment originating at that time.

# CHAPTER 8

## The Carbon-Dating Fiasco

On Friday, October 13, 1988, representatives from the University of Oxford and the British Museum made their now-famous announcement regarding the results of carbon 14 testing on the Shroud of Turin: the date range was from AD 1260 to 1390, and with 95 percent confidence the Shroud was declared a fake.

It was a demarcation point that effectively put any additional testing on hold and dampened enthusiasm for further research. For the many scientists, historians, theologians, and researchers, myself included, it meant confusion and disbelief. This was especially troubling given that so much of what had been discovered up to that point indicated a much earlier date, along with compelling evidence supporting the authenticity of the Shroud.

But there was much more to the story yet to be told. Questions surrounding the entire process soon began to arise. These concerned

Carbon 14 test results written on a blackboard, presented by Oxford's E. "Teddy" Hall, Michael Tite from the British Museum, and Robert E. M. Hedges, Oxford Lab's chief scientist. (*Daily Telegraph*, October 1988)

such critical aspects as the protocols established and then ignored, in-fighting and competition among the many players involved, the choice of testing methodologies and sample locations, and even questions of whether all pertinent data on the findings had been released. The expectation of those involved in Shroud research was for an outcome that was reliable, within the known limitations of carbon dating, whether that indicated a first-century origin or not. But almost like a spy novel, there turned out to be ins and outs and twists and turns that impacted the entire enterprise.

By highlighting some of these many facets, I believe we can put the relevance, or perhaps irrelevance, of carbon dating in its proper perspective.

*The lead-up to the carbon 14 testing.* As early as 1961, the prospect of carbon dating the Shroud had been a topic of discussion across various scientific disciplines. Potential drawbacks were also examined. P. J. Anderson of the Harwell C-14 laboratory (UK) mused that "the effect of the fires and subsequent drenching with water [...] and the possibility of contamination during early times, would, I think, make the results doubtful." He also described potential problems arising from damp conditions with fungi, molds, etc., given the history of the Shroud.[1]

A case in point is an artifact that resides at the Manchester Museum in England. Dr. Rosalie David, head of the Department of Egyptology at the Museum documented the curious case of Mummy no. 1770 excavated in the 1890s. Dr. David sent samples out for carbon dating. Surprisingly, they found the bones to be from 1000 BC, but the wrappings dated to AD 380, a variance of 1,380 years. The discrepancy was believed to be either rewrapping done at some later date or "the resins and unguents used in mummification may affect the bandages and bones in ways which affect the carbon dates. (...) From our experience, carbon dating of mummified remains and their associated bandages has produced some unexpected and controversial results."[2]

In 1979, three STURP members published a paper titled "Radiographic Examination of the Shroud of Turin—a Preliminary Report." The late Swiss archeologist Maria-Grazia Siliato, citing this report, noted that they looked at the corners of the Shroud, and that "they had seen that the homogeneity of the cloth presented considerable disparities...that is to say heavily restored." This information would suggest the inadvisability of taking samples from these precise areas.[3]

Two years before the 1988 testing, a workshop was held in Turin to discuss a second round of tests proposed by STURP. These included a variety of new testing methodologies for consideration, with carbon dating being just one of them. This was the first gathering of what would be a long series of meetings, correspondence, and negotiations involving the Pontifical Academy of Sciences, numerous scientists, both Italian and American, as well as representatives from laboratories, the Vatican, and elsewhere, each with their own interests and agendas. This would finally culminate with the carbon dating itself.

For those tests, a unified decision was made to require multiple samples from at least three different locations on the cloth. Seven prominent testing laboratories would be involved: four would employ the older proven, proportional counter method while the other three would accomplish their work using the newer nuclear accelerator (AMS) process.

The protocol offered a maximum number of checks and balances between samples and dating technologies. In addition, the tests were to be blind. The labs would not know what samples were from the Shroud versus a control sample, nor were they supposed to know the age of the control sample. Lastly, there was to be no communication between the labs prior to dating to prevent collusion.[4] The protocols were well thought out, however, as we shall see, in the intervening time from the initial conference to the actual testing, they were abandoned altogether.

*Infighting affects the process.* It wasn't long before politics entered the picture and polluted the entire affair. Infighting arose between the labs as to which ones would be finally chosen. In addition, there was a palpable tension between the Italians and the American scientists who comprised the STURP team, which had a poisoning effect on the project.[5] Many Italians were still angry over how much attention the Americans received during the first round of tests in 1978, which led to their desire to cut STURP out of the next examination completely. Harry Gove, from the University of Rochester and lead developer of the nuclear accelerator testing methodology, was heavily involved with planning, and he too wished to see STURP out of the picture. He felt they were "true believers" in the Shroud's authenticity and therefore could not be impartial—a sentiment completely at odds with reality.

Personalities, reputations, and egos—all were on full display throughout the process of deciding which tests to do, how they would be done, and who would actually do them. In other words, human nature played a large role in the increasingly messy endeavor.

The Pontifical Academy ultimately decided to eliminate any of the other proposed testings and proceed only with carbon dating. This circumstance meant that carbon dating became the decisive litmus test for authenticity for the next decade and a half. This is despite all the historical and scientific work already amassed that did not comport with a medieval date.[6]

*Testing laboratories eliminated.* In another twist, in 1987, the decision was made to eliminate all four labs that utilized the proportional counter methodology. This proven standard for the prior thirty years converts organic material to carbon dioxide gas and then counts each molecule of radioactive C-14 over several days. It is a long process but very precise.[7]

There was great concern among the carbon-dating laboratories over the decision to reduce the number of laboratories involved from seven to three. In fact, on July 5, 1987, a cable was sent to Cardinal Ballestrero of Turin, signed by all seven laboratories and the British Museum expressing the potential dangers:

> It is our collective impression that Cardinal Ballestrero has received very unwise scientific advice… The procedure that the Cardinal of Turin is suggesting is bound to produce a result that will be questioned in strictly scientific terms by many scientists around the world who will be very skeptical of the arbitrarily small statistical basis when it was well shown that a better procedure was recommended.

> *Rather than following an ill-advised procedure that will not generate a reliable date but will rather give rise to world controversy, we suggest that it would be better not to date the Shroud at all.*
>
> The new procedures…will, if implemented, yield a result for the date of the Shroud that will certainly be vigorously challenged.[8] (Emphasis added)

The nuclear accelerator mass spectrometry (AMS) method was the methodology ultimately accepted by the Italian team. It converts organic material to a carbon pellet and counts all the carbon atoms instead of just the C-14 atoms. It is a much quicker process and requires only a small amount of material, which was obviously appealing.

From today's viewpoint, this may sound reasonable; but the nuclear accelerator was a new technology and did not have the track record of proportional counter labs. This added to the concern expressed to the cardinal. The objection, however, gained no traction. The three labs chosen were in Zurich, Oxford, and Tucson; and it was the first of a cascade of poor choices that began the downward slide of the entire operation.

The next involved the Turin authorities deciding that instead of allowing three samples from different areas of the cloth, as proposed by STURP, they would limit the number of samples to one to be cut from a single location. This sample would subsequently be cut into three pieces, one for each lab—a

Location of the samples cut from the Shroud in 1988 showing how sample was divided among the three carbon 14 laboratories (Image courtesy of nuclear engineer Robert Rucker)

decision that removed all the carefully planned safeguards. All told, the most significant carbon-dating event in history would hang on the results of one sample.[9]

It soon became apparent the tests could not effectively be blind. The three control samples—two were Egyptian, one dating from AD 200 and the other, AD 1100, and the third came from the cloak of Louis IX of France dating to the mid-1200s—were all easily distinguishable from the very distinctive 3/1 weave of the Shroud. This obviated the protocol recommendation of conducting blind tests.[10]

*The sample locations selected.* But the most consequential decision was yet to come—the location of the one sample. It strains credulity that on April 21, 1988, after they spent fourteen hours observing and deliberating, the decision was made to cut the sample from the outside corner edge of the cloth, next to a small area cut in 1973 by textile expert Gilbert Raes. The selected area was chosen for one reason only—the aesthetic appearance; it would be neat and tidy.[11]

❖

The drawings and sketches below are only a small representation of the centuries of recorded exhibitions of the Shroud to vast throngs held in churches, public venues, and private showings.

*Example etchings in silk and copper showing how the Shroud was held and displayed during public exhibitions through the centuries*

Three of the scores of etchings made throughout the centuries that show church prelates and nuns exhibiting the sacred linen to crowds during special occasions. Note the manhandling and potential for contamination and damage from the hands grasping the cloth at the upper edge, the most vulnerable section of the cloth, particularly at the corner where the sample was cut for the carbon 14 tests. (All photos are in the public domain.)

The selected location had an enormous effect on the entire testing process and not on the positive. Over the centuries well over 250 public and private exhibitions occurred. May 4 was declared the official feast day of the Holy Shroud. Officials displayed it every year in Turin from 1578 to 1706 and, prior to that, every year in Chambéry from 1453 to 1577. Dozens of sketches exist showing the Shroud displayed full-length with clergy standing behind, each grasping the cloth by the corners, most notably in the precise location cut for carbon dating—the most handled and well-worn section of the entire fabric. Experts warn against sampling the edges of an artifact, which are most susceptible to contamination and possible repairs over time. This is especially true for fabric, which is highly porous and more likely to absorb contaminants, unlike solid materials such as wood or bone.[12]

*Alternate dating test reported.* Another word of caution came from archaeologist Bill Meacham, who attended the meeting in Turin in 1986 and warned of the pitfalls of C-14 if they failed to sample it correctly. He described a previous test, not formally authorized, that found dating differences within a single thread; variations in the samples could clearly present problems. Following the announcement of the dating results, Meacham issued a press release:

Shroud Dated 200–1000 AD in Secret Testing:
Results Inconsistent with Recent Dates

A closely guarded secret testing of the Shroud of Turin in 1982 by an American C-14 laboratory yielded conflicting dates of 200 AD and 1000 AD, an American archaeologist involved in Shroud research claimed today.

Mr. William Meacham of the University of Hong Kong said that members of the US scientific team which examined the Shroud in 1978 informed him that a single thread was later tested at the University of California nuclear accelerator facility.

He said separate ends of the thread gave quite different results, and the presence of starch was also detected during the pretreatment. These findings were never published because the C-14 testing did not have the approval of the Turin Authorities at the time.[13]

*Chemical evaluation protocol eliminated.* The original carbon-dating protocol required chemical evaluation of any sample removed to verify if it was consistent with the rest of the cloth. These tests were not conducted. Only visual observation was permitted. This may seem insignificant, but when the carbon tests were reduced to just one sample site, chemical analysis became critical to be certain it represented the entire cloth. Chemist Ray Rogers made the following statement in 2001:

> It is very unfortunate that the C14 samples were not better characterized because the evidence shows that it is highly probable that the samples were not characteristic of the Shroud and were spurious.[14]

*The video protocol circumvented.* There is one more piece of scientific dereliction that occurred. All the hours spent with the cloth were carefully recorded on video, including the cutting of the sample, which was done under the supervision of the overall coordinator, Dr. Michael Tite head of the scientific laboratory at the British Museum. But strangely and incomprehensively, the samples were then taken out of view of the camera into an adjoining room where they were deposited into stainless steel containers for transfer to the labs. This surprising incident conjures images of secrecy and sample switching—all because the most critical part of the procedure was not filmed[15]

There was no evidence that anything untoward occurred during this lapse, but it serves to highlight the bungling of the entire testing process. Scientists establish protocols to prevent this very thing, to eliminate questions and suspicion, yet here they were completely overlooked.

Harry Gove in his 1996 book *Relic, Icon or Hoax? Carbon Dating the Turin Shroud,* wrote of being very dissatisfied with the whole affair, even though he believed the Shroud to be medieval. He summarized all that went on during the carbon dating saga, describing it as a "shoddy enterprise,"[16] while also taking time to complain about his lab at Rochester being eliminated from the running for dating the cloth. In addition, he recounted a conversation with Teddy Hall, head of the testing lab at Oxford, who voiced his own thoughts about the sampling.

Hall thought representatives from the labs should have been at least in the next room when Tite supervised the cutting, and that they should have received the samples right there and then. He was particularly concerned that the British Museum be protected against the charge that Tite substituted samples.[17]

This anxiety over the switching of samples, or the appearance of having done so, was clearly top of mind; and yet they took the samples into another room, away from the cameras anyway.

*The results are announced.* Between April and October 1988, anticipating the announcement of the results, the media drove the story with a plethora of articles and newscasts. Every headline implied, in so many words, that the authenticity of the Shroud would soon be known. When the testing laboratories released the results on October 13, 1988, the Catholic Church, not wishing to appear anti-science, accepted the results as accurate. With so much media fanfare, they could not possibly challenge the results. After all, to blame it on the sample location or the number of samples taken would be to blame themselves.

It was nothing short of a complete fiasco. Had this been the test of a more common artifact, with questionable results or methods, an archeologist could likely order another test, or even multiple tests in different locations. The original findings would be set aside until further examination could either confirm or reject them. However, none of this was possible with the Shroud. Not only were samples limited, but for the church, there had been far too much buildup, the die was cast, and there was no choice but to publicly accept the result without challenge. Over thirty years later, there are still no plans for a reexamination.

*Cynicism on display?* Several months after the announcement of the results, on Good Friday, March 24, 1989, Oxford University made public that forty-five businessmen and wealthy benefactors had donated one million British pounds (five million dollars in today's world) to create a chair of Archaeological Sciences and Director of the Research Laboratory for Archeology. This was one of the three labs that dated the Shroud and was originally established by Dr. Edward "Teddy" Hall. No doubt the notoriety of Hall's role in the dating process was a factor in promoting the financial appeal, with the advancement of the AMS facility as a major focus. The first person to fill the chair was to be none other than Dr. Michael Tite, former head of the research laboratory of the British Museum.[18] He had fulfilled his role as the "impartial" guarantor of the carbon dating process, sharing the stage with Hall, in front of the blackboard showing the medieval dates. Tite's appointment to the chair, in light of all that went decidedly wrong surrounding the carbon dating of the Shroud, could be seen as an unfortunate irony.

It should also be noted that the sentiments expressed by Dr. Hall following the testing couldn't help but bring his professionalism as a scientist into question. In regard to the prospect of further investigation of the Shroud, he said:

> This assumes that I'm interested in solving these remaining mysteries in the first place and I'm not, to be quite honest. I haven't given it much thought, and I certainly don't intend to now that I know it's a fake. I actually find it totally uninteresting now.[19]

In addition, his response to the question of how the image on the Shroud was made was characteristically flippant: "Someone just got a bit of linen, faked it up and flogged it." He also famously derided anyone who believed in the Shroud's authenticity as flat-earthers.[20] It would be hard to imagine a greater display of cynicism and superiority.

Teddy Hall passed away in 2001, with his reputation as a strict man of science firmly intact, as described in his obituary from *The Independent* in August 2001. It was said about his role with the Shroud that "he also took pleasure in, as he saw it, the debunking of any conviction that could not be rationally demonstrated," and that, "He suspected what the answer would be, being a firm non-believer, but prejudice was never allowed to interfere with science." I think it is safe to say a lack of prejudice from Prof. Hall has been difficult to discern.

As for Michael Tite, he too showed an absence of ongoing interest. At a symposium on the Shroud held in Paris in 1989, he was interviewed for a Parisian radio program, *Radio Courtoisie*. When asked if he would be interested in further testing to solve the remaining questions, he replied, "I do not feel the need."[21] Then concurrent with a 1990 exhibition at the British Museum about the carbon dating titled "Fake," he gave a conference with the same title for the Museum Society of Haslemere. A Mr. David Boyce reported that Tite, when pressed about the image formation, "put forward the grotesque hypothesis of a Crusader crucified by the Saracens in the fourteenth century, whose decomposing body vapors would have left an imprint on the cloth in which it was buried." Such a fanciful explanation ignored all the science compiled by STURP, as well as Tite's earlier agreement at the conference that the image has three-dimensional qualities.[22]

However, in the years since retiring from his position at Oxford in 2004, Michael Tite has actually made some remarkable admissions. In an interview on the BBC program "Witness," his response to a question about what is seen in the image was quite accurate, even though he maintains his belief that the cloth is medieval. Perhaps time has opened his eyes just a little:

> Well, I think that, I mean, there is no real evidence for paint. The other oddity is, if you look at every painting from the Middle Ages and later in the Renaissance, they always paint Christ with the nails going through the palm of the hands and through the top of the foot, sort of thing. Whereas, in reality, if you are going to crucify someone, in order that they stay on the cross, you'll have to put the nails through the wrists...[23]

The foregoing incidents illustrate the all too common hubris and arrogance that permeates much of the scientific profession. This is especially apparent when dealing with topics that stray outside an adamantly held materialistic worldview. *A priori* bias and innate skepticism replace objective, fact-based inquiry for anything deemed "religious." Rather than allowing research to lead where it may, the desire to control the outcome can taint the whole process. Sadly, carbon testing the Shroud was an easy fit in this category.

*New areas of inquiry emerge*

As word leaked out about the violation of the sampling protocol along with the questionable location of the sample, legitimate skepticism began to emerge over the veracity of the results. By the mid-1990s, Dr. Alan Adler, one of the blood chemists who worked on the Shroud, analyzed spectroscopic data from the sample corner. The results showed it was not chemically consistent with the rest of the cloth. He stated:

> There is a clearly evident chemical compositional difference between the sample area and the non-image areas of the cloth.[24]

*Repair or reweave suspected.* In the year 2000, researchers Sue Benford and Joe Marino analyzed high-resolution images of the sample corner and noticed anomalies in the weave. Knowing that the Shroud had undergone various repairs that were documented over its history, they wondered if there hadn't also been additional undocumented repairs, including in the sample corner, which could account for the anomalies. They suspected a mending or repair had occurred near the corner cut for the sample, possibly utilizing a process called French invisible weaving. This process was often performed during the Middle Ages to mend expensive tapestries and clothing. It involves painstaking weaving by hand to intertwine new threads with the old for a seamless meshing of the two.[25]

Professor Raes, who examined the Oxford sample from 1988, said he observed cotton contained inside the Shroud threads, possibly accounting for their larger diameter.[26] Italian researchers Orazio Petrosillo and Emanuela Marinelli believed that the heavier, blended material may explain why the C-14 sample apparently weighed about twice as much as expected. Also, Professor Teddy Hall, head of the Oxford lab, noticed fibers that looked out of place upon microscopic examination of the Oxford C-14 sample. A laboratory in Derbyshire determined that the rogue fibers were cotton of "a fine, dark yellow strand." According to Peter South of the lab, "It may have been used for repairs at some time in the past…"[27] In addition, Giovanni Riggi, who cut the original sample, noted the size as being 8 square centimeters. However, "because fibres of other origins had become mixed up with the original fabric," it was trimmed to approximately seven square centimeters.[28]

Benford and Marino also showed photographs of the Zurich C-14 sample to three different textile experts, not divulging the identity of the sample. Each expert described various inconsistencies, such as a disparate weave pattern, different thread sizes, and evidence of mending, perhaps to prevent unraveling.

These were some of the factors that formed the basis for Benford and Marino's report on the skewing of the carbon date. Especially considering evidence of a possible "invisible" repair with foreign material, they felt strongly that the dating results would have been impacted.[29]

They submitted their hypothesis to chemist Ray Rogers, for his analysis. Rogers was decidedly skeptical, believing them to simply be over-enthusiastic zealots. But still, he was persuaded to assess Benford and Marino's findings as to the validity of their proposal.

Rogers obtained a thread from the middle of the carbon-dating sample—part of the reserve portion held back in case more material was needed in the future. He already possessed a thread from the main body of the cloth from 1978, when he was hands-on as part of the STURP team. Chemical and spectroscopic analysis clearly showed the threads were not the same. Rogers found cotton mixed in with the flax of the reserve sample. Benford and Marino appeared to be right. The corner chosen for carbon dating was not the same as the rest of the cloth and could not produce an accurate date.

Alan Adler had earlier commented,

> You have no way of knowing if the area you took the C14 sample from represents the whole cloth. That's an area which has obviously been repaired. There's cloth missing there. It's been rewoven on the edge. They even cut part of it off, because it was obviously rewoven on the edge. The simplest explanation why the date may be off is that it's rewoven cloth there. And that's not been tested.[30]

In his ongoing testing of Benford and Marino's evidence, Rogers also detected a madder root dye, perhaps used to blend in the lighter color of new cotton threads with the darker yellowed linen threads of the original cloth. In addition, he found the presence of starch, echoing the same revelation from the unauthorized testing in 1982. The starch was likely used to stiffen the threads to perform a repair. He even observed a splice where the cotton and flax threads were connected. All the ingredients needed for a medieval repair became evident.[31]

Rogers published his results in a peer-reviewed chemical journal in January 2005, along with issuing a press release on his findings. Among those findings was Rogers' discovery of vanillin, a chemical component found in the polymer lignin which gives structure to the flax fibers used to weave linen. Vanillin disappears over time at a predictable rate. A medieval-aged cloth (circa 1200) should have over 30 percent vanillin remaining whereas time would deplete the vanillin content of a first-century linen. Curiously, threads taken from the cloth body have no vanillin remaining in the lignin. Yet the radiocarbon sample from the outside corner has over 30 percent vanillin remaining. This is a powerful indicator that the C-14 sample area is younger than the rest of the cloth. Sadly, this significant story got little media attention. Had it been Easter week, secular journalists might have taken more notice. How did this not make front-page news?[32]

In March 2005, just two months after the journal published his paper, Ray Rogers died of cancer. However, before he died, Barrie Schwortz, the documenting photographer for STURP, spent four hours filming and interviewing him. The resulting video became part of Schwortz's compendious archive on his Shroud.com website, the world's largest and most comprehensive resource for Shroud research. There is not a documentary made that does not include Schwortz or his images.

Sue Benford and Joe Marino put together a significant Shroud conference in 2008 at Ohio State University in Columbus. A producer for the Discovery Channel was there and interviewed them for a documentary. Their work, and that of Ray Rogers taken from Schwortz's interview, went worldwide in the noted film, *Unwrapping the Shroud: New Evidence*. Sadly, only a few months later, Sue Benford also died from cancer. From any perspective, the combined contribution of Rogers and Benford in exposing the likely cause of the aberrant carbon date was tremendous and timely.

*Reweave questioned*. There are several Shroud researchers who take issue with the reweave theory because it has only been confirmed through intense magnification and is not apparent to the naked eye. Physicist John Jackson examined x-ray images of the corner that were taken in 1978 and was unable to discern where the repair was made. Of course, all researchers are hamstrung with limited or no access to the linen or any new material to examine. But the fact remains that there has been no reexamination of the cloth to specifically assess the possibility of a medieval repair in the sample corner.

Textile expert Mechthild Flury-Lembert played a primary role when, in 2002, the Shroud was "restored." At that time patches were removed, burn holes were trimmed to remove all charred fibers, and miscellaneous debris were vacuumed, all of which sits in vials in Turin, awaiting hoped-for future testing.[33] While involved in that process, Flury-Lembert claimed that she saw no evidence of a repair. Intriguingly, in the documentary, *Unwrapping the Shroud: New Evidence*, heavily magnified images of that sample corner appear to show a slight misalignment in the weave, one of the clues that captured the attention of Benford and Marino, as well as the three textile experts they consulted.

There have been, and continue to be, competing theories and hypotheses surrounding the characterization of the sample corner, but the combination of Benford and Marino's research with the chemical analysis and fiber examination by Ray Rogers created an especially compelling argument. At the very least, there has been more than enough evidence presented to conclude that the area chosen for carbon dating was not representative of the entire cloth.

*New alternate testing renders first-century date*. In 2013, scientists with Padua University in Italy, led by tireless researcher Giulio Fanti, took an innovative route for dating the Shroud. Fanti's team started by collecting samples of linen with known dates spanning five thousand years. The scientists analyzed a dozen representative samples, measuring the amount of chemical decay in each. They used two methods—Fourier transform infrared spectroscopy and Raman spectroscopy. Both tests measure how a substance reacts when subjected to electromagnetic radiation and creates a chemical signature specific to the substance being measured.

In addition, multiparametric mechanical tests were conducted to assess mechanical decay—i.e., the tensile strength of the samples. Fabric becomes weaker and more brittle as it gets older. Fanti and his team established a plotline of predictable chemical and mechanical decay for all their samples.

The linen samples included two modern fibers, two from the Middle Ages, one from the first century, two from around 200 BC, and three with dates ranging from 1000 to 3500 B.C. The same three techniques were used to assess fiber samples from the Shroud. By comparing the amount of chemical and mechanical decay of Shroud fibers to that of the known linen samples, it was found that the comparative results aligned with a five-hundred-year date range of 280 BC to AD 220, with the first century right in the middle.[34]

Critics of this study take issue with the methodology not having been previously used for this application, namely dating ancient cloths. However, I applaud Fanti for his resourcefulness when facing the reality that the Turin authorities have not allowed further direct access to the Shroud. His results, in turn, helped raise more questions about the accuracy of the carbon dating.

*Lack of full disclosure of C-14 results.* Perhaps the most striking revelation following the 1988 testing was the fact that not all the data were provided with the report of findings published in the scientific journal *Nature,* in 1989. The British Museum, represented by Michael Tite, was the clearing house for all the raw data.

For the past thirty years, various researchers have requested that all raw data be released for review, but remarkably to no avail. Finally, in 2017, as a result of several Freedom of Information Act (FOIA) requests to the British Museum and the carbon labs, the data became available. The museum provided some 200 pages, (unfortunately, not organized in any coherent manner), to French researcher Tristan Casabianca, and colleagues. Casabianca subsequently visited the museum where he was able to scan an additional 500 pages, creating a compendium of information. Of course, this begs the question, why wasn't all of the data published in 1989, and why did it take a FOIA request to obtain it? The answer lies in the coveted claim by the labs of having a "95 percent confidence level" for their carbon dating results. Casabianca et al. proceeded to investigate.

The carbon labs each had enough sample material to run multiple tests. Arizona ran forty separate measurements, Zurich also performed forty, and Oxford conducted five measurements. All told, there were eighty-five separate measurements.

When assessing the complete data, Casabianca and his team analyzed differences in raw data reported by the individual labs versus data included for publication in *Nature*. The statistical analysis revealed not only the complex procedures involved that varied between labs but also the question of possible outlier dates and how they were reported...collectively, individually, weighted? Some of the variables included computer errors for which adjustments were made, as well as the discovery by both the Oxford and Arizona labs of foreign material on some subsamples. These included threads of different colors, a thread identified as cotton, as well as various debris. Interestingly, while the dates of the Shroud samples showed wide variations, the control samples of known age did not.

The overall results, factoring in all the raw data, showed there to be up to a 190-year age difference for the Shroud between the three labs, and a 161-year age difference within the same lab. This is highly significant. The industry standard when comparing the results of multiple labs is to have greater than 60 percent agreement between them for reliability. However, when all data was factored in, the overall agreement between the labs dropped to 28.4 percent. A similar phenomenon was seen within the individual labs. A study of the Arizona data shows an overall agreement index of 34.6%, well below the standard. Defenders of the C-14 tests would say it is expected to find variation between labs due to differences in equipment or calibration settings. However, that doesn't explain how there could be such a large difference in the results of the same lab measuring the same sample.

Casabianca worked in collaboration with important scholars including Emanuella Marinelli, author of several books on the Shroud; Giuseppe Pernagallo, a data analyst at the University of Catania; and Benedetto Torrisi, associate professor of economic statistics at the University of Catania.[35] Together they determined that an overall lack of precision suggests the need for retesting with strong protocols. Their landmark paper, "Radiocarbon Dating of the Turin Shroud: New Evidence from Raw Data," was published in the October 2019 issue of *Archaeometry*, with the following statement:

> Without this re-analysis, it is not possible to affirm that the 1988 radiocarbon dating offers "conclusive evidence" that the calendar age range is accurate and representative of the whole cloth.[36]

Later, in a 2020 interview with National Catholic Register, Tristan Casabianca said,

> Secular media called carbon dating a triumph of science over religion. Instead, it was a failure of the scientific process.[37]

*More challenges to carbon dating—wide-angle x-ray scattering (WAXS).* The latest research, published in 2022, adds yet another obstacle to the defense of the medieval carbon date. A new examination, using a Shroud fiber from an area away from the questionable sample, near the front image of the feet, assessed the amount of natural aging of the cellulose in the linen. The test was carried out by Dr. Liberato de Caro, et al, of the Institute of Crystallography, a division of the National Research Council in Bari, Italy, using wide-angle x-ray scattering (WAXS). This new method is considered superior to carbon dating for determining the age of linen. In an interview with the National Catholic Register, de Caro made the following observation regarding carbon dating difficulties:

> Molds and bacteria, colonizing textile fibers, and dirt or carbon-containing minerals, such as

limestone, adhering to them, in the empty spaces between the fibers that at a microscopic level represent about 50% of the volume, can be difficult to completely eliminate in the sample cleaning phase, which can distort the dating.[38]

The new tests used the wide-angle x-ray technology on both the Shroud sample and a variety of textile samples with verified ages spanning five thousand years, from the current era back to 3000 BC. Thus, comparisons could be made. Multiple calculations and tests were performed on all samples using the X-ray dating method. In the case of the Shroud, they also considered historical environmental factors of the types noted above, along with temperatures and humidity, in drawing conclusions. The sample that had the best correlation with fibers from the Shroud was a piece of fabric from the Siege of Masada (Israel) and is known to date from AD 55 to AD 74.

The WAXS examinations showed that the amount of natural aging seen in fibers from the Shroud far exceeds what would be possible in the mere seven centuries claimed by the carbon labs.[39] It also corroborates the spectrographic method of measuring decay pioneered by Giulio Fanti in 2013. The report of the results by de Caro, et al, was subjected to peer review and published in the journal *Heritage* on April 11, 2022.

*Conclusion*

The carbon-14 dating in 1988 was seen by many as the last word on the possibility of the Shroud being the authentic 2000-year-old burial garment of Jesus of Nazareth. With 95 percent confidence, the labs made their declaration, punctuating it on the blackboard with an exclamation point, implying that the book was now closed, with no need to ever open it again. In addition, public statements afterward from prominent players such as Teddy Hall and Michael Tite revealed the contempt in which they held many of the Shroud scientists and researchers.

But the circumstances outlined in this chapter, from the complications and wrong turns surrounding the testing to the significant work that has been done since, both in evaluating the veracity of the conclusions and introducing newer dating methods, serve to bring perspective to that controversial project.

Beyond the surrounding drama, serious Shroud scientists and researchers are well aware of the shortcomings of C-14 as a single source for dating; typically it is combined with other tests to arrive at a reasonable result. The hoped-for goal was always to establish, if possible, a reliable, conclusive time frame for the Shroud, understanding that first-century dating was not necessarily a foregone conclusion.

A multi-disciplinary approach continues to be the guide in the quest to answer the many unsolved mysteries that remain. Carbon dating is but one element in the toolbox, and having been shown to be far from the last word, its relevance continues to diminish.

For those who believe that the Shroud is the work of a medieval artist, however, the testing has bolstered their argument. For them, the mystery is solved and the answer was there all along. Only, it might not be that easy. As a coda to part 1, which began by looking at various attempts to replicate the Shroud, chapter 9 will take a look at how well the medieval artist theory holds up by looking at examples of fourteenth-century art and copies of the Shroud from later centuries.

This will be a natural segue to part 2, which will introduce significant historical documentation that further challenges a medieval date of origin. Beginning before the Middle Ages, the long historical trail will help to amplify the "preponderance of evidence" in favor of authenticity.

# PART 2

The Long Winding Road:
Following the Historical Trail

CHAPTER 9

---

The Challenge of Art History

Up to this point, we have covered the scientific research performed on the Shroud including the forensics of the body, the blood chemistry, the nature of the image, and the nature of the Shroud as an ancient textile. The previous chapter, the saga of the troubling carbon dating, brings us back to our fundamental either-or proposition: if it isn't the authentic burial shroud of Jesus, then it must be manmade, and for that scenario, a medieval artist must fit the bill. But could such an artist have created the image and blood flow patterns seen on the Shroud? Is there anyone in the fourteenth century who had the skills and knowledge necessary?

Here we will look to art historians to give us a crash course on medieval art, the conventions, the expectations, and actual examples, to illustrate why this theory faces serious challenges not easily explained away. Then we will look at a number of later copies of the Shroud to see if they hold any place in the discussion of fakes or forgeries.

*Thomas de Wesselow—the Shroud image is foreign to its historical epoch.* Thomas de Wesselow studied art history at Edinburgh University and went on to earn his master's and PhD at London's Courtauld Institute of Art. He served as an art historian at King's College in Cambridge, and has been engaged in ongoing research on the Shroud. As someone well-versed in that topic, as well as the world of medieval art, he made the following observation:

> One might have expected study of the Shroud to take on a new complexion after 1988. Accepting the carbon dating, art historians should have leaped on the Shroud as one of the most fascinating visual creations of the medieval period, a true masterpiece of devotional imagery. Strangely though, they have remained almost entirely silent. The reason is simple: the negative photo of the cloth is an unmistakable sign that the Shroud's famous image could not have been created by a medieval artist. Technically, conceptually, and stylistically, the Shroud makes no sense as a medieval artwork. The discipline of art history has had over a century to study the Shroud since it was first photographed, and in all that time no art historian has ever ventured to attribute it to a medieval artist.[1]

De Wesselow makes the case that something as profound as the Shroud would not have entered the mind or imagination of a fourteenth-century artist. The analogy would be like finding a seven-hundred-year-old painting in a style like Salvador Dali in a French Gothic cathedral. But why not? All the paint materials were available. The answer is that art evolves. Dali's style derives from artistic knowledge built upon Renaissance artists, neoclassicists, Romanticists, realists, Impressionists, and eventually the many schools of modern art. Dali's work is the culmination of all these periods of artistic expression. To suggest the Shroud is the effort of a medieval artist is as unlikely as the same artist producing a Dali-style painting at a time when nothing was remotely similar.

# SHROUD ENCOUNTER

Elaborating on this theme, de Wesselow states:

> The sense of the uncanny that emanates from the cloth is due, above all, to its singularity, its radical dissimilarity from anything else known. The sensation of being in the presence of a bona fide mystery, something so anomalous that it defies, to some extent, the human capacity to understand, is one that no mechanical reproduction can possibly convey.[2]

*Specific imagery of the body.* To illustrate some of the remarkable features of the Shroud, de Wesselow looks specifically at the bloodstain patterns and how they defy the artistic convention of that era. He addresses each area of the body.

*The head wounds from the crown of thorns*

Indeed, the bloodstains on both the frontal and dorsal images of the head look like no artistic representation of blood that I know—medieval or otherwise. It is extraordinarily difficult to disguise habitual methods of depiction, and when artists try to simulate blood flows the results are always more-or-less formulaic.[3]

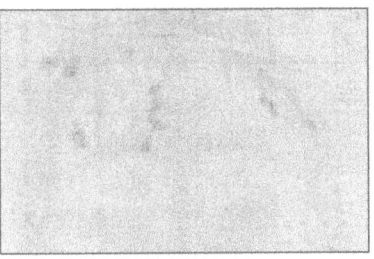

Natural image of the head wounds
(Image courtesy of Barrie M. Schwortz collection, STERA Inc.)

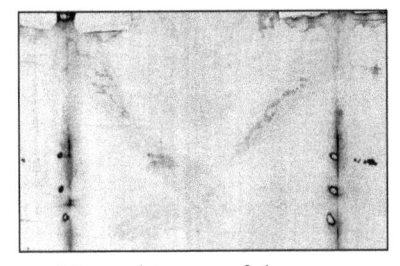

Natural image of the arms
(Image courtesy of Barrie M. Schwortz collection, STERA Inc.)

*The arms*

> Medieval artists never depicted such blood flows on the body of the dead Christ. They imagined blood dribbling from the hand wounds but left the forearms clean... The likelihood that the forearm stains are the work of a medieval painter is virtually nil.[4]

*The whip marks*

> The vast majority of medieval images of the dead or dying Christ fail to depict any scourge marks at all. This may be because it was generally assumed that the flogging only affected Christ's back. There are a few paintings that depict the scourging, but they are all crude and show no knowledge of the Roman flagrum. To attribute the marks on the Shroud to a provincial unknown working in the mid-fourteenth century is therefore ridiculous.[5]

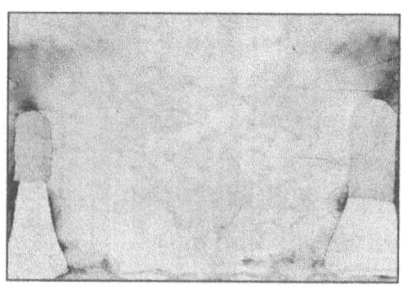

Natural image of the scourged back (Image courtesy of Barrie M. Schwortz collection, STERA Inc.)

Furthermore, it was virtually unknown for an artist to venture outside the creative convention of the time. De Wesselow explains that to do so:

> would have been nonsensical and shocking—even unthinkable—in the Middle Ages, when artists were bound by theological and devotional requirements.[6]

As a result, during this period, the nail wounds were always shown in the palm of the hand. If the Shroud were a medieval painting, then it would have been an unheard-of break with convention to depict the wound in the wrist. Besides, this was long before any awareness of medical experiments that would show the necessity of that location to hold the weight of a body for any length of time.

*The pool of blood across the lower back*

No medieval artist ever painted anything resembling the dorsal pools on the Shroud… Christ was the manifestation of the divine on earth, and no one would have ever represented his Holy Blood as a messy puddle, unconnected with his wounds… More than any other mark on the cloth, the blood and water across the back are inconceivable as part of a medieval forgery.[7]

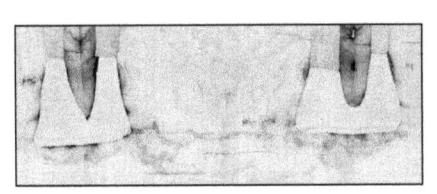

Natural image of lower back as seen on the Shroud (Image courtesy of Barrie M. Schwortz collection, STERA Inc.)

With the combination of the preceding elements, De Wesselow clearly challenges the concept of a medieval artist having created the Shroud. He explains that the depiction of the dramatic blood spatters alone represents an insurmountable contradiction for that time in history:

It stretches credulity to think that in the Middle Ages, an era of rigid stylization, anyone could have designed such a convincing spattering…or even wanted to. To regard these haphazard dabs and runnels of blood as fourteenth-century brushwork is to ignore the limits of medieval art and to misunderstand the whole tenor of medieval thought.[8]

*Isabel Piczek.* A refugee from Hungary, Isabel Piczek was an artistic prodigy. At the age of fourteen, she painted, along with her sister, a four-hundred-square-foot mural in the Vatican's Pontifical Biblical Institute. She became highly knowledgeable in all forms of art and became known for creating large-scale works of art that reside in nearly five hundred buildings around the world. She was also a dedicated Shroud researcher. As for the Shroud being a painting, she explains:

> No painting will yield more knowledge than the painter has put into it, yet the Shroud yields more and more knowledge with each new examination.[9]

Here, Isabel details more of what constitutes a painting, negating, also, some of the arguments discussed earlier in chapter 1.

> First and above all, a painting always is the result of an educated, conscious, and intelligent activity. It is never a strange, single item. It faultlessly fits into the cultural era of its time, either as its member or as its consequence, creating the next necessary step. The Turin Shroud does not fit this definition at all.
>
> In spite of what lay people hold to be true, a painting does not depend on paint particles. It thoroughly and solely depends on the paint mediums, binders in liquid forms, mediums that tie the paint particles to each other and to the paint background. This creates a continuous film that alone carries the image consciously willed by the painter to appear on a surface. By natural law, it can only be a visible and continuous image while the medium film remains intact. Once it

begins to disintegrate, chunks of the image or the painting will be missing.

The image on the Turin Shroud is an intact, continuous image without any continuous paint medium film. This is the strongest and most definite proof that the Shroud is not a painting.[10]

In de Wesselow and Piczek, we have two experts in the field of art, and particularly the era of the Middle Ages. Their accounts of how the Shroud stylistically differs from all the elements expected of a medieval artist, including known artistic materials and mediums, serve to reinforce the extreme unlikelihood of its having been created in the fourteenth century. In addition, de Wesselow's telling observation bears repeating that due largely to the undeniable significance of the photographic negative, almost no art historian in the last century has seen fit to attribute the Shroud to a medieval artist, except one.

*Skeptic and art historian, Dr. Gary Vikan.* Contrary to our experts' learned opinions, art historian, Dr. Gary Vikan, offers a different spin on the topic. Dr. Vikan, former director of the Walter's Art Museum in Baltimore, asserts that the Shroud is a fourteenth-century hoax, and published his theory in his 2020 book, *The Holy Shroud: A Brilliant Hoax in the Time of the Black Death*. Declaring that "this is not a clever painting,"[11] Vikan elevates the Shroud image to the very pinnacle in the realm of art:

> An artistic achievement without precedent in the history of art. The Shroud's creator was more than a technical genius—he was a gifted artist, working at the intersection of art and science.[12]

Dr. Vikan's declarations echo those who choose to disregard the contradictory historical and artistic evidence, as outlined above, as well as the abundance of scientific data. His unique contribution, however, is that he has gone so far as to name the artist he believes was responsible: Naddo Ceccarelli, (d. 1360) a devoted student of Italian artist Simone Martini (1284–1344), master of the Sienese style of art originating in Siena, Italy. Coming from an art historian, this would seem to warrant some acceptance. However, we will see that, based solely on de Wesselow's principles of artistic style in the Middle Ages, Vikan's hypothesis is woefully misguided. (I will note that Vikan's complete explanation makes for entertaining reading of the absurd, for anyone who would like to consult his book.)

The following sequence of Ceccarelli's known paintings provides a stark comparison of how his artistic composition and anatomical details radically differ from the Shroud image.

*Ceccarelli artistic style comparison with the Shroud*

Fourteenth-century crucifixion scene painting—artist, Naddo Ceccarelli (public domain)

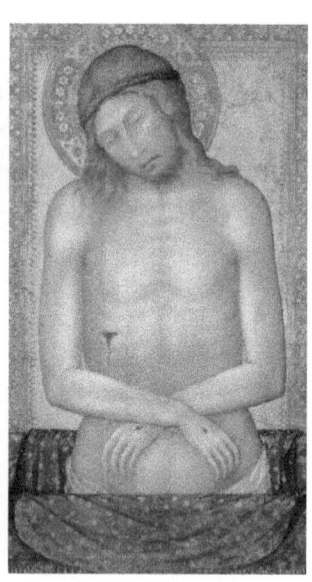

*Christ as the Man of Sorrows*—artist, Naddo Ceccarelli, ca. 1347 (Liechtenstein collection)

The above side-by-side large images are Naddo Ceccarelli's cruxification scene (ca. 1350) and *Man of Sorrows*, painted around 1347. The following close-ups of the head, hands, arms, torso, and side wound can be compared with the Shroud images and the critique offered by Thomas de Wesselow.

*The head image.* Notice no obvious crown of thorns, no puncture wounds, and no blood rivulets on the head or face as seen on the Shroud.

*The side wound.* The blood is crudely spewing like a faucet from Jesus's side wound with no evidence of "water." Blood would not spurt without the heart pumping. The Shroud shows blood that oozed with a clear separation of blood and serum, thought to be water by the apostle John. Ceccarelli's *Man of Sorrows* shows only a miniscule amount of blood flowing from the side wound and no serum separation.

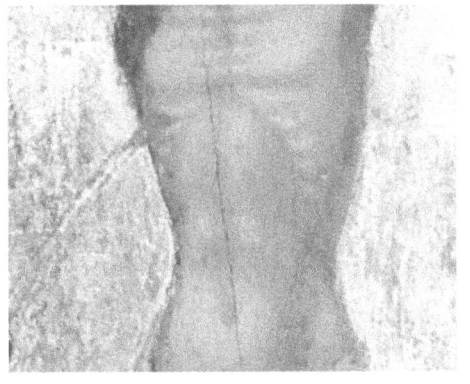

*The chest.* Again, referring to the close-up of the torso showing the side wound, there is a complete absence of scourge marks. Yet the Shroud image shows numerous scourge marks on the chest and thighs. Most medieval artists assumed the whipping was applied only to the back.

*The hand.* The nails are clearly in the palm, consistent with the artistic standards of the time. The Shroud, as we know, shows the wound in the wrist.

*Arm and hand.* In the large crucifixion scene, notice that the blood pours straight down into the angel's chalice. On the Shroud, the blood oozes down the arm naturally and pools at the elbow.

*Position of arms and hands.* Not seen in the crucifixion painting above but clearly viewed in Ceccarelli's *Man of Sorrows*, the arms are crossed over the lower chest, not the pelvis as seen on the Shroud. The burial linen shows far more realistic evidence of foreshortening with the shoulders and knees drawn up, allowing the hands to naturally cover the groin area.

*Loincloth.* As with all sacred art from the fourteenth century, Jesus is depicted in a loincloth or modesty cloth. The Shroud shows a man clearly naked.

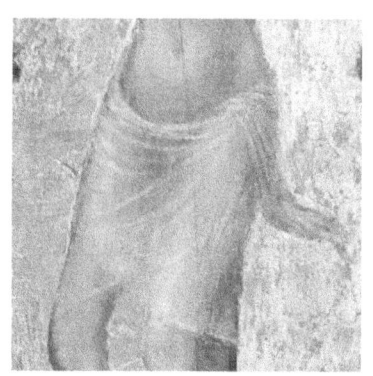

*The feet.* The only part of Ceccarelli's crucifixion painting that compares with the Shroud is the position of the feet with one foot placed upon the other secured by a nail.

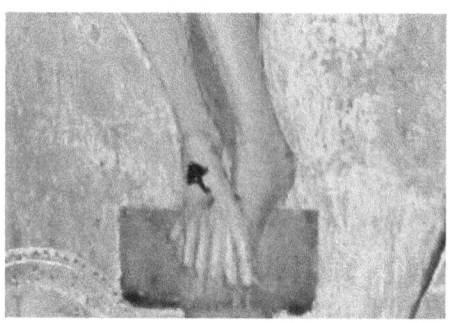

*Commentary on the artistic comparison of Ceccarelli and the Shroud image.* Does it seem remotely plausible that an artist who has spent a lifetime developing an artistic style with respect to the depiction of Jesus, following the artistic principles of the time, would suddenly abandon all his training, and mysteriously develop a completely new representation? Would he utilize an entirely different painting mechanism using an unknown technique to create a faint body imprint while incorporating medical knowledge not known at the time? And all intended to pull off the fraud of the millennium? In the case of the alleged painter Ceccarelli, this scenario simply has no foundation. In the end, the theory presented by Dr. Vikan, an art historian, appears to have all the ingredients of a good story rather than applying the demands of professional rigor.

*The history of Shroud copies from the sixteenth to the eighteenth century*

Beginning in the sixteenth century, copies of the Shroud started being produced not as nefarious frauds but rather as devotional art, which was common in an era in which photography did not exist.

Shroud skeptics often point to these examples and pose the cynical question, with all the known copies, how do we know the Shroud of Turin is the real deal and not just a copy itself? The answer will become obvious.

Don Luigi Fossati was born in Turin in 1920 and was a beloved priest and devoted scholar of the Shroud. He conducted a comprehensive study and comparison of all the known copies of the Shroud created from the sixteenth through the eighteenth centuries. He included only those done on cloth and close in size to the original, with a special focus on the different face images with comparison to icon images known for their artistic beauty.

Some of the copies were done directly from the original and are noted either on the cloth itself or in the documents of authentication signed by the bishop of Turin. Others were made indirectly from models or previous renderings. These were authorized copies created as gifts to be presented to monasteries, convents, prelates, and nobles, as well as relatives of the royal Savoy family, owners of the linen from 1453 to 1983. Most notably, each one had been placed in direct contact with the Sacred Shroud, pressed to the cloth's surface, face-to-face, thereby elevating the work to venerable status as a sanctioned relic. This practice, as we have seen, would also leave microscopic paint particles on the original linen, to be found by scientists hundreds of years later.

Of these painted copies, some show a Shroud that is much darker than the original, yet others portray a faint image as seen today. The bloodstains do not appear to be exaggerated in their depictions, countering claims the blood was more vivid and more visibly red in earlier times.

For the most part, these copies are crude and simplistic. None of them appear lifelike, nor are they able to capture the subtleties of the twentieth-century photo-negative image. All of them appear as obvious manmade efforts, and cursory examination would reveal the substances used. Their value was derived from all having touched the original. They were meant to represent what was known about the Shroud image at that time, even painting in the burns and subsequent patches sewn onto the original in 1534. But not one came close to emulating the wonderful realism of the Turin Shroud. Fossati could readily see that none of the examples bore any likeness to the traditional artistic representations, as seen in the devotional art of Naddo Ceccarelli, which conformed to accepted portrayals that often looked to classical models for inspiration. All told, we can see that these copies, which differ so markedly from the Shroud's realism, could never be mistaken for the original.

Full-length copies of the Shroud dated from 1571 to 1653
(Image attribution: Luigi Fossati, *Shroud Spectrum*, public domain)

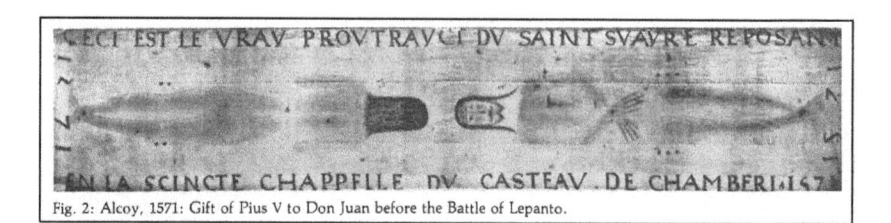

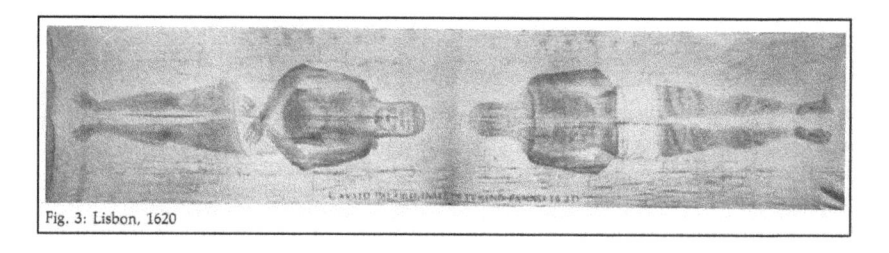

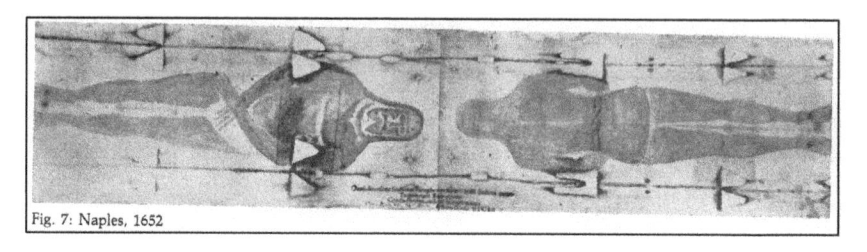

Fig. 2: Alcoy, 1571: Gift of Pius V to Don Juan before the Battle of Lepanto.

Fig. 3: Lisbon, 1620

Fig. 7: Naples, 1652

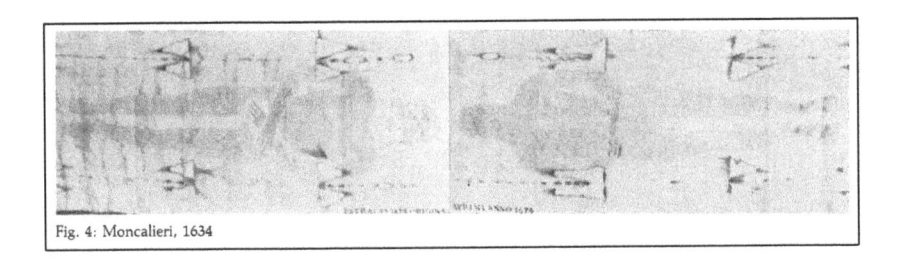

Fig. 4: Moncalieri, 1634

The following are representative of face images from the Fossati studies of full-length Shroud copies dating from the sixteenth to eighteenth centuries. (Image attribution: Luigi Fossati, *Shroud Spectrum*, public domain)

*The faded-image allegation.* The characteristic faintness of the image on the Shroud has given rise to common allegations related to the medieval artist theory. The argument is that it was painted, and the paint has obviously flaked off over the last few centuries, leaving the faint residue we see today.

To counter this skeptical view, it is particularly helpful to consult contemporary sources who viewed the Shroud centuries ago. These firsthand reports also give strength to the understanding that the image has no outline, as from an artist's brush.

When St. Charles Borromeo made his pilgrimage to Turin in 1578 to venerate the Shroud, Francesco Adorno was in his company and wrote in a letter how no outline to the image can be seen:

> One sees the frontal and dorsal sides of Christ, and in a really remarkable way, one discerns all the parts of his most holy body, even though *one cannot see how the lines of the figure were drawn.*[13] (Emphasis added)

The saint's biographer, Charles Bascapé Barnabite, was also with him in the pilgrimages of 1578 and 1582. After the second journey, he wrote:

> Of no use here the master hands of Buonarotti or Titian, for these holy forms, even if *they resemble most a first faint sketch than a finished work*, are as far above whatever artwork, be it ever so perfect and rare, as death and artificial images are surpassed by truth and life.[14] (Emphasis added)

Another friend of St. Charles, Agostino Cusano of the Marquises of Somma, remembering the Turin celebrations of 1578, described how obscure and faint the image seemed to be:

> The whole figure is rather obscure, like the first sketch of a painting, that now you see it, now you don't.[15]

Well before the sixteenth century, there were accounts of the Shroud image appearing very faint. Shortly after 944, a lengthy *Narratio de Imagine Edessena*, a narration, was written under the auspices of Constantine VII, in which the image was described as extremely faint and appearing "as a moist secretion without pigment or painter's art." This echoes what STURP determined in 1978.[16]

In addition, the Byzantine Greek historian, Symeon Magister, writing his *Chronographia*, asserted that Constantine VII, himself, could see the faint image, while his two brothers-in-law could "barely make out an outline." These reports not only add confirmation of the faintness of the image very early on but also chronicle the Shroud's existence over a thousand years ago.[17]

*Commentary:* Our enlightening evaluation of medieval art directly confronts the contention that an artist of that period could have, or even would have, had the inclination or ability to create the Shroud. The examination of a specific artist as a candidate exposes the dubiousness of that suggestion. In the end, the continuing desire by some to hold to this belief and ignore the historical evidence, common sense and, importantly, the findings of science, represent a bridge too far.

In addition, by reviewing and comparing the known copies of the Shroud it's easy to see that they bear no resemblance to the original, except in subject matter. To try to claim that any one of them could be the "real" shroud rather than the linen cloth residing in Turin is an absurdity. These were devotional works meant to be given as gifts. As such, they reveal heartfelt efforts to honor a divine and mysterious subject.

Finally, both tenth-century and sixteenth-century narratives confirm the faintness of the image as a well-documented feature—not easily explained.

After giving the artistic theory a fair hearing, we venture now into the historical trail of the Shroud to further our discoveries.

# CHAPTER 10

## Clues from the Early Centuries
## Piecing Together the Historical Trail

After covering all the missteps of carbon dating and new data that challenges the 1988 results, it behooves one to examine other dating evidence found in the historical trail. To put this in perspective, the oldest carbon date for the cloth is 1260, as published by the British Museum. However, there is strong contradictory evidence that indicates a much earlier origin.

Due to the ravages of fires, floods, war, and natural decay, historical documents become sparse as the historian searches further back in time for elusive clues. The distant past becomes murky due to the interplay between the historical record and the received wisdom of the various legendary accounts. As a result, following the Shroud trail in the early centuries is less tidy than documenting its history from the Crusades forward. But there are powerful threads one can follow to discern its early history. It is the historian's job to research, separate truth from fiction, and end up with a plausible sequence of events, and that is what Ian Wilson and others have done so admirably over the past decades. With their discoveries as guideposts, we will illuminate this fascinating trail, which begins in Edessa.

*Eusebius, Jude, and King Abgar V.* The writings of Eusebius, the official historian for the emperor Constantine is a good place to start the historical journey. He lived from AD 260 to AD 340 and became the bishop of Caesarea in ancient Israel. He was the first to tackle the history of the early Christian church in his ten volumes of *Ecclesiastical History*, circa AD 325, a work of enormous importance to scholars of antiquity. While researching for his first volume, he travelled to the city-state of Edessa in Syria and transcribed documents kept in the record office there—records that had been there long before Eusebius's arrival. Located four hundred miles north of Jerusalem, the city was formerly part of Syria but is now called Şanlıurfa in southern Turkey. It has been in Turkish control since the Ottoman Empire conquered the area in 1637.[1]

Edessa was a prominent city along the trade route known as the Silk Road, between the Near and Far East. Traders would pass from ancient Israel through Edessa on their way to India and China and back again. Word of Jesus traveled with the traders, who related the stories of an amazing teacher-prophet performing miracles around Jerusalem.

It is from the pages of Eusebius's accounts that the story of King Abgar V appears, the monarch of Edessa, which incorporates the apostle Jude. First described as "Judas, Not Iscariot," his name was shortened to Jude to avoid confusion with the one who betrayed Jesus. He is also referred to as Thaddaeus or Addai in Aramaic and sometimes Jude Thaddaeus.[2]

Eusebius began his account of Jude's sojourn in Syria by documenting the great number of people who had heard of Christ's miracles and how they traveled to Judea in search of the prophet who healed the sick and raised the dead. The historian described how King Abgar V heard of these accounts and was hopeful for relief of his own suffering from a terrible physical disorder, possibly leprosy. He sent a messenger to Jerusalem, Ananias, with a letter crafted by the king as an appeal to Jesus. The following is the text of the Abgar's letter as recorded by Eusebius.

> Abgar, ruler of Edessa, to Jesus, the good physician who has appeared in the country of Jerusalem, greeting. I have heard the reports of you and of your cures as performed by you without medicines or herbs. For it is said that you

make the blind to see and the lame to walk, that you cleanse lepers and cast out impure spirits and demons, that you heal those afflicted with lingering disease, and raise the dead. And having heard all these things concerning you, I have concluded that one of two things must be true: either you are God and having come down from heaven you do these things, or else you, who does these things, are the son of God. I have therefore written to you to ask you if you would take the trouble to come to me and heal all the ill which I suffer. For I have heard that the Jews are murmuring against you and are plotting to injure you. I have a very small yet noble city which is great enough for us both.[3]

Ananias returned to Edessa with the following reply conveyed from Jesus.

Blessed are you who have believed in me without having seen me. For it is written concerning me, that they who have seen me will not believe in me, and that they who have not seen me will believe and be saved. But in regard to what you have written me, that I should come to you, it is necessary for me to fulfill all things here for which I have been sent, and after I have fulfilled them thus to be taken up again to him that sent me. But after I have been taken up, I will send to you one of my disciples, that he may heal your disease and give life to you and yours.[4]

As recorded by Eusebius, following the ascension of Jesus the apostle Jude traveled to Edessa and began preaching and working miracles among the people. Word of Jude's presence in the city reached Abgar, who reasoned that he was the disciple Jesus had promised would come to heal him. The king sent for him, and as Jude entered the king's court, Abgar experienced a "great vision" on the apostle's countenance and prostrated himself on the floor. The nobles who were present were stunned by the king's reaction as none had seen Abgar's vision.

When Abgar asked Jude if it were true that he was the disciple of Jesus who was sent to cure him, Jude's response was in keeping with the apostle's mission:

> Because you mightily believed in him that sent me, therefore have I been sent unto you. And still further, if you believe in him, the petitions of your heart shall be granted according to your faith... Therefore I place my hand upon you in his [Jesus's] name.

Immediately Abgar was cured of the disease and of his suffering.

Eusebius's account in the *Ecclesiastical History* also reports that all of Jude's healings and miracles were done with the laying on of hands, using the authority that Jesus gave his apostles, without the use of herbs and medicines. The document further records that Jude cured "many other inhabitants of the city with his wonders and marvelous works."

Upon King Abgar's healing, he commanded the citizenry of his realm to hear the preaching of Jude Thaddeus. In gratitude, he was offered gold and silver, which were firmly turned down by the apostle, who felt God's work did not require monetary gifts.

Regarding Eusebius's transcription of Jesus's letter that gives rise to this encounter, some critics say it incorporates things written in the Gospels, which came later. However, the Gospel accounts of what Jesus said and did began very shortly after his death as oral accounts and were compiled as a written record in the ensuing decades. In addition, Eusebius has been considered the greatest historian of the early Christian church, which adds credence to his reporting.[5]

The Gospel of Matthew lends additional credibility to the Abgar-Jesus letter when it describes the fame of Jesus throughout Syria, encompassing the city-state where King Abgar made his throne:

> News about him spread all over Syria and people brought to him all who were ill with various diseases—those suffering severe pain, the demon-possessed, those having seizures, and the paralyzed—and he healed them. (Matthew 4:24 NIV)

Further still, people living in Şanlıurfa today (formerly Edessa) are very familiar with the Abgar story and passionately believe it dates to the time of Christ. It is part of their ancient cultural tradition.[6]

*A second version of the Abgar story.* A later version of the story emerged in the early fifth century that came from a source named the *Doctrine of Addai*. Addai, as mentioned, was the name of Jude in Aramaic. This story, known as the "picture version," has the same core as the fourth-century Eusebius-Abgar-Jude story but with an interesting addition that interjects a cloth that takes on the characteristics of the Shroud. The tale goes that as Ananias was trying to convince Jesus to come to Edessa, he was told it was not possible due to Jesus's committed destiny with the cross. As consolation, he attempted to paint a picture of Jesus for the king but was unable to capture his likeness from the "brilliance of his being." As a remedy, Jesus took Ananias's cloth, pressed it to his face, and miraculously transferred his image, which cured the king.[7] This

Icon of King Abgar holding the Mandylion, the image of Christ (encaustic, tenth century, St. Catherine's Monastery, Mount Sinai; public domain—Creative Commons)

version with Jesus pressing his face to the cloth is associated with a Greek account of the story; however, the Syriac version has Ananias painting the image of Jesus using "choice paints."[8]

In the sixth century, yet another version of the *Doctrine of Addai* emerged that described Jude as the person delivering the miraculous image of Jesus to King Abgar, which resulted in his healing. Some scholars believe that the "vision" the king experienced in the previous telling was the folded Shroud showing just the face. However, this would have been readily seen by those in attendance, making this version seem unreasonable. The Doctrine of Addai is likely a blending of the two accounts. For more context, there is compelling circumstantial evidence and educated inference for another scenario of how the Shroud arrived in Edessa.[9]

*Dangerous lands—the Shroud secreted out of Jerusalem to Edessa.* In order to lay a foundation connecting the early church with the Shroud and its movements, it is important to look at the unfolding historical events in the region during the tumultuous first century. Scholars believe that Peter went to Antioch and later returned to Jerusalem prior to AD 44. At the time, Herod Agrippa had been aggressively suppressing followers of Christ. The Christian community was in disarray.

It is not unreasonable to believe that Jude also returned to Jerusalem from his travels in Syria, rejoining others to share encouragement and support at this time of constant danger. With this backdrop, the church leaders would have felt a great urgency to preserve and protect anything related to Jesus, with the Shroud being especially vulnerable to destruction from both the Jewish and Roman authorities. But where could they hope to take it?

It is recorded that as Jude and Simon the Zealot traveled throughout Syria as a team, they converted over sixty thousand people to the faith, which offered the increasing security of numbers in a hostile world.[10] King Abgar, too, had become a faithful follower through the ministry of Jude and was the leader of a well-fortified city outside the reach of the Roman Empire. Edessa was a perfect choice for preserving the Shroud. The city was situated in a neutral zone between the Roman Empire and the Parthian Empire of Persia.

It remained an independent city, controlled by neither power, until 239. Not until then did the Romans end the Abgar monarchy and absorb the city into the Roman province of Osroene.[11]

Some researchers believe the Shroud was taken to Antioch, however, the city was annexed by Rome in 64 BC and was the capital of Roman-occupied Syria. It was the third largest city of the empire, and while it's true that many Christians lived there, the strong ongoing Roman influence meant safety for the Shroud would be questionable. Edessa, on the other hand, was, at that time, a haven, far away from the Jews and the Romans who were intent on persecuting Christians.

The belief that Jude made a second journey to Edessa, this time to secret the Shroud to safety, is not out of the question, and also makes a distinction between his two meetings with Abgar, the first time for healing, the second time for safekeeping of the Shroud. It may also explain why Eusebius makes no reference to an image bearing cloth but only of Abgar's healing by the hands of Jude. A second journey for delivering the sacred cloth into the hands of a newly converted king may explain its lack of mention. Further still, historian Ian Wilson believes the cloth brought to Edessa was, in fact, the Shroud folded up in such a manner as to allow only the face image to be visible. Early writings referred to the cloth as a "tetradiplon" meaning doubled in four. Such a folding pattern would show only the neck and face, as depicted in several artistic representations of the True Likeness, beginning in the sixth century. As for the legends of Ananais, either painting the picture of Jesus or receiving the cloth that Jesus imprinted with the image of his face, they combine with others of a similar nature in telling an embellished story of how a mysterious image of Jesus arrived in Edessa. These later legends were perhaps a conflation of the two journeys of Jude.[12]

*St. Jude of lost causes.* As I reflect on the role of Jude in the safekeeping of the Shroud, I am struck by the fact of his being the apostle who became known as the patron saint of lost causes. In 1988, the Shroud truly became a lost cause with the announcement of the carbon date. Not until seventeen years later, in 2005, did the tide turn back. With the publication of Ray Rogers's investigation

St. Jude Thaddeus, patron of lost causes (Frank C. Turner artist) (HomeShrineIcons.com)

showing how a repair or reweave may very well have affected the validity of the carbon date, research and interest in the Shroud revived like a phoenix rising from the ashes. What poetic irony to think St. Jude might still be looking after the Shroud he brought to Abgar almost two thousand years ago. Although only one short book, a letter, is assigned to Jude in the Bible, the Gospel of John reports him asking an intriguing question that could bring the Shroud to mind. This was what he asked Jesus at the Last Supper, "Lord, how is it that you will manifest yourself to us, and not the world?" (John 14:22 ESV). Fittingly, the stunning photo-negative of the image of the Shroud has circulated across the globe, not to mention the numerous icon images based on the True Likeness that have graced the walls of thousands of churches and millions of homes over the centuries. Indeed, Jesus has been made manifest to the world by the very cloth carried by Saint Jude to the city of King Abgar.

*The Holy Mandylion, the Keramion, and the True Likeness.* Subsequent to King Abgar's conversion to Christianity, he tore down a prominent pagan idol over the tunnel entrance to the palace at the Western Gate of the Citadel and replaced it with a mosaic tile with the same face image of Christ visible on the Shroud. This was known as the Keramion, or the "Isa" Tile, and bore the inscription, *Christ the God. He who hopes in thee is never disappointed.*"[13] The cloth image later became known as the True Likeness. It is also noted in the historical record that the cloth had different names at different points in history, including the "Image of Edessa" and the "Holy Mandylion." The facial features included long hair, a full beard, large eyes, a long nose, and hair parted in the middle—all features seen on the Shroud.[14]

*The death of King Abgar and the Shroud hidden away.* In AD 50, King Abgar V died. His eldest son took the throne, only to die shortly after. His second son, Manu VI, took the throne in AD 57 but rejected the Christian message, reverted to his familiar paganism, and restored the worship of idols as before. The hostile king brought persecution upon the nascent Christian Church in Edessa, and all emblems of the faith were put in jeopardy. Fearing the cloth would be destroyed, a concerned bishop hid the mysterious treasure inside an interior wall at the tunnel entrance and blocked it up, concealing it from view.[15] Hidden away with the cloth was the Keramion tile and an oil lamp. Interestingly, it was an ancient tradition to place a burning oil lamp in the tomb with the deceased.[16]

ISA Tile—the Keramion (used with permission by PED)

As the generations who knew about the hidden relic passed on, the cloth remained tucked away and forgotten for almost 450 years until 525, when a severe flood struck the city, killing thousands and destroying most of the buildings. As the city was being rebuilt, workers rediscovered the cloth along with the Keramion tile and the oil lamp. It was now two hundred years past the reign of Constantine who established Christianity throughout his realm, making it safe to be a Christian. As the city was being rebuilt, workers discovered the repository of hidden items. The newfound image became known throughout the entire Byzantine Empire as the aforesaid Image of Edessa, described as the "true Likeness of Christ, not made by human hands." From this point on, nearly all Orthodox icon images of Jesus changed to conform to the features seen on the True Likeness.[17]

*The Persian attack thwarted.* Subsequent to the rediscovery of the cloth in 525, it achieved superstar status when it was credited for saving Edessa from the attack of Chosroes, king of the Persians in 544.

Enemy forces had constructed a great tower just outside the city wall, enabling the Persian soldiers to shoot flaming arrows directly into the city from a higher position. To ward off the attack, the Edessans recited aloud the letter from Jesus to King Abgar from the top of the wall, in hopes of invoking divine assistance; but no immediate help arrived. At the same time, Edessan soldiers were digging a tunnel from underneath the city wall, hoping to set fire to the tower from below. Due to lack of air in the tunnel, the fire would not kindle. But suddenly, Edessans received a miraculous intervention—the cloth with the sacred image was brought forth, and suddenly the tower burst into flames and crumbled into a blazing ruin. Smoke could be seen from twenty miles away. The attack of the Persians was thwarted, and all credit went to the Image of Edessa. With supernatural power now attributed to it, the legend of the image quickly spread far and wide.[18]

In 1994, researchers translated two sixth-century documents originally from Sinai. They tell of two Assyrian monks, Theodosius from Edessa and Isadore from nearby Hierapolis. Theodosius was the overseer of "the image of Christ in Edessa," and Isadore took care of the Keramion. The monks travelled together to what is the modern-day Republic of Georgia to paint icon images based on the True Likeness to be given to new churches being built as Christianity spread. The documents are testaments to how icon images proliferated so quickly during the sixth century. These Assyrian artist-monks were acting as missionaries, spreading the Gospel through the message of the icon. Indeed, for an illiterate population and for people who grew up worshiping pagan idols, an icon of the True Likeness made Christ real. It served as a bulwark against people returning to their familiar idols and affirmed the biblical story of Jesus.[19]

*Harrowing times for sacred icons.* The Image of Edessa transformed the portrayals of Jesus in Byzantine Orthodox art to one that strongly reflected the Shroud image. In the following centuries, the Byzantines endured two periods when icon images fell out of favor and were thought to be a form of idolatry. These iconoclast movements brought on widespread destruction of all sacred images starting in 726 with Emperor Leo III and lasted until 787 and the

Second Council of Nicaea. The iconoclasts then regained power under Emperor Leo V from 815 to 843, after which the destruction ended for good.

In 787, the True Likeness, kept in Edessa, was the principal justification for restoring veneration of holy icons as a valid religious practice as declared at the Second Council. A powerful advocate of icons was St. Theodore the Studite, who referenced the Shroud "in which the Christ was wrapped and laid down in the sepulcher." Theodore described the significance of the apostle Jude having brought the sacred cloth to King Abgar:

> To clearly grant us His divine features, our Savior who had been covered with it, imprinted the form of His own face and portraying it touching the cloth with His own skin.[20]

Reinforcing the decision for restoring images to their revered status was the following statement from the Council:

> In the two years preceding the destruction of Jerusalem by Titus Vespasian, the faithful were warned by the Holy Ghost to leave Jerusalem and go to the kingdom of Agrippa, still allied to the Romans. Thus, going forth from the city, they took with them their most precious objects; this is how the images and other sacred objects were taken to Syria and were to be found there.[21]

The Jewish uprising against the Romans began in AD 66, leading to the destruction of the temple four years later and the great diaspora of the Jewish people. The warnings to leave Jerusalem and the Holy Land was paramount, resulting in the precious relics being carried off to such places as Beirut, Pella, and Edessa.[22]

Tracing the journey of the Shroud from Jerusalem to Edessa and beyond has combined historical research with the interpretation of ancient documents, along with reasoned suppositions. The legends of King Abgar V are many, but all have overlapping elements pointing to both knowledge of Jesus and the arrival of a mysterious cloth. Most telling is the dramatic shift in the depiction of the face of Jesus after the discovery of the True Likeness and the Image of Edessa. A banner bearing this sacred image was credited with thwarting the Persian attack on Edessa after its being hidden away in a wall awaiting discovery in the sixth century. These incidents speak to the existence of the Shroud in Edessa from the first century and, as we will see in more detail, its well-documented seizure from there in 944, which resulted in its removal to Constantinople. As we move on we will build on this foundation with even more and varied historical validation.

# CHAPTER 11

## The Trail of Ancient Icons

From the second through the fifth centuries, artists often pictured Jesus in a variety of ways. He is seen with a lamb on his shoulders as the Good Shepherd, as a clean shaven and beardless youth, in profile as a side view looking to the left or to the right, sometimes with short hair, other times with longer hair, yet still with no beard. However, after 525, it all changed to picture Jesus only one way—with features based on the Image of Edessa, later known as the True Likeness. From that point on, artists could only depict Jesus as front facing with long hair, full beard, enlarged eyes, and a long, flattened nose. Icon painters would not even consider painting a picture of Jesus that did not conform to the True Likeness.[1]

Painting of the beardless Christ from the catacombs (public domain)

The Sinai icon, kept in the Monastery of St. Catherine in southern Egypt, is the first known icon based on the Edessa Image. Crafted in AD 550, it is a magnificent painting and one of the few early Pantocrator icons to survive the iconoclast movement of the eighth century. Pantocrator is a Byzantine-Orthodox artistic style that depicts Christ as ruler of the universe. If the Shroud face is laid over the Sinai icon, 180 points of congruence can be counted. In other words, the images almost perfectly line up, a remarkable pattern indicating a strong correlation between both images. With so many similarities, many researchers believe the True Likeness and the Shroud are one and the same and the source of inspiration from which the icon images are derived.[2]

Paul Vignon, a scientist and philosopher, studied and wrote about the Shroud during the 1930's until his death in 1943. He was also intrigued with the similarities of the Shroud and True Likeness. In his pioneering research published in 1937, he wrote:

Christ Pantocrator icon, Monastery of St. Catherine, Sinai, Egypt, ca. sixth century (public domain)

> There are many representations of Christ, notably the Image of Edessa, which could be derived only from the Shroud. A careful study of these copies, which I have recently completed, shows that the…face visible on the Shroud served as a model for artists… The artists did not copy slavishly, but tried to interpret the face, translating the mask-like features into a living portrait, which was still a recognizable copy of the original.[3]

The icon images incorporate features derived from the original and include the following:

- Long hair parted in the middle yet slightly shorter on his right side
- Always front facing
- Pronounced eyebrow arches and a V-shaped mark on the bridge of the nose

- Large deep eyes, wide orbits, and a long, straight nose
- Pronounced cheekbones
- A small mouth not hidden by mustache and a hairless area between lower lip and beard
- A medium-length beard appearing plucked at the chin[4]

In the early years of the Byzantine Empire, coins were minted with images of Jesus. The first such coins date from AD 437 to AD 450 and showed him beardless with short hair.[5]

*The Justinian coins show the True Likeness–Shroud connection.* In 692, Emperor Justinian II ordered the minting of coins with an image of Jesus. Not to be too humble, he placed his own image on the reverse side. Interestingly, Jesus is now front facing and clearly based on the features of the True Likeness.

Points of congruence are comparable to the Sinai icon but with a major difference. The coins pick up a fold on the Shroud that appears as a double line across the neck. Many men may have had long hair and a full beard, but the double line across the neck was a fold mark unique to the Shroud. This is powerful evidence showing that the True Likeness and the Shroud are the same. The coins are nearly six hundred years older than the oldest carbon date of 1260. It appears the engravers who created the mold for the coins had direct access to the Edessa Image to use it as a reference model. There are too many precise details incorporated into the coins not possible otherwise. Coins minted in later centuries would likely have been based on the original molds.[6]

Both sides of a Byzantine (Justinian) coin from AD 692 showing True Likeness on one side and Emperor on the other. (Alexander Marinescu, Vilmar Numismatics LLC)

Ian Wilson and other historians believe the True Likeness/Mandylion was the Shroud simply folded in such a way that when viewed, only the face could be seen. Some criticize this belief, saying the Edessa image was only a small towel-like cloth bearing simply a face image and not connected with the Shroud. However, historical descriptions beginning in the eighth century describe a full-body image and even reference the side wound.

*Gradual revelation of the full body image.* There are many historical accounts that show how the Shroud transitioned from being known as only a facecloth to a long burial cloth bearing the full-body image of Jesus. This is reported from the eighth century:

> Christ spread out his entire body on a linen cloth that was white as snow. On this cloth, marvelous as it is to see…the glorious image of the Lord's face, and the length of his entire and most noble body, has been divinely transferred. (Pope Stephen III)[7]

Another reference from the eighth century states, "King Abgar received a cloth on which one can see not only a face but the whole body."[8] This is an intriguing reference as it connects the cloth brought to Abgar by the apostle Jude as bearing the features of the entire body of Christ, not just a face image.

In the tenth century, another legend arose to account for the full body image seen on the Shroud. The story was later included in *Otio Imperiala*, written by English canon lawyer Gervase of Tilbury. (ca. 1210–1214):

> When the Lord our redeemer was hanging on the cross, with his clothes stripped from him, Joseph of Arimathea came up and said to Mary the Lord's mother and to the other women who had followed the Lord to his passion: "Alas, this plight shows how much indeed you loved this righteous man! For though you see him hanging naked on a cross, you have not covered him." Moved by this rebuke, the Lord's mother and the rest of the women who were with her quickly

bought a spotless linen so large and long that it covered the whole body of the crucified Christ. And when the body hanging on the cross was taken down, there appeared imprinted on the linen an effigy of the whole body.[9]

An eleventh-century version called the Latin Abgar legend shows the following response from Jesus to King Abgar's request for him to come to Edessa to heal the king:

But if you wish to see my face in the flesh, behold I send to you a linen, on which you will discover not only the features of my face, but a divinely copied configuration of my entire body.[10]

Another version of the Latin Abgar legend is from Ordericus Vitalis, who wrote *Ecclesiastical History* circa 1141:

A precious linen, on which he had wiped off the sweat from his face, and on which an image of this same Savior shines forth, miraculously painted: this image shows to whoever looks upon it the appearance and size of the Lord's body.[11]

The above references, over and over, not only mention a full-body image, but also a cloth both large and long, describing how the image is derived from covering the entire body. Collectively, these individual reports, which perfectly correspond with the Shroud, span five centuries before its appearance in France during the Middle Ages—and all of them long predate the oldest carbon date of 1260.

Echoing the Latin Abgar legend is another quote from Gervase of Tilbury, circa 1213:

The story is *passed down from Archives of Ancient Authority* that the Lord prostrated himself with his entire body, on the whitest linen, and so by divine power there was impressed on the linen a most beautiful imprint of not only the face, but the entire body of the Lord.[12] (Emphasis added)

This last reference is extremely important. It carefully points out how the Lord's full-body imprint was not a new idea in 1213, when the passage was written, but something passed down over the centuries.

*Conflating of images.* The folded-up Shroud showing only the face was sometimes called the Mandylion. During that time, painted copies of the face were also described as *the Mandylion*. They were given sacred status because they were based on the original, which was rarely seen. Which one is real? Ian Wilson recounts how, in 944, when the Shroud was taken from Edessa and brought to Constantinople, there were "no fewer than three Edessan versions of the Image, including one kept by the Nestorians." A local bishop, Abraham of Samosata, was tasked with determining the "true unpainted picture" to be brought back to the emperor.[13]

Given that all these painted versions featured only the face image, it is easy to see how the original image (folded up showing only the face) and painted copies of the same could become conflated over time as being the same thing. Adding to the confusion, in Constantinople, they become listed separately, as the burial linen bearing the divine image and as a separate cloth showing only a face image—likely one of the painted copies. As the pages ahead will document, the burial linen, known as the "sindon" in Greek and Latin, disappeared in 1204 following the Fourth Crusade while the Mandylion remained in Constantinople. It was listed in the inventory of relics sold in 1247 to the king of France, Louis IX. The sacred image, most likely a painted copy of the original Shroud face, was brought to Paris for display above the altar of the Sainte-Chapelle Church, built by the king to display his new relic collection.[14] Sadly, whatever sacred items were brought to Paris in 1247 were destroyed by fire in 1737, which ended the trail of the Mandylion.

*Commentary.* The cloth "doubled in four," as described by Ian Wilson, goes a long way toward explaining how the full-length image remained hidden for years, even centuries. Numerous historical references also give credence to the explanation that a singular face image…was only a portion of a folded full-body cloth. The concept of the cloth "doubled in four" makes perfect sense and explains the initial confusion of what was on the cloth, and the eventual understanding of what it truly contained. Taken together, the historical trail of the Shroud, the emergence of the Image of Edessa, known as the True Likeness, and the church mandate of universal conformity seen in countless icons provide a convincing relationship illustrating the existence and influence of the Shroud, beginning in Edessa.

# CHAPTER 12

## The Intrigues of Medieval History

By 944, Edessa had fallen to Islam. With his throne in Constantinople and concern about the safety of the Church's most revered relic, known then as the Mandylion, Emperor Romanos I took decisive action. In August of that year, the emperor sent the entire Byzantine Imperial army six hundred miles to Edessa. Soldiers surrounded the city, but their purpose was not to fight. On the contrary, they brought bags of silver and two hundred prisoners of war to offer as a trade for the sacred linen. The Muslims, now in control, had no need for the cloth and agreed to the deal despite opposition from Christians still living in Edessa. It seemed the prudent thing to do to avoid a war.[1]

Shortly thereafter, the army returned to Constantinople with great fanfare and delivered the cloth to the Church of Saint Mary of Blachernae for reflective veneration by the faithful. The next day, it was transported through the streets of the city where it entered the Hagia Sophia and afterward the Pharos Chapel inside the imperial palace. During the procession, they proclaimed, "For the glory of the faithful, for the safety of the emperors, for the preservation of the entire city and the way of life of the Christian empire."[2] Invoking "safety" and "preservation" harkens back to 544 when the cloth was credited with saving Edessa from the attack of the Persians.

The most important relic of all was safe in the capital city of the empire. Originally built in the fifth century, the Hagia Sophia (Holy Wisdom) was the religious center of the city and one of the largest freestanding dome structures in the world. Gregory, the archdeacon of the cathedral, delivered a sermon that night in the palace.

> The splendor has been impressed uniquely by the drops of agony sweat sprinkled from the face…These are truly the beauties that produced the coloring of Christ's imprint, which has been embellished further by the *drops of blood sprinkled from his own side…blood and water there, sweat and image here.* (Emphasis added)[3]

The reference to the side wound and the appearance of blood and water match what is seen on the Shroud, except today it is known to be the separation of blood and serum, which appears clear like water. This is another important historical reference added to the ones discussed in the previous chapter that show the cloth bore more than just a face image but also a full body image, as demonstrated by Gregory's mention of the side wound. The use of the word *sweat* as a cause of the image indicates a natural process, not a painted creation.

During this same ceremony, the cloth was laid out on the emperor's throne with his crown laid upon it—a perfect symbolism for something believed to have wrapped the King of Kings. John Skylitzes, a Greek historian from the eleventh century and a skilled artist, crafted an important painting of the return of the Shroud, showing the general of the returning army presenting the True Likeness (Mandylion) to the

Image of the Mandylion being presented to the Byzantine Emperor Romanos I in Constantinople by the general of the returning army in 944 from Edessa. Picture made by Greek historian, John Skylitzes, in the 11th Century. (Wikimedia commons—Public domain)

emperor. The painting clearly depicts a long cloth, with a portion draped over the general's back. The emperor is seen holding the other end of the cloth, which is folded over his arms several times, clearly showing it was not a small facecloth.

In between the general and the emperor is a third face, the face of Christ, positioned in the center of this long cloth, where the face appears on the Shroud.[4]

For 260 years, the Shroud remained in Constantinople. In 1201, Nicholas Mesarites, overseer of the relic treasury in Constantinople, wrote, "In this place the naked Lord rises again, and the burial linen can prove it."[5]

Interestingly, after the Shroud was taken to France in the fourteenth century, all artistic depictions or copies of the Shroud modestly added a loincloth or sometimes a covering resembling a bath towel or shorts. However, the man on the Shroud is naked, matching the above description.

In 1204, another reference to the Shroud was made by a known chronicler of events happening at the time, the French knight Robert de Clari:

> But among the rest [of the churches in Constantinople], there was also another which was called Saint Mary of Blachernae, within which was the shroud wherein Our Lord was wrapped. And on every Friday that shroud did raise itself upright, so that the form of Our Lord could clearly be seen. And none knows—neither Greek nor Frank [French]—what became of that shroud when the city was taken.[6]

This is an important reference demonstrating that a linen shroud bearing a full body image was there in 1204 and yet disappeared during the Fourth Crusade, "when the city was taken." This weekly occurrence in which the Shroud "did raise itself upright" may have been a liturgical device allowing people to see the full-body image in four different stages. The sequence that seems the clearest would begin at the first hour of the day, 6:00 a.m. on Friday, when clerics raised the Shroud a couple of feet, representing Christ as a baby. At 9:00 a.m., they raised it a little more, showing Christ as a child. At noon, the cloth was raised even more, depicting Christ as an adolescent. And at 3:00 p.m., the fourth and final stage, the Shroud was raised all the way up to reveal Christ the crucified Lord, the hour the Gospels say Jesus gave up his Spirit.[7]

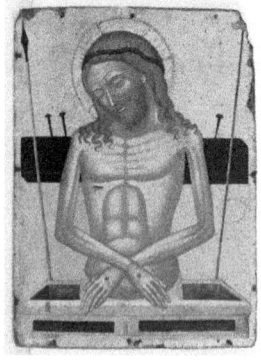

This ritual provides interesting insight into a significant icon from Constantinople called the Man of Sorrows or the Man of Pity, which shows the image of Jesus emerging vertically from a box.

In 1978, physicist John Jackson, a leading member of STURP, applied raking light to the Shroud to reveal all the various fold marks. Jackson suspected there might be a cluster of folds where the cloth wrapped around a square dowel to raise the cloth out of a box, as depicted in the Man of Sorrows icon. The fold marks were indeed there. Jackson was right, which further validates the belief of many experts that the Shroud was preserved, protected, and venerated in Constantinople prior to 1204.[8]

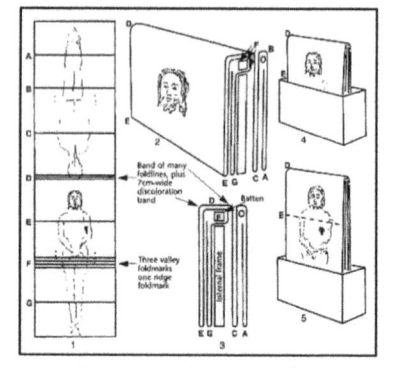

Painting of the Man of Sorrows, late fifteenth century. (Public domain)

*The Fourth Crusade.* In 1201, Pope Innocent III authorized the Fourth Crusade to retake Jerusalem from Muslim control. This would prove a great tragedy for Christendom. Most of the Crusaders were from Northern Europe and had developed a strategic ally with the doge (duke) of Venice and his famous Venetian navy. The Crusaders convinced the doge they would gather thirty-five thousand

Diagram showing the fold marks corresponding with how the Shroud was exhibited in Constantinople. (Courtesy of Ian Wilson)

men and provide compensation of eighty-five thousand marks, an enormous sum, in exchange for transport to Egypt. The Crusaders would proceed on foot from there to Jerusalem. When the time came for their departure, the Crusade had only collected a third of the men and money promised; however, the doge held to his part of the bargain. The Venetians had suspended most commercial operations for a year to build a massive fleet of ships that comprised troop transports, horse transports, and battle galleys sufficient for thirty-five thousand men. The Crusaders owed him a tremendous debt.[9]

An opportunity presented itself to financially bail out the Crusaders, which only required a detour from their original itinerary. Prince Alexius Angelus was the nephew of the current emperor of Constantinople, Alexius III, and was a suitor to the throne. Constantinople, under control of the Greeks, represented the Eastern arm of the Holy Roman Empire and was known for its vast wealth and treasure. The crusaders were led to believe the sitting emperor was unpopular with the people and that his nephew would be welcomed with open arms. The package deal was for the Crusaders to sail the prince to Constantinople and install him as the new emperor. In return, the prince promised to provide compensation of more than enough to cover the debt.

Unfortunately, when the Crusaders arrived in 1203, the citizens of Constantinople failed to greet Alexius Angelus with the expected overtures of acceptance. Instead, they rallied around the current emperor, Alexius III. The gambit had failed. The Crusaders' only alternative, as they saw it, was to turn to war and the plunder of fellow Christians in order to cover their "debt" despite the threat of excommunication by the pope. During the medieval period, it was common European practice to pillage and demand tribute from conquered nations or cities to offset costs and amass wealth; however, those laws were specifically directed at Muslim and Jewish communities. It was forbidden to attack another Christian city, and the pope's threat of excommunication was normally a powerful deterrent in the medieval world. Sadly, on this occasion, it was not successful.[10]

Here is the backdrop of the great city the Crusaders encountered and hoped to profit from: There were thirty churches in the city, but only three of them were honored with preserving and venerating prominent relics at the highest level, most notably the Pharos Chapel, which was beautifully ornate and attached to the royal palace. This chapel laid claim to the crown of thorns and two nails of the crucifixion along with the Keramion tile and a painted copy of the Mandylion. The Hagia Sophia was graced with the True Cross, assembled from three pieces of wood. The third location was the Church of Saint Mary of Blachernae, where the Shroud of Christ was displayed.[11]

Beautiful reliquaries made of gold and silver and decorated with jewels and pearls contained the sacred relics that were carried in procession as expressions of liturgy. This occurred once per year when Christians brought revered items of the passion to the Hagia Sophia in solemn celebration during Easter week. In times of crisis, they would also march these relics in their glorious reliquaries around the city to invoke God's protection and favor. Unfortunately, these rituals offered little help in 1204.[12]

In an attempt to avoid war, negotiations took place, attempting to strike an agreement for compensating the doge. In the meantime, certain Crusaders were allowed to move about the city as they waited. But the obvious wealth of Constantinople—with its gold, silver, and many relics—only whetted the appetite for looting. The city was a plum ripe for the picking. The Crusaders, having lost their senses, set a mosque on fire, and strong winds caused it to get out of control and consume the center of the famed city. Much hatred was stirred between the Latins and the Greeks. When the awaited deal to compensate the Crusaders failed to materialize, war was inevitable.[13]

*The battle for Constantinople.* The battle for Constantinople began on April 12, 1204, pitting the crusaders against Alexius III's Byzantine army. Feeling secure behind three concentric walls as high as sixty feet, it should have taken months to breach the defenses. However, the Venetians found an old entrance to the city down by the water and proceeded to break through the walled-up opening and were inside within a day. Less than a hundred Crusaders came through the opening, but their sudden appearance spread fear and panic throughout the city. The Crusaders opened the main gate and allowed thousands more troops waiting outside to flood into the city.

Shocked and overwhelmed, the Byzantine army broke, and resistance quickly ended. The citizens of Constantinople expected the Western force to install a new emperor and that life would go on, never dreaming the Venetians and the French would plunder the city and carry off their treasures. Nearly everything of value was stolen or destroyed. The city would never be the same, and the division between the East and West became irreparable.[14]

Conquest had not been the goal when the Crusaders diverted to Constantinople, but when events spiraled toward war, the die was cast. What followed were three days of horror played out in excessive violence, rape, and uncontrolled looting. The medieval tradition for conquered territory was to allow for three days of pillage, after which order must be restored. In the case of Constantinople, three days was plenty of time for wholesale destruction to occur.[15]

In 1205, Pope Innocent III received a letter of protest from the emperor's brother, Theodore Angelus of Constantinople, that read,

> In April last year, a crusading army, having falsely set out to liberate the Holy Land, instead laid waste the City of Constantine. During the sack, troops of Venice and France looted even the Holy Sanctuaries. The Venetians partitioned the treasures of gold, silver, and ivory, while the French did the same with the relics of the saints and... *Most sacred of all, the linen in which our Lord Jesus Christ was wrapped after his death and before the resurrection.* We know that the sacred objects are preserved by their predators, in Venice, in France, and other places, *the sacred linen in Athens.* (Emphasis added)[16]

*The aftermath of the Crusade.* Pope Innocent III was devastated not only by the destruction and debauchery but, combined with a battle of Christian against Christian, his dream of reconciliation between East and West was shattered.

In a letter widely distributed, Innocent made his displeasure known to all.

> How will the Greek Church…return to ecclesiastical unity and devotion to the Apostolic See, a church which has seen in the Latins nothing except an example of affliction and the works of Hell, so that it rightly detests them more than dogs? It was not enough for them (Latins) to empty the imperial treasuries and to plunder the spoils of princes and lesser folk, but rather they extended their hands to church treasuries and, what was more serious, to their possessions, even ripping away silver tablets from altars and breaking them into pieces among themselves, violating sacristies and crosses, and carrying away relics.[17]

The pope clearly blamed the loss of God's favor on the unwarranted pillage of the Eastern capital of Christendom and ordered the immediate return of the sacred relics to the Greeks under threat of excommunication. Without repentance and absolution, only hell and damnation awaited those found guilty. However, few relics would ever be returned. Instead, fanciful stories were crafted called *translatio* narratives to explain how a relic arrived at a new location in the West. Anonymous hagiographers were hired to memorialize recently acquired relics and, thereby, exempt them from papal scrutiny. Relics that were found with no known origin also needed stories. These were called *inventio* narratives.[18]

*The lure of relics*. Much of the lure and power of relics came from these origin stories. People wanted to know the saint identified with the relic, what they were known for, how it arrived, and the miracles associated with it (miracles provided proof of authenticity). There had to be a story even if it was invented from the mists of fiction that floated all about. Purported miracles for a relic could be divided into three categories: *by contact*—someone was healed upon touching it, *by travel*—a ship was doomed to sink until the passengers appealed to the saint associated with the relic and were thus saved, and *by installation*—a miracle occurred after the relic was securely in place, which was seen as a demonstration of God's favor. In the medieval mind, these narratives helped integrate the relic into the fabric of the community and had far greater value than random relics stolen from another location with no surrounding story.[19]

*The pope's concern over fake relics.* When the French and Venetian Crusaders returned from their pillage of Constantinople, loaded with stolen booty, it set off a gold rush for even more Byzantine relics. It was a demand satisfied by the creation of thousands of fakes, which were used to attract gullible pilgrims and their money to cathedrals and churches all around Europe.[20]

In Venice alone, one could find "fragments of the True Cross, drops of milk from the Virgin, an ampule of Christ's blood, a piece of the column of the Flagellation, and other relics pertaining to the life of Christ."[21]

So pervasive was the abuse of bogus relics that Pope Innocent III, fearing a scandal would discredit the church, directed the Fourth Lateran Council in 1215 to adopt Canon 62:

> The Christian religion is frequently disparaged because certain people put saints' relics up for sale and display them indiscriminately. In order that it may not be disparaged in the future, we ordain by this present decree that henceforth ancient relics shall not be displayed outside a reliquary or be put up for sale. As for newly discovered relics, let no one presume to venerate them publicly unless they have previously been approved by the authority of the Roman pontiff. Prelates, moreover, should not in future allow those who come to their churches, in order to venerate, to be deceived by lying stories or false

documents, as has commonly happened in many places on account of the desire for profit.[22]

The essence of Canon 62 was that no public veneration of a relic would be permitted if it had not been venerated prior to 1215. Any new relic required papal approval prior to public display for veneration—a clear effort to stem the tide of fakes, a growing industry. It was also to prevent the merchandising of relics stolen from Constantinople. This Canon law remained in force until 1563 when the Council of Trent allowed for a bishop to approve the veneration of a new relic.

The Council was an extraordinary event. Pope Innocent III and his advisors spent years planning for what would be the first such international gathering of the church since the Second Council of Nicea in 787. The question of relics was one of many issues covered. The pope's main concern was uniting East and West once again with hopes of restoring the Holy Roman Empire. Only then did Innocent believe God would grant them control of the Holy Land. However, that hope was fading fast as the Greeks had no desire to consolidate under the Latin pope, especially after the wholesale pillage of their beautiful city and desecration of their holy sites.[23]

*The "missing years."* In 1356 the Shroud was seen once again. It was on exhibition in Lirey, France. Without a fully documented path after the sack of Constantinople, this period is often referred to as the missing years. However, there are intriguing hints that connect some of the dots with likely explanations as to why it went underground.

During the sack of Constantinople, elite knights were given authority over certain areas of the city including the churches under their jurisdiction. One prominent theory involves Othon de la Roche, a French knight and renowned nobleman from Burgundy. He was a major figure during the Fourth Crusade and received command of the District of Blachernae, where the sacred linen was publicly venerated.

Othon de la Roche is written about in a notable book that was published in 2011, *The Untold Story of the Holy Shroud*. It was commissioned by Vittorio Emanuele di Savoia, the crown prince of Italy and duke of Savoy, whose family were custodians of the Shroud before its arrival in Turin. The book was written by Carlos Evaristo, who was described by the crown prince in the foreword as "a world-renowned relic expert, Vatican Museum Patron, and a member of the Dynastic Royal Orders of the Savoy Royal Family." From the Savoy archives, Evaristo writes,

> The Holy Shroud's undocumented first century in Europe (France), following the sack of Constantinople, is perhaps resolved in the light of the contemporary tradition of the arrival, from the East, of another claimed Relic of the Burial Cloth of the Christ, said to have been first venerated at the Cathedral of Saint Stephen in Besancon, France up until the year 1349. Local tradition claims that during the Fourth Crusade, Othon de la Roche, Duke of Athens and Sparta, who was in command of the District of the Blachernes, in Constantinople, where the Holy Shroud was publicly venerated by Imperial permission, after the Sack, received (or stole) a Burial Cloth of Our Lord (most probably the very Holy Shroud) as part of the recompense for services rendered in the line of Battle.[24]

After the Crusade, Othon was appointed the duke of Athens, with the city as his fiefdom. The letter of Theodore Angelus to Pope Innocent III in 1205 mentioned earlier states clearly,

> We know that the sacred objects are preserved by their predators, in Venice, in France, and other places, the sacred linen in Athens.

Knowing what happened and how it happened is important for understanding how a knight—not a king, a prince, or a bishop—came into possession of the Shroud. Blame the fog of war and the blur of three days of unbridled carnage that caused hundreds of relics, all carefully collected over the centuries, to suddenly disappear in a whirlwind. Amid the flood of relics and wealth leaving the city, no accounting was possible; but after the passage of time, the reality of the specific looting became apparent, with some relics like the Shroud going underground to avoid the new owner getting excommunicated and other relics escaping scrutiny by claiming newly invented stories regarding its origin.

*Where did it go?* According to historian Daniel Scavone, the linen was sent to Château de Ray-sur-Saône, Othon's chateau in Burgundy, in either 1206 or 1219. Count Hubert de Salverte, who published a monograph in 1936 on the ancestry of the castle of Ray-sur-Saône, records that Othon de la Roche became the owner of the castle when he married Isabelle, the baroness of Ray, in 1205. To this day, the castle boasts the possession of a wooden box that encased the cloth when it was transported from Athens. The box is labeled with the following description:

> 13th Century coffer in which was preserved in Ray Castle the Shroud of Christ brought by Othon de Ray from Constantinople.[25]

In 1253, documents indicate a linen cloth was used as part of the Easter liturgy at St. Stephen Cathedral in Besancon, within the province of Othon's Burgundy chateau. Scavone believes it was the Shroud. If true, we could surmise that Othon or his later family members allowed for its display during Holy Week. The trail picks up again a hundred years later in Besancon in 1350 as property of Othon's direct descendant, his great-great-great-granddaughter Jeanne de Vergy.[26, 27]

Another version of events notes Othon as having sent the cloth to Besancon in 1208, where it remained, with annual displays in St. Stephen's Cathedral. It was known as the Relic of the Burial Cloth of the Christ.[28] It is reasonable to assume Jeanne de Vergy inherited the sacred cloth and continued the tradition of allowing its exhibition in St. Stephen's Cathedral. According to Evaristo, who had access to the Savoy archives, "the relic was exposed for veneration on each Easter Sunday up till the year 1349 when fire broke out in the Cathedral."[29] Not being Easter Sunday, the Shroud would have been safe and sound in Othon's chateau.[30]

Evaristo offers us another tantalizing clue for the Shroud/painting conundrum:

> After the Cathedral of Besancon was restored or perhaps whilst its restoration was still underway, the Bishop of Besancon…lamented the decision to move the *Major Relic* and failing to recover Custodianship of the Shroud, two years later, had a painted copy *Relic Replica* exhibited in the Cathedral, to the satisfaction of the local devotees… Canon Dom Chamart found conclusive evidence that the Shroud exhibited at Besancon, after 1352, was only a painting, but a painting never-the- less that was a replica of the genuine *Holy Shroud* by then in possession of the Charney Lord (in Lirey).[31]

This explanation offers a reasonable scenario to answer critics who allege the Shroud is only a painting. Evaristo's account shows that, in fact, a painting of the Shroud was crafted as a replacement for the genuine linen taken from Besancon after the church burned down in 1349.

*Geoffroi de Charny*. Within the next few years, Jeanne de Vergy married Geoffroi de Charny, who was described as "the most loyal and valorous of all knights." This great knight of the realm was known to have impeccable integrity, selected by two French kings to carry the battle flag into war and so committed to his faith that he even carried a portable altar into battle and authored a book on chivalry at the request of King John II of France. Many believe Jeanne offered the Shroud to Geoffroi as a dowry for marriage, an antiquated concept today; however, it was a way of protecting the bride in the medieval world. Should the marriage end because of abuse, the dowry would return to the woman. Should the husband die, the dowry could help provide a retirement for the widow.

After their marriage, Geoffroi and Jeanne moved to Lirey, France, and began building a small collegiate church. Geoffroi had petitioned Pope Clement VI for his blessing on the church he intended to build there.[32] The couple publicly exhibited the Shroud in 1356 and had a medallion cast for the event, featuring the double image found on the Shroud as well as the distinctive herringbone-pattern weave of the cloth. Jeanne's direct ownership is nearly as certain as the medal cast for pilgrims, which bore the crests of both the de Vergy and de Charny families.[33] The wife of a prominent knight would not be represented in medieval times unless she was the rightful owner. Geoffroi became a co-owner through marriage.

The 1356 Exhibition medallion showing double image and family crests of Geoffroi de Charny and Jeanne de Vergy. (Courtesy of Niels Svensson)

Before Geoffroi could exhibit the Shroud in Lirey, he would have had to receive papal approval from Pope Innocent VI in accordance with Canon 62, codified in 1215, regarding the display of relics. Geoffroi's claim of Byzantine provenance, when coupled with Crusader Robert de Clari's report of having seen the cloth displayed for veneration in Constantinople every Friday in *St. Mary of the Blachernae* circa 1203–1204, would have been enough to satisfy the requirement.[34]

This introduces an interesting series of events. With de Charny securing papal approval, akin to the Shroud's validation, it would have been significant news. One might expect a papal bull to be issued, validating the cloth as the authentic burial shroud of Jesus, a relic formerly displayed in Constantinople that could now be seen and venerated in Lirey, France. So why didn't this happen? The answer is clear: the Eastern emperor, John V Palaeogus, based in Constantinople, would have certainly laid claim to the Shroud as a stolen relic and demanded its immediate return. The only solution was to quietly accede to Geoffroi's request to exhibit the cloth as genuine without creating international fanfare. In fact, to keep this from blowing up into a scandal, furthering the divide between East and West, the Pope imposed an edict of perpetual silence on de Charney, his family, and his advisors regarding the Shroud's origin.[35] This mandate for silence only makes sense if the sacred cloth was stolen from Constantinople in 1204.

Because the Shroud had been relocated to Lirey, church officials in Besancon were no doubt upset over the cloth's departure, especially since records show it to have been part of their Easter tradition for over a hundred years. To recompense, Jeanne agreed to have a painted copy of the Shroud (the front image only) sent to the church in Besancon. This reiterates the report from Evaristo describing the substitute painting received by the bishop of Besancon to replace the *"Holy Shroud* by then in possession of the Charney Lord." Jeanne had likely already committed the original Shroud to her husband for display in Lirey.

*The Knights Templar.* Historian Ian Wilson has theorized the Shroud may have been in the possession of the Knights Templar for some time during the "missing years," which, given their prominence at that time, could provide a possible scenario.

Originally known as the Order of the Temple of Solomon, Templars were called warrior monks and came into being around 1090. In their initiations, they took vows of poverty and chastity with full allegiance to the pope. Their original headquarters was set up in the Al-Aqsa Mosque, built over the Temple Mount in Jerusalem, where Solomon's Temple once stood. As a papal-sanctioned charity, the monks received tax-free donations from all over Europe. Over the course of two hundred years, the Templars became a formidable fighting force and amassed enormous wealth and power

    consisting of hundreds of castles and outposts that could be found in every part of the Christian world. Their military reach encompassed all of Europe, the Mediterranean and lands along the Atlantic Ocean. Because of the popularity of their mission and their high public standing, they attracted large donations, both from members of the order, and from bequests left to it by wealthy lay families. As their wealth grew, the Templars developed a banking system issuing notes of credit to travelers in order to ensure the availability of their funds in foreign lands, a strikingly modern innovation which contributed to the order's ability to raise the capital it needed.[36]

The Templars also offered the service of preservation of assets and belongings of wealthy land barons during the many months away on pilgrimage. Paintings, jewelry, tapestries, clothing, and anything that might get stolen by thieves in their absence were brought to a local Templar castle for protection until they returned.[37] It is this service that could have played a role in protecting the Shroud.

The most direct link between the Shroud and the Templars is through Othon de la Roche, who is believed to have become a preceptor of the Knights Templar in 1225 after he returned to Burgundy once his duties as duke of Athens came to an end. A preceptor was part of the Templar chain of command.

From his castle stronghold, it is believed that Othon likely allowed the Shroud to be periodically displayed on Easter Sunday at Saint Stephen's Cathedral in Besancon, as described earlier. Reflecting the reputation and influence of the Templars, the Shroud's protection from theft would have been a top priority for Othon and his family. And so even though this remains to be proven, it is certainly a tantalizing possibility that serves as food for thought about the missing years.

The historical journey of the Shroud picks up with Jeanne de Vergy, a fifth-generation descendant of Othon. Her marriage to Geoffroi de Charny, as recounted earlier, transferred the Shroud to the de Charny family; and we know it was displayed by the couple in 1356. Geoffroi died in battle shortly thereafter. With concerns about the Shroud's safety, Jeanne relocated it to the castle of Montfort-en-

Auxois, owned by the de Vergy family, where it remained from 1360 to 1389.[38]

Geoffroi and Jeanne's son, Geoffroi II, petitioned the pope in 1389 for permission to exhibit the Shroud again in Lirey. This was the catalyst for a document, the "d'Arcis Memorandum," which will be discussed in the next chapter.

*Further evidence of early dating.* Two early depictions of the Shroud contain significant markings that date from before the fire in 1532, described in chapter 1, which produced the water stains and patches that we see today.

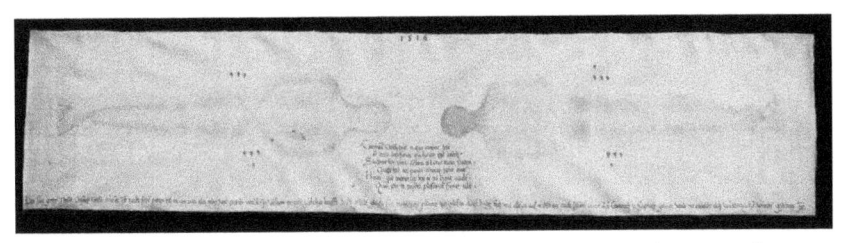

Copy of the Shroud from Lierre, Belgium (c. 1516), showing the L-shaped burns that pre-date the 1532 fire. (Courtesy of Aldo Guerreschi)

The first, shown above, is a cloth on which is painted a copy of the Shroud from Lierre, Belgium, (c 1516). It is known that there were annual exhibitions of the Shroud in Chambery, France, beginning in 1502; and it is reasonable to assume that the artist saw it during one of these events.

The Lierre copy clearly depicts the faint image, front and back, known from the Shroud. Significantly, it also shows a distinctive L-shaped pattern of burn holes in four uniform locations. It is believed these were caused by hot coals accidentally escaping a censer used during a liturgical ceremony as the cloth lay folded on the altar. This feature stands out all the more because of the overall simplicity of the artwork.

Stepping back in time, we take up the second example that pre-dates the Lierre copy by over three hundred years. The Hungarian Pray Manuscript is the first book ever written and bound in the Hungarian language. It comprises a collection of writings as well as five picture codices depicting the crucifixion and resurrection of Jesus, a picture codex being a fine-line painting used to depict a story. The material was accumulated over several decades and bound as a book in 1192. It is famous for being a documentary source on the ancient history of the kingdom of Hungary. Named after Gyorgy Pray, who discovered it in 1770, it is kept in the Budapest National Library.[39]

The stunning revelation when seeing these drawings of the crucifixion and resurrection is the presence of the same L-shaped holes found on the Lierre copy, which are clearly seen on the Shroud. Given the latest date of 1192, when the manuscript was officially bound, it is easy to assume the existence of the Shroud before that time.

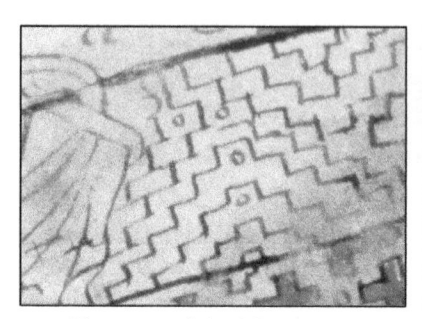

Close-up of the Hungarian Pray Manuscript painting of the resurrection in 1192 AD (*above*) with the zigzag pattern of the linen and the matching four L-shaped holes that burned through the folded Shroud (*below*).

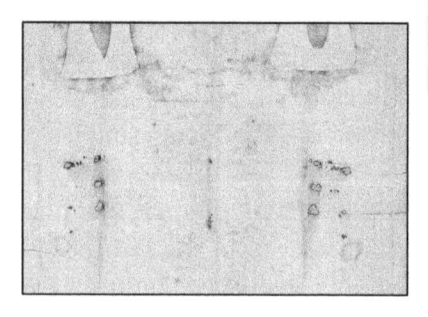

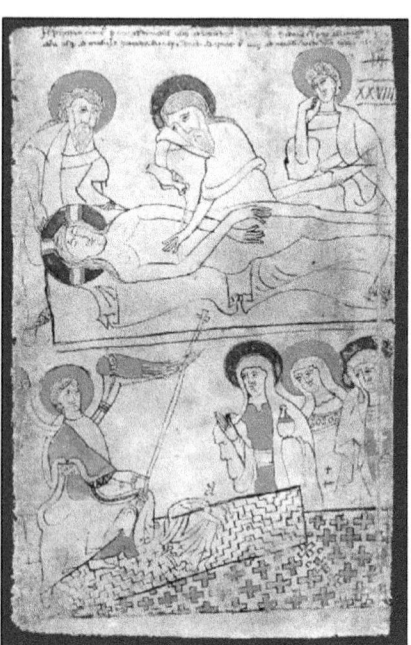

The Hungarian Pray Manuscript comprises a collection of writings and pictures assembled over several decades and bound into a book in 1192.

But perhaps even more convincing are the additional attributes found in these pictures. The depiction of Christ in the burial scene (top half) shows the following:

1. A naked man
2. Arms crossed over the pelvis
3. Elongated fingers
4. No thumbs
5. Long hair
6. Outline of a beard

The depiction of the resurrection scene (bottom half) shows the following:

1. A long, narrow linen cloth folded over depicting an empty shroud.
2. Zigzag lines depicting the distinctive herringbone weave
3. Four burn holes seen in an L pattern
4. Proportions of length and width of the long rectangular cloth are identical to what is seen on the Shroud
5. The last clue may be the most important. Pictured in the scene on the far left is the angel. In the middle are the three women who came to anoint the body on Sunday morning. Mary Magdalene is depicted directly in the center of the picture holding a vial of oil in her left hand, while on her right, the artist has superimposed a face image, indicating that there must be an image inside the shroud.

There are eleven unique attributes of the Hungarian Pray Manuscript that perfectly align with the Shroud of Turin. The odds are astronomical that these eleven correlation points are merely accidental. They are equivalent to matching fingerprints.

Skeptics argue that the L-shaped holes are merely decorative and that the depiction of the folded cloth is not a linen but a gravestone. These implausible assertions are reminiscent of the contortions undertaken to evade anything associated with the Shroud prior to the medieval date assigned by the carbon labs.

To give context for the Hungarian Pray illustration, we turn to King Bela III of Hungary, who reigned from 1172 to 1196. As a young man, from the year 1163, he served in the imperial court at Constantinople for ten years. He was a guest of the emperor, was given the designation of *despotes* (lord or prince) and became engaged to the emperor's daughter. With such high status, it is reasonable to think that at some time, he would have been allowed to see some of the holy relics of the great city including the most important one of all, the Shroud. It is known that the Shroud was displayed in the Church of Saint Mary of Blachernae, where one of his entourage could have crafted the artistic record that later became one of the entries in the Pray Manuscript.

It must be noted that this is nearly one hundred years older than the oldest carbon date of 1260, and it was known to have been venerated in Constantinople since 944 after retrieving it from Edessa. The Hungarian Pray Manuscript is like a DNA match. There is no reason for the artist to have incorporated the eleven specific attributes of the Shroud into the picture, especially the L-shaped pattern of burn holes, unless he was depicting exactly what he was seeing. The manuscript definitively links the Shroud of Turin to the cloth stolen in 1204.[40]

These distinctive connections to Constantinople are, to my mind, the game changer. Additionally, the Shroud's prior residence in Edessa is nearly certain, which dates the cloth to at least 544 when it was credited with saving Edessa from the attack of the Persians. The legend of King Abgar and the involvement of St. Jude traces it all the way back to the first century and the time of Christ.

*Historical trail, fifteenth century to the present day.* Geoffrey de Charney II had a daughter, Margaret, who inherited the Shroud. By 1438, she was widowed for the second time and had no children from either marriage or heirs to inherit the Shroud. Even though her deceased husband promised the canons of Lirey to return the sacred cloth, it would not be so. With deep concern for the cloth's preservation, Margaret sought someone with the means to keep and protect it. The duke of Savoy expressed great interest in acquiring the relic and gave Margaret his promise of safekeeping for future generations. As compensation, they paid to Margaret the revenue of two castles—quite a statement of value.

In 1502, the Savoy family gave the Shroud an honored home in the Sainte-Chapelle in Chambery, France, where it was put into a silver case placed behind the high altar in a special cavity carved out of the wall. For added safety, they protected it with an iron grill secured by four locks, each opened by separate keys, two of which were in possession of the duke. This proved to be disastrous.[41]

As it happened, in 1532, a major fire broke out, believed by many to have been arson. Because the keys were in different places, they frantically called upon a locksmith to pry open the grill. But it took too long; and by the time the silver box was retrieved from the burning wall, the cavity had become an oven, resulting in silver from the top of the box falling onto a corner of the Shroud and, because of its folding pattern, creating an origami-type burn pattern seen on the Shroud today.[42]

The fact that the Shroud survived this tragic incident, leaving the entire image (minus only the elbows) completely intact, was seen as an act of divine providence. The Shroud took on all-new significance as the cloth's preservation was seen in 1532 as a validation of its authenticity.[43]

The nuns at the Poor Clare Convent, in 1534, were tasked with sewing patches onto the front of the cloth to cover up holes made from the burning silver. They also attached it to a fine backing cloth made in Holland to strengthen the cloth for public veneration.[44]

The ailing Cardinal Charles Borromeo was planning a walk from Milan to Chambery in 1578 to offer thanks to the Holy Shroud for sparing his city from the plague. To accommodate the elderly cardinal, Duke Emmanuel Philibert ordered the Shroud moved to Turin, which was much closer to Milan, with no mountains in between. With a sacred ceremony and a solemn procession, they transported the revered cloth to the royal courtyard where they constructed a large platform. It was placed on exhibit for forty hours, and about forty thousand people came to venerate the holy relic and celebrate its arrival in Turin, where it would stay.[45] Cardinal Borromeo's subsequent visits to venerate the holy image were in 1581, 1582, and right before his death in 1584. Seeing the pious veneration of this beloved leader of the church fostered comparable devotion among the populace, with the Shroud drawing thousands during annual exhibitions. Fueling this mass devotion was the cardinal's belief that the Shroud somehow intervened and helped dispel the ravages of the black death that continued to impact Europe from time to time and in various locations after it emerged in 1348.[46]

Until 1694, it was displayed every year in the royal courtyard, with large crowds gathered on balconies and rooftops and completely filling the entire area. Forty thousand showed up in 1606, and in 1647, multiple deaths were reported as people swarmed to see it. In 1653, over sixty thousand people came and in 1676, the crowds were so large, the city could not accommodate them all.[47]

Beginning in 1578 with the first public presentation of the cloth in Turin, the exhibitions became officially known as *ostentiones*, a word meaning "the raising up of the relic for display and veneration." They chose this word to reference the Bible verse "And I, if I be lifted up from the earth, will draw all men unto me" (John 12:32 KJV).[48]

In 1694 the Shroud was given a permanent home in a specially designed altar positioned in the center of the Chapel of the Holy Shroud, designed by architect Guarino Guarini. Located between the Turin Cathedral and the Royal Palace, it became known as the Guarini Chapel. The Shroud remains there to this day.[49]

With only a few hundred at a time able to be let into the new chapel, the number of visitors dropped considerably. The lack of electric lighting also made the image difficult to see. The last annual exhibition was held in 1697 with only four documented exhibitions held in the eighteenth century.[50]

By 1898, the Shroud had become an obscure occasional object of veneration. But then Secondo Pia took his now-famous photograph and discovered the Shroud's distinctive features, seen only in photo negative. What was faint and difficult to see in the chapel because of poor lighting was now revealed to the entire world with more clarity than ever seen before.

King Umberto II of the house of Savoy, the last king of Italy, was exiled to Portugal in 1947 following WWII. He had one son, Victor Emmanuel; but at age thirty-three, Victor broke forty-four generations of tradition that required the crown prince to always consult the king on his future bride. Instead, he was married in a civil ceremony in Las Vegas without consulting either parent. Reeling from this unthinkable insult, King Umberto formally disinherited his son. In 1983, with no reliable heir, the king willed the Shroud to the current living pope, the office of which continues its custodianship.[51]

CHAPTER 13

---

The d'Arcis Memorandum

The two most prominent arguments presented by Shroud skeptics to prove their case for inauthenticity are the carbon test results of 1988, which we have discussed, and, second, what is commonly referred to as the 1389 d'Arcis Memorandum, which is a document that requires thorough examination as to its purpose, validity, and surrounding events.

In 1389, Bishop Pierre d'Arcis of Troyes, France, was upset that a cloth bearing the purported image of Jesus was being displayed twenty miles away in a modest church in Lirey, a parish within his diocese, an attraction that was diverting paying pilgrims away from his cathedral, which boasted several relics but nothing comparable to the Shroud.[1] But he was stymied because the collegiate church was under the aegis of the cardinal, the papal legate, who was a higher authority.

A review of the background on this matter is crucial to understanding the story. As presented earlier, the fabled knight, Geoffroi de Charny, petitioned the pope to build the church at Lirey in 1349 in the precise middle of the fearsome Black Death as a pious offering of devotion. Sometime around 1354, Geoffroi married Jeanne de Vergy, who claimed possession of the sacred linen as a fifth-generation descendant of Othon de la Roche, who absconded with the cloth from Constantinople in 1204. In 1356, the couple chose to display the Shroud to the public in their new church; but shortly after in the same year, the great knight was killed at the Battle of Poitiers carrying the king's personal banner, the fork-tongued oriflamme that legend tells descended from Charlemagne.

Following the 1356 exhibition, Geoffroi's wife removed the cloth from the Lirey church, with concerns about the Shroud's safety, and brought it to the castle of Montfort-en-Auxois, owned by the de Vergy family. Over three decades later, in 1389, Sir Geoffroi's son, Geoffroi II de Charny, petitioned Pope Clement VII to put it back on display in Lirey. The pope approved the request and issued a papal bull, declaring it to be the burial Shroud of Christ.

All feuds begin or can be rekindled with a single definable event, and here was no surprise. During the 1389 exposition in Lirey, calamity struck when the entire nave of Bishop d'Arcis's Troyes Cathedral collapsed.

Shortly after, the rose window in the north transept fell out. Not only were decades of fundraising and construction work ruined, d'Arcis now had a roofless cathedral filled with rubble and broken stained glass.[2]

*An ulterior motive?* Suddenly Bishop d'Arcis needed funds for repairs, and his attention turned to the Lirey church and the linen that was vexing him. As the plague had abated for a few years, pilgrims were free to journey great distances to seek blessing and favor at the locations displaying sacred relics, which provided a significant source of revenue. Seeking a solution to his precarious financial problems, the bishop devised a way intended to steer pilgrims away from Lirey and over to his cathedral.

To counter the Shroud's prominence, the bishop drafted a memorandum that was intended to be sent to the pope disparaging the mysterious linen. But curiously, it was never signed, nor is there any record of it being sent. Nevertheless, the bishop's sentiments became apparent. In the memo, d'Arcis alleged that his predecessor, Bishop Henry d'Poitiers, had reportedly seen the cloth thirty-three years earlier during the first Lirey exhibition and had supposedly questioned an artist who had made a "full confession" as to his creation. Bishop d'Arcis also recollected d'Poitiers's statement that the Shroud was "nothing but a piece of common cloth cunningly painted," essentially naming it a fake. It appears that if he couldn't have the cloth for his church, he wanted it gone but couched in verbiage that elevated himself as a man standing against the sin of idolatry—a paragon of virtue.

In the bishop's memo, the artist was never identified, nor was there a documented confession of any kind to prove d'Poitiers's original allegation. Adding to this, d'Poitiers's description of the cloth, that it was "cunningly painted" and made with "common cloth," did not reflect the Shroud we know as it was obviously an expensive linen with a rare herringbone weave and no evidence of paint or any other artistic substance on the cloth.[3] This trail of inaccuracies and questionable evidence, on top of D'Arcis's financial problems, not only started him down a slippery slope, but puts the entire story in a dubious light. Even so, the battle lines were drawn with d'Arcis on one side and the dean and canons of the Lirey church; Geoffroi II de Charny; his mother, Jeanne de Vergy; and, for that matter, Pope Clement VII on the other—all of this amidst the circulating rumors and innuendoes of d'Arcis's ulterior motives fueled by greed and jealousy rather than the piety he professed.

If there were any credence to this "confession" made to d'Poitiers by the alleged artist, it might have been the authorized painted copy that Jeanne de Vergy commissioned and presented to the church at Besancon to console the church clerics when their beloved Shroud had been removed to Lirey; what is more likely—d'Arcis's hidden motive that money was being drawn away by pilgrims, bypassing his church for Lirey. It also obscures the important fact that the "evidence" d'Arcis was relying upon was purely hearsay, which casts doubt over the bishop's protestations.

Adding to d'Arcis's flimsy case was the glaring problem that Bishop Henri d'Poitiers was unable to be deposed as he had conveniently died nineteen years earlier in 1370. He left no documentation, no copy of the alleged confession, no name of the superlative artist, and a verbal description that does not match the Turin Shroud. In fact, there was no known clerical support within the church hierarchy to uphold the story.

The hypocrisy of Bishop d'Arcis's was his ability to condemn the sin of idolatry regarding the Shroud while overlooking the sin of theft on display at his own Troyes Cathedral. Among the many items exhibited were several gruesome relics, including the arm of St. James the Greater, the head of St. Philip, and the body of St. Helen of Thyra, all stolen from Constantinople by a former bishop of Troyes in 1204, who was killed during the same inglorious Fourth Crusade.

After 1215 and Pope Innocent's publishing of Canon 62, which forbade stolen or unauthorized relics from being exhibited or sold, the succeeding bishops seated in the cathedral at Troyes were, in effect, complicit in the knowledge they were displaying artifacts stolen from the Byzantines. No hands were clean in regard to the relics at Troyes; but most certainly, after disparaging the Shroud, the good bishop d'Arcis would have been willing and grateful to reposition the sacred cloth it at his church.

Even the skeptic and art historian Gary Vikan, whose theory of a medieval artist we dismissed in chapter 9, had his doubts about this whole incident. His musings call into question the character of the participants.

> But at the same time, I believe both Henri d'Poitiers and Pierre d'Arcis were being less than truthful as to *why* they were taking the actions they took. It was not simply because they were so eager to put an end to idolatry, as they professed, but also, as their detractors claimed, because they wanted to get their hands on the Lirey Shroud and the wealth it represented for themselves. Their cathedral was literally falling apart on Christmas Day 1389.[4]

In a direct appeal to the pope, d'Arcis again expressed his convictions regarding the cloth. The following year, to appease the bishop, Pope Clement VII, issued a second papal decree requiring the cloth in Lirey to be referred to as a "representation and not the authentic burial shroud of Jesus." The canons of the Lirey church, however, continued with their belief that the cloth was authentic, albeit privately.

*Papal statements regarding authenticity*

In 1912, noted Catholic theologian, Herbert Thurston was ambivalent about the Shroud as Secondo Pia's photographs from 1898 were considered fakes by many. Nonetheless, he acknowledged that for centuries, even after the papal bull of 1390 was issued to appease bishop d'Arcis that the Shroud could only be referenced as a representation, the cloth was clearly revered as the authentic burial Shroud of Christ.

> That the authenticity of the Shroud of Turin is taken for granted, in various pronouncements of the Holy See cannot be disputed. An Office and Mass "de Sancta Sindone" was formerly approved by Julius II in the Bull "Romanus Pontifex" of 25 April, 1506, in the course of which the Pope speaks of "that most famous Shroud (*præclarissima sindone*) in which our Savior was wrapped when he lay in the tomb and which is now honorably and devoutly preserved in a silver casket." Moreover, the same Pontiff speaks of the treaties upon the precious blood. Composed by his predecessor, Sixtus IV (1471–1484), in which Sixtus states that in the Shroud "men may look upon the true blood and portrait of Jesus Christ himself."[5]

Critics of the Shroud allege that the papal bull of 1390 is proof the church knew the Shroud was a fake but fraudulently continued to exhibit the cloth for the income derived from gullible believers. However, this allegation does not comport with the facts. Even Thurston, a known skeptic of the Shroud (quoted above), counters this claim.

Additional statements by popes affirming the authenticity of the Shroud of Turin are compelling and convincingly refute any complicity by the church of promoting a fraud. To be more specific, over thirty popes have affirmed the authenticity of the Shroud. Below are the last seven spanning the past one hundred years.[6]

*Pope Francis (papal term, 2013 to present).* On April 9, 2020, Pope Francis wrote the following to the archbishop of Turin to commemorate a televised viewing of the cloth on Holy Saturday:

> I too join in your supplication, turning my gaze to the Man of the Shroud, in whom we recognize the features of the Servant of the Lord that Jesus realized in His Passion: "A man of suffering, and familiar with pain… Surely He took up our pain and bore our suffering… But He was pierced for our transgressions, He was crushed for our iniquities; the punishment that brought us peace was on Him, and by His wounds we are healed" (Is 53:3–5)… As Christians, in the light of the Scriptures, we contemplate in this cloth the icon of the Lord Jesus crucified, dead and risen again.[7]

It should be noted that in translating from Italian to English, the use of the word *icon* is often used to mean "image." There is no implication the cloth is merely a devotional painting.

*Pope Benedict XVI (papal term: 2005–2013).* In May of 2010, upon visiting Turin during a public exhibition of the Shroud, Pope Benedict XVI, considered a theological giant among recent popes, described the cloth, as having "wrapped the remains of a crucified man in full correspondence with what the Gospels tell us of Jesus."

He went on to say that it was "an icon written in blood; the blood of a man who was whipped, crowned with thorns, crucified, and injured on his right side."[8]

In March of 2013, Pope Benedict became the first pope to resign in nearly six hundred years. His last act as pope was to authorize a ninety-minute televised exhibition of the Shroud and described by the Vatican as his "final gift to the Roman Catholic Church."[9] It is improbable to believe the last act of an outgoing pope would be to publicly exhibit a known fake.

*Pope John Paul II (papal term: 1978–2005)*. On May 24, 1998, Pope John Paul II arrived in Turin as a pilgrim to venerate the holy image. He knelt in the "Turin cathedral, where the Holy Shroud, the most splendid relic of the passion and the resurrection, has been housed for centuries" and went on to pronounce those unequivocal words:

> The Holy Shroud, a most singular record of Easter, the Passion, Death and Resurrection a mute, yet surprisingly eloquent witness.[10]

*Pope Paul VI (papal term: 1963–1978)*. Pope Paul VI declared it "the most important relic in the history of Christianity."[11]

*Pope John XXII (papal term: 1958–1963)*. Pope John XXIII observed the sacred linen and declared, "The finger of God is here."[12]

*Pope Pius XII (papal term: 1939–1958)*. Pope Pius XII also revered the sacred image:

> Turin, city of the Most Holy Sacrament, guards as a precious treasure the Holy Shroud, which displays, both to move and comfort us, the Image of the lifeless body and the tortured Face of Christ.[13]

*Pope Pius XI (papal term: 1922–1939)*. Pope Pius XI said:

> They are the pictures of the Divine Son of Mary; they come, in fact, from that object known as the Shroud of Turin; still mysterious, but certainly not the work of any human hand.[14]

Even hinting about deceit from the long line of popes from the Middle Ages to the present is not only in bad taste but repugnant and patently untrue.

After 1390, the Lirey clerics remained quietly committed to the Shroud's authenticity (with no credible evidence otherwise), disdaining Bishop d'Arcis's unremitting protestations, which led to yet another appeal, this time to King John II of France. It appears the king acquiesced to d'Arcis's complaint. Overstepping the pope, he sent his bailiff to collect the Shroud with a command that it was to be sent to the king or one of the local churches (undoubtedly it would have been the cathedral at Troyes). The cannons of Lirey were able to forestall the cloth's abduction by pretending they were unable to find the key to the treasury and ultimately persuading the bailiff to leave, putting an end to the matter.

Detractors of the Shroud will forever point to the d'Arcis Memorandum as their case-closing "smoking gun." However, for most researchers and historians, this incident displays the hallmarks of jealousy, resentment, financial desperation, and false accusations based on unsubstantiated claims. The result is nothing more than an elaborate ruse that fails in making its case.

(See note 1 below.)

1. David M. Perry, author of *Sacred Plunder: Venice and the Aftermath of the Fourth Crusade*, on page 34, writes authoritatively on the subject:

    During the 4th Crusade, Papal legate Peter Capuano, concerned with appearing to offer papal approval to the sack, held back and did not participate in the pillaging of Constantinople. However, after the city fell, he was happy to "take advantage of the sudden windfall on behalf of the pope." He took control of a cache of relics collected by Bishop Garnier of Troyes who did not survive the battle. Capuano arranged to have the stolen treasure sent back to Troyes which included the arm of St. James the Greater, the head of St. Philip, and the body of St. Helen of Thyra.

# CHAPTER 14

## Confirming the Historical Trail through Pollens-Minerals-DNA

In part 1, we reviewed the science employed to examine the body, analyze the blood, and explore the cause of the image on the Shroud. In part 2, we have been examining the historical trail and found convincing evidence for the Shroud's origin far earlier than 1356, when it first appeared in Lirey, France. As an intriguing adjunct that bolsters the likely origins and travels of the Shroud, we turn to such disciplines as botany, geology, and archeology, thereby adding more layers and pieces to fill in the story. We begin with evidence gleaned from pollens.

*Max Frei's pollen evidence.* Max Frei was a Swiss botanist and criminologist who often worked with Scotland Yard to help solve complex crimes. In 1973 and 1978, Frei employed his expertise when given access to the Shroud. Pressing sticky tape onto its surface he collected various particles and debris, which included dirt, insect parts, mites, and pollen. The pollen in particular provided quite significant data. Frei initially identified

Max Frei lifting pollen samples from the Shroud with tape (courtesy of Barrie M. Schwortz collection, STERA Inc.)

fifty-eight different pollen species, twenty-two being from plants that grow primarily in parts of Turkey that correlate with the Shroud's time in Edessa and Constantinople. He also found seven species of plants that only grow in Israel. This was the first confirmation that the Shroud could have originated in the Holy Land.[1]

Just as Heller and Adler removed particles from the tapes of Ray Rogers for analysis, Frei removed the pollen spores from the tape onto slides. He was meticulous in his documentation and confident of the various identifications of spores. Years later, when samples were analyzed by other botanists, deterioration of the spores as a result of contact with the glue from the sticky tape made it difficult to confirm all of Frei's findings, leading some critics to question his results, and even hint at possible fakery. In contrast, other respected botanists utilized the Frei samples to add to their own unique findings, as noted further on. Without a doubt, Frei's body of work and data from the Shroud has been an invaluable source for ongoing research.

*Danin and Baruch—pollens and flowers.* Israeli botanist Avinoam Danin was a professor of botany in the Department of Evolution, Systematics, and Ecology at the Hebrew University of Jerusalem, who worked extensively on Shroud pollens before his death in 2015. One of his several books also dealt with Near East plant images found on the cloth. Working closely with Danin was palynologist (expert in pollens and spores), Uri Baruch. Together they conducted extensive research on specific pollens unique to areas around Israel.[2]

The two botanists documented spores of *Gundalia tournefortii*, a thorny thistle plant, and *Cistus criticus*, a flower with rounded petals from samples taken from the Shroud. Both are native to desert areas around Israel, and both bloom in April and May. One of their significant discoveries from high-resolution photos of the Shroud was the presence of flowers in areas of the cloth around the head. They appeared somewhat wilted and were clustered together, indicating their having been placed on the cloth. Even more curious is the high concentration of pollen from similar areas around the head, another clear sign that flowers were laid on the surface of the Shroud.

Regarding their plant identifications, some palynologists question whether specificity can be made down to the species level, as pollen of related species may look alike. However, both plant types noted above, when even more broadly defined to encompass related species, are native to desert areas consistent with the surrounds of Jerusalem. Of particular note here is the fact that there are no deserts in Europe, where most skeptics are convinced the Shroud originated. Had the Shroud originated in Europe in the fourteenth century, and remained in those environs until its permanent placement in Turin, there would have been no opportunity for it to collect pollen native to the Middle East.[3]

To further validate the pollen evidence, in 1998, Dr. Baruch, using a light microscope at 800X magnification, confirmed nineteen of the pollen spores identified by Frei in 1973 with no sign that any of his identifications were faked or fraudulent, as some critics had alleged.[4]

Dr. Danin further identified images on the Shroud of the flowers corresponding with the above two pollens, as well as the distinctive image of *Zygophyllum dumosum*, a flowering bean caper plant native to Israel.

He confirmed an additional twenty-eight flower images of different plants that all grow in that locale. Flowers emit coronal radiation in the process of decay, and Danin's images show portions of imprints that can be seen using high-contrast photography. This phenomenon is known to schoolchildren and scientists alike by putting a fresh flower or a green leaf between the pages of a book. A few days later, natural radiation will imprint the image of the flower onto the paper.

As a testament to Danin's expertise, his résumé shows seven books on the flora of the Holy Land, as well as the discovery of several new plant species. At the time of his death in 2015, he was Associate Professor Emeritus of Botany at the Hebrew University in Jerusalem. His eighth and final book was *Botany of the Shroud*. So familiar was he with his subject that he could identify a flower with just a glance. Regarding the Shroud, he made the following statement:

> Using my database of over 90,000 sites of plant distribution, the place that best fits the

assemblage of the plant species whose images and often pollen grains have been identified on the Shroud is 10–20 km east and west of Jerusalem.[5]

Based on his research, Danin was even more specific: the Shroud originated from an area between Jerusalem and Hebron, as that was the only area containing these species of plants that could have conceivably been gathered and placed around the body. Additionally, these plants flower from March through April, which coincides with Passover and Easter.[6]

As with other instances of data analysis, there are critics who make objections, often saying the findings are too subjective. Rather than dismiss such evidence, I believe we give credence to the researcher's experience and body of work as a reputable expert and, at the very least, remain open to further validation from complementary studies.

As an example, there is the interesting work done by long-time researchers, Dr. Alan Whanger and his wife, Mary. Alan pioneered the use of polarized image overlay that allowed him to compare the Shroud image with those found on various icons and coins, determining the points of congruence. He placed the Shroud face image in one slide projector and an icon image in another and lined them up to exactly overlay one to the other. Switching from vertical to horizontal polarity and back again, Whanger observed specific markings or attributes they had in common. The same technology allowed him to confirm various other items on the Shroud, most notably several flower images seen using high-contrast photography. He made side-by-side comparisons of the images with flower and plant drawings found in *Flora Palaestina*, a noted reference book of the botany

Ossuary from the Louvre, Paris, France—typical of Jewish burials containing bones of the deceased (public domain)

of Israel. Additionally, the overlay technique provided further confirmation including data linking the flowers to that geographical area. One of his slides clearly shows the outline of a chrysanthemum, an ornamental flower that grows in the Middle East, and elsewhere. He also found a distinct stem and berry formation for *Pistacia*, an aromatic spice plant, among many others.[7]

Close-up image of chrysanthemum flower that compares with the ossuary flower images (picture by Alan and Mary Whanger, courtesy of Evidentiary Research Institute)

The possibility of flowers having been laid within the burial shroud is quite interesting. Although the use of flowers in this way is not specified as part of ancient Jewish burial customs, they do appear as a common motif. In an earlier chapter, we described how Jewish families used ossuaries to preserve the bones of their loved ones. These were made of limestone allowing for the deceased's name to be etched on the outside. Decorations were also carved on the sides, with various flowers, large and small, being quite common. Comparing these carvings with Dr. Whanger's chrysanthemum shows a similarity worth noting when considering flower images on the Shroud.[8]

*The presence of limestone.* In 1978, microanalyst Giovanni Riggi vacuumed debris from the underside of the cloth, the side opposite the image. The particulate matter included many pollen spores. However, unlike the spores taken by Frei from the front side of the Shroud, where the image is visible, about 50 percent of Riggi's pollens were covered with a calcium-based mineral coating. No such coating appeared on pollen taken from the image side of the cloth. The underside of the cloth would have been the surface to come into direct contact with the stone resting place for the body. Limestone is composed of calcium carbonate, so such a slab from a cold and damp tomb could account for this observation.[9]

Looking further, microscopic limestone particles are found across the whole of the Shroud. The late researchers Joseph Kohlbeck, an optical crystallographer with the Hercules Aerospace Center in Utah, and Eugenia Nitowski, an archaeologist, analyzed the particles and determined they were specific to travertine aragonite limestone.

Using a high-resolution microprobe, they compared the spectra of the limestone particles taken from the "bloody foot" on the Shroud with samples of limestone collected from ancient tombs around Jerusalem. The chemical spectral signature was nearly identical, including trace amounts of strontium and iron, validating a close match.[10] While this type of limestone exists in other parts of the world, the significance here is the amount and widespread distribution of these particles found all over the cloth.

*The presence of magnesium.* A recent study published in 2019 offers more interesting clues. In addition to the particles of carbonate materials, including calcite, aragonite, gypsum, and limestone, there are also particles of magnesium. Adler and Heller could not explain the magnesium particles and assumed they were just environmental contaminants. However, the ratio of magnesium to calcium and carbon is like that of dolomite found in a particular area of Jerusalem. Dolomite is a sedimentary carbonate rock that contains a high percentage of the mineral also known as magnesium limestone. The tomb where they laid Jesus after death, known as the Tomb of the Holy Sepulcher, is part of a system of over nine hundred tombs cut into the bedrock. There are five primary geologic formations within the vicinity of Jerusalem. Some are soft and chalklike while other formations are much denser.

The Tomb of the Holy Sepulchre is within the Shivta formation, which is made of dense limestone and dolomite and poses the most difficulty for stonemasons for carving a tomb. People with small financial means could only afford a tomb carved out of softer rock whereas wealthier people could cover the higher cost of carving a tomb from harder rock. Laying the burial cloth out on the floor of this limestone-dolomite tomb would explain the array of particles seen on the Shroud, including the magnesium. We are reminded too that Joseph of Arimathea was a "rich man," as described in the Gospels, and well able to afford an expensive tomb.[11]

*DNA from dust particles.* As we know, in 1978 and 1988, scientists vacuumed dust particles from the space between the Shroud and the backing cloth sewn on after the fire in 1534 to strengthen it for public display. The dust comprised pollen, mites, spores, and mineral particles. Human DNA can attach to any of these particles. Anyone who touched the cloth left genetic traces that can be tested. In 2015, authorities in Turin gave researchers access to this particulate matter to conduct DNA analysis on plant debris as well as any residue of human DNA.

As expected, several species of plant DNA are from the Mediterranean area, Asia, and the Middle East. Findings from human DNA also provided quite fascinating data. This included genetic sequences from people of varying ethnic origins clustered into several Western Eurasian haplogroups. A haplogroup is a genetic population of people that share a common ancestor through their mother or father. DNA from other haplogroups found on the Shroud included the Near East, the Arabian Peninsula, and the Indian subcontinent. The geographic areas represented are compatible with the presumed historical trail of the Shroud originating in the Near East (Jerusalem, Edessa, Constantinople, France, and Italy), and coincide with the origins of plant DNA mentioned above. We know that people who lived in these parts of the world over the centuries handled the cloth in a variety of ways: handheld public exhibitions, transporting of the cloth, private veneration services, and other incidental occasions.[12]

Lead scientist on the project, geneticist Gianna Baraccia, described a fascinating discovery in an interview with Live Science:

> One of the most abundant human mitochondrial haplotypes, among those discovered on the Shroud, is still very rare in western Europe, and it is typical of the Druze community, an ethnic group that has some origin in Egypt and that lives mainly in restricted areas between Syria, Jordan, Lebanon, Israel and Palestine.[13]

The discovery of significant traces of human DNA from a rare ethnic group identified only with the Middle East adds further weight to the Shroud's presence in that part of the world, not to mention the correlation with pollens, limestone, and magnesium evidence discussed earlier.

*The mystery of the burn patterns and water stains.* Shroud researchers Aldo Guerreschi and Michele Salcito presented a paper at the Dallas Shroud conference in 2005 that was both inspired and fascinating. Over years, they developed a theory regarding the burn pattern and water stain patterns seen on the Shroud. Based on extensive experimentation, they developed an explanation that offers strong support for a first-century Middle East origin.[14]

The major burns occurred in 1532. We can clearly see eight prominent burn clusters and corresponding holes from the fire. The image lies between what appears to be parallel lines, which are scorch marks connecting the burn holes. Photographs taken between 1931 and 2000 show the familiar pattern of patches covering the holes; but in 2002, the patches were removed, revealing the new backing cloth seen through the burn holes.

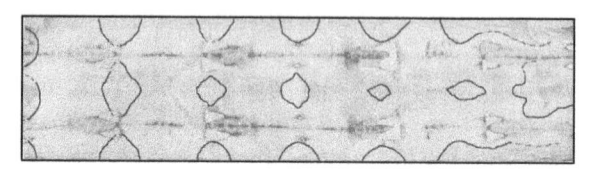

Shroud stains outlined showing nineteen locations (image courtesy of Aldo Guerreschi)

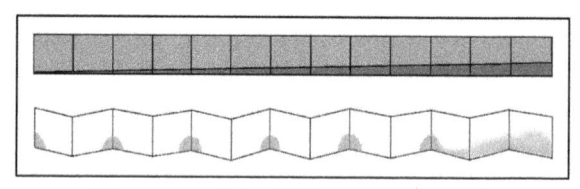

Diagram of the folding pattern and water stains seen in the folded position (image courtesy of Aldo Guerreschi)

Using a replica of the Shroud, Guerreschi and Salcito reconstructed the folding pattern used in 1532 by lining up the burn holes. At the time of the fire, keepers of the linen folded it into a square of sixteen layers and partly folded it over itself to form thirty-two layers.

We can see a uniform pattern of nineteen large water stains over the entire cloth thought to have occurred when they doused it with water to extinguish the fire. However, there is a problem. This particular water stain pattern does not match when lined up with the burn holes. It should be an easy correlation—matching up the burn holes should automatically match up the water stains if they occurred at the same time. Surprisingly, evidence shows the large water stains have nothing to do with the fire. It's the many smaller water stains that appear more randomly across the Shroud that can be attributed to the fire event.

Surmising that a different folding pattern could help solve the mystery, the challenge was undertaken to find the pattern that correlates with the large water stains and determine their origin. They folded the cloth in half lengthwise and then folded it again, creating four layers that were then folded like an accordion into fifty-two segments measuring about 12.6 × 13.4 inches (32 × 34 cm). This method did not quite match but was getting closer. To completely replicate the water stain pattern, they needed to take the folded cloth, partially roll it, and place it in a round container that would hold it vertically. As shown in the illustration, the stains are located uniformly along one edge, indicating the vertical orientation. When looking for such a container that might have been used in the distant past, the only candidate was an earthenware jar like those that contained the Dead Sea Scrolls found at Qumran, Israel. It was the exact size needed. They could fully simulate the water stains by assuming a small amount of water had seeped into the jar with it tipped at a slight angle. The stains are visible because of calcium and other minerals the cloth absorbed from the clay pot. A wooden or metal box would not have produced these stains as the cloth would have laid flat, nor would it form a calcium ring.

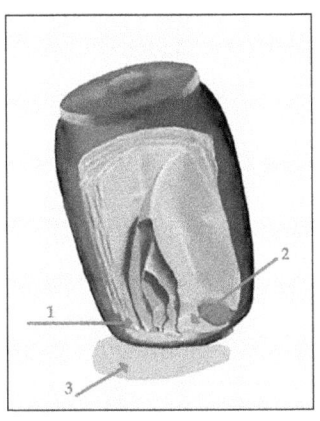

Drawing depicting a first-century clay jar with the folded Shroud inside and water intrusion that would have been able to create the repetitive stain pattern seen on the Shroud (image courtesy of Aldo Guerreschi)

This insightful theory of the Shroud being folded and stored in this way certainly adds an additional argument for its origination in the Holy Land, as well as the use of clay pots for storage being a uniquely Middle Eastern practice. [15] Could it be possible that the linen was hidden in a jar of clay while in Jerusalem, and then transported to Edessa? Did a rainstorm along the journey cause the water stains, long before the fire of 1352? The words of 2 Corinthians 4:7 could be seen as a veiled hint: "But we have this treasure in jars of clay..." Altogether, Aldo Guerreschi and Michele Salcito's work is both exciting and very compelling.

*Summary.* In this chapter, we have looked at six scientifically validated points of evidence that corroborate the historical trail of the Shroud and its probable origination in the Middle East, circa the first century. These include pollen, flower images, DNA traces, limestone, magnesium, and water stains. Combining these elements with key data from previous chapters, the picture becomes even more persuasive:

*Putting it all together*

- Illustrations from the Hungarian Pray Manuscript—eleven points of comparison to the Shroud, firmly placing it in Constantinople prior to 1204.
- Icon images based on the True Likeness beginning in the sixth century
- Historical descriptions from the sixth to the thirteenth centuries.
- Justinian coin minted in 692 with hair and facial features that match the Shroud along with the distinctive double line across the neck.
- Pollen along with flower images native to the Middle East
- Mineral-coated pollen from the outside of the cloth, suggesting contact with a limestone tomb
- Traces of DNA from people groups outside of Western Europe, including the Middle East

- Evidence of limestone particles (travertine aragonite) characteristic of the hills and tombs around Jerusalem
- Magnesium characteristic of a limestone tomb carved out of dolomite known as magnesium limestone
- Water stain pattern consistent with storage in a clay jar like those found at Qumran in Israel
- Alternative dating methods based on chemical and mechanical decay of a dozen other linen fragments give the Shroud a comparative date range of 280 BC to AD 220.
- Wide Angle X-ray Scattering shows how the amount of natural aging found in fibers from the Shroud compares with cloth fragments found at Masada circa first century.

The above points of evidence clearly indicate that critics are looking in the wrong century for their elusive artistic genius who most probably never existed at all.

# CHAPTER 15

## Hitler's Quest for the Shroud

As a concluding chapter on the historic trail of the Shroud, we highlight a twentieth-century saga that reads like a thriller while also illustrating the power of this ancient relic to stir an obsession in the heart of one man to possess it as his own. And once again, we witness a miraculous escape for this special linen cloth. The fate of the Shroud of Turin—having survived the Crusades, fires, water damage, and more—was once again challenged during World War II. As there was fear for its safety from potential bombing, according to the official account, it was moved out of Turin in 1939 to the Abbey of Montevergine, near Avellino, Italy. This is a beautiful hilltop monastery 150 miles south of Rome with links to the Savoy family for generations.

As it happened, the location proved providential, considering that Pope Pius XII thought it best to move the Shroud to the monastery at Monte Cassino, a location he felt was potentially more secure. However, as the war moved into Italy, in 1944, Monte Cassino was bombed to rubble after Allied forces tried to prevent it from becoming a Nazi stronghold. The Shroud would have been in great peril.

However, the timing involved is somewhat puzzling. Italy was not involved in the war until June of 1940, so the specter of bombs had not arisen. Yet the Shroud was moved in September 1939. What could be the answer to this?

*A startling revelation.* In early April 2010, on the eve of the Shroud's six-week exhibition, which attracted over two million visitors, a Benedictine monk, Reverend Andrea Cardin, library director of the Abbey of Montevergine, made a startling discovery that added another layer of intrigue to the Shroud's many captivating mysteries.

Cardin, upon preparing a Shroud exhibit for his abbey library, came across a document providing proof that King Umberto, in September of 1939, only weeks after Great Britain's declaration of war on Germany, secretly moved the Shroud from Turin to hide it from none other than Adolf Hitler. Clandestinely it was hidden under the altar of the Chapel of the Night Choir, a small chapel off the main sanctuary. Not even the Archbishop of Turin was aware of the move.[1]

The document found by Rev. Cardin contained information from Archbishop Maurilio Fossati, named Royal Custodian of the Sacred Relic by the king following the war in 1946. He referenced a visit by Hitler to Turin in May 1938, only two months after invading Austria. Hitler did not see the Shroud, but the party of men accompanying him asked unsettling questions about the cloth and its location, garnering much concern from the Savoy family.[2]

Fossati wrote in a church document that hiding the Shroud had been the right thing to do because "…the invader had been in a hurry to ask questions." He also added,

> It was indeed wise to have taken the Holy Shroud away from Turin, since even if it had been respected by the bombs, it would not perhaps have been respected by *the invader, who lost no time in trying to find out where it was.* (Emphasis added)[3]

Hitler now became part of the story.

*Hitler's world vision leads to the Shroud.* Hitler's closest boyhood friend, August Kubizek, in his book, *The Young Hitler I Knew*, offered a treasure trove of information and insight about Adolph's formative years. Hitler had intense interest in the arts and music, especially in composer Richard Wagner. It was the influence of Wagner's operas that played a major part in the future rise of the National Socialist German Workers' Party (Nazis). The martial pageantry, music, banners, and torchlight parades were all elements of Wagner's genre emulated by Hitler, concluding with his rousing speeches.[4]

Kubizek painted the picture. When he (Hitler) listened to Wagner's music, he was a changed man: his violence left him; he became quiet, yielding, and tractable; his gaze lost its restlessness; and his own destiny, however heavily it might have weighed upon him, became unimportant. He no longer felt lonely and outlawed, misjudged by society. He was intoxicated and bewitched. Willingly he let himself be carried away into that mystical universe, which was more real to him than the actual workaday world. From the stale, musty prison of his back room, he was transported into the blissful regions of Germanic antiquity. That ideal world was the lofty goal for all his endeavors.[5]

German WWII propaganda poster showing Hitler raising a flagpole in the posture of Parsifal's Spear of Longinus, with the "dove of peace" above his head in the form of a war.

It was Wagner's opera *Parsifal* that became Hitler's guiding light. Loosely crafted from an epic poem, Wagner's adaption was first shown in 1882 and features a young man, Parsifal, who safeguards the fabled Spear of Longinus, believed to have pierced the side of Christ, and restores the knights who protect the Holy Grail. It completely captivated Hitler. He even informed members of the Wagner family who had become some of his closest friends that he would build a "religion" out of *Parsifal*, and he did. It was a bizarre mixture of Christianity, Buddhism, and mystical idealism that was, in essence, a partial blueprint for the Third Reich, replete with its message of honor, glory, power, purity, redemption, and even a vindication of WWI dishonor.[6]

Hitler saw himself as a biblical prophet who, by sheer force of will, would awaken the German people not only to their hallowed ancestry a thousand years before—to Charlemagne; Henry the Fowler, founder of the medieval German state; and Frederick Barbarossa, the twelfth-century Holy Roman Emperor. He also devoted great energy to educating the German people about the superiority of their Germanic "Aryan" bloodlines, which would provide the wellspring of the glorious Third Reich. One can almost hear the reverberations of a wildly ecstatic opera crowd at the close of Wagner's *Parsifal* at Bayreuth (pron. "Bi-roit") and the image of a raised arm in the manner of a victorious Parsifal ultimately grasping the magical Spear of Longinus.

Knowing that the purported Spear of Longinus was held in the Hofburg museum in Vienna must have filled Hitler with an unquenchable desire to have it. The authenticity of the relic, however, is a complicated matter; a forensic analysis is difficult for an object of steel. Other "Spears of Destiny" exist, including one remnant in the Vatican archives. Ultimately, the spear's authenticity is secondary to the psychological importance to Hitler because of its association with his beloved Richard Wagner and the opera *Parsifal*, which would transport him into a trance-like state fostering delusions of world conquest and domination.

And then we come to the Shroud. It is not hard to imagine the impact the Shroud would have had on Hitler. One need only be reminded that Giuseppe Enrie's mysterious 1931 photo-negative images of the Shroud were soon circulating around the world, gaining increasing interest from medical experts, scientists, historians, and great numbers of the religious community right at the time of Hitler's rise to power. Enrie's higher-resolution photos completely vindicated any accusations of fraud made against Secondo Pia's 1898 images. There was no longer any doubt that the cloth and its provocative image revealed special and unexplained qualities that could no longer be dismissed—mysterious qualities that would appeal to the German führer's dark imagination.

Hitler recounted to Albert Spear, his architect and confidante, a view of religion that conveyed a brutal dismissiveness toward

Christianity, a version that offers insight into how he could have ordered so many diabolical acts against church clergy; the public execution of Polish priests and civilians in the Bydgoszcz Old Market Square in 1939 and the one thousand Jesuit priests sent to the Dachau death camps are graphic examples. Hitler's statement to Spear shows how the führer saw religion fitting into his societal aims:

> It's been our misfortune to have the wrong religion. Why didn't we have the religion of the Japanese, who regard sacrifice for the fatherland as the highest good? The Mohammedan religion too would have been more compatible to us than Christianity with its meekness and flabbiness.[7]

It was Hitler's mystical universe, as described by Kubizek, that justified his campaign to possess the great public and private art of Europe as well as holy relics held in the churches, thus the dogged pursuit of the Shroud, the Holy Grail, and the Spear of Longinus. He was driven by a kind of madness to find links to history, archaeology, and mythology to prove to the world the supremacy of the German people.

*The Spear of Longinus.* The name Longinus was reputed to come from the Roman centurion who lanced Jesus in the side to confirm his death on the cross, the wound that produced the "blood and water" noted in John's Gospel and possibly the same stains found on the Turin Shroud. It is also known as the Spear of Destiny or the Holy Lance, and Hitler was finally able to obtain the object of his obsession in 1938, when he looted it from the Hofburg museum in Vienna.

Hitler's fanatical interest in Wagner's *Parsifal* gave the spear a special place in his heart. Even more importantly, it was part of the Imperial Regalia, which had been stored in the treasury in Vienna's Hofburg Palace since 1804, all important components of the magisterial symbols of office of the ancient Frank dynasties from the medieval era and beyond.[8] This magical collection, all part of the grand theft, which included the royal crown, the royal orb, and the scepter that denoted kingship and royal authority. The regalia was so important that after obtaining it, Heinrich Himmler, Hitler's closest ally, had it secretly transported by armored train to Nuremberg, where it was stored in an underground vault not discovered until after the war.

As for the Shroud, it would have held an even loftier position in Hitler's mind. One can only imagine the effect the Shroud, believed to bear the actual blood of Christ, would have on the Nazi leader if he had been able to possess it. Thus began a zealous search by special SS groups to locate it.

The quest for these artifacts was no idle mission. It was all part of Hitler's utopian idealism that expanded proportionally through the '30s with his power and rise in world stature. His totalitarian ambitions were even fanned by his appearance on the front page of *Time* magazine in 1934 and 1936 and was capped off by *Time* shamefully naming him Man of the Year in 1939.

*Heinrich Himmler's "contribution."* Heinrich Himmler was the perfect executor of Nazi insanity. He joined the Party in 1925 and emerged incrementally from the lower ranks into Party leadership in the early '30s. In succession, he rose from *Reichsführer* of the SS to head of the secret police, the Gestapo, and soon after arrived at the pinnacle: second in command of the Third Reich.

Himmler was the prime architect of the Holocaust and a devotee of an amorphous ideology described by some as "philosophical mysticism," similar in ways to Hitler's philosophy. Himmler left a legacy that resulted in a cold-blooded, fanatical adherence to Nazi racist ideology and the death of millions.[9]

As a paramilitary adjunct to the SS, Himmler organized the Ahnenerbe, a multifaceted body of scien-

Adolph Hitler and Heinrich Himmler Reviewing a parade in 1940. Himmler is wearing the "Death Heads" insignia of the SS (Schutzstaffel) on his cap. (Public domain: *Israeli Times*)

tists, historians, archeologists, and others that, among their many objectives, was in charge of the worldwide procurement of the religious and mystical artifacts described above. Another prime objective was researching the world's archives and developing a field of pseudoscience and history whose purpose was to justify Nazi goals. They compiled a massive library on witchcraft trials and executions, all stolen from repositories throughout Europe, which delved deeply into the world of black magic and the occult.

Unlike Hitler, Himmler subscribed to many occult ideas that went beyond their shared incorporation of secrecy and mysticism.[10] He also performed nighttime occult masses in castles throughout Germany for SS initiations. He envisioned the Third Reich as a revival of the Arthurian legend of Camelot with the Knights of the Round Table (presumably SS leaders), with Hitler replacing the good King Arthur. To facilitate this, Himmler confiscated a castle in Wewelsburg, Germany, to be an SS headquarters and renovated it to receive the Holy Grail once it was found, a Holy vessel that only those of a pure Aryan bloodline could drink from and be granted eternal life. Others, less pure, would die.[11] It is not inconceivable that the Shroud would have ended up there too.

One of the historians conscripted into the Ahnenerbe was Otto Rahn, an expert in Holy Grail legends who was ordered to commence a comprehensive search for the Holy Grail. By 1939, Rahn had exhausted all leads and clearly failed in his mission. He resigned from the SS after witnessing the atrocities of a Nazi concentration camp and was later found frozen to death in the Austrian Alps.[12]

*The SS search of Montevergine Abbey.* Himmler's SS search party showed up in Turin in April 1943, intent on seizing the Shroud, only to be told it had been moved.[13] For the Nazis, events were moving fast and not in a positive way. By September of the same year, the Allies had already taken back Sicily, and Patton's Seventh Army corps was advancing quickly north from the southern boot of Italy. Hitler feared he would lose Italy and end his quest to find the Shroud.

It is unknown how Hitler's men found their way to the remote Montevergine Abbey or whether they knew of the Shroud's presence there. What is known is that his henchmen stormed the monastery in the dead of night and demanded to search the premises, claiming only to be looking for spies.[14]

Once again, Providence appeared to be in the wings. With the Nazis on their way up the mountain, the abbot ordered the monks to gather in the choir chapel for prayer, where, unbeknownst to them, the Shroud was hidden under the altar. The gambit worked. After searching room by room, the soldiers arrived at the choir chapel, also known as the Sanctuary of the Madonna,[15] so named for the beautiful icon painting measuring twelve feet tall and six feet wide, mounted on the wall directly behind the altar, dominating the room with its beauty. Amazingly, the Nazi officer leading the search said, "Don't bother the monks…let them pray," and the soldiers left empty-handed. A miracle had taken place. The Shroud lay only twenty feet away from being discovered.[16]

It is interesting to consider whether the tranquil Madonna rising high above the altar, witnessing this imminent tragedy, acted in her role as protector and consoler just when she was needed.

*Treasures returned.* In 1943, the Roberts Commission was formed to counter the abomination of the Western world's art being pillaged by Nazi special squads. Working closely with the US Army, a monuments, fine arts, and archives unit nicknamed the Monuments Men was formed. Working within the war zone, at great peril, the group eventually retrieved over one thousand troves containing an estimated five million artworks and cultural items.

The icon of the Black Madonna hung above the altar at the side chapel of the Abbey of Montevergine where the Shroud of Turin was stored between 1939 and 1946. (Courtesy of Creative Commons)

The biggest cache was in an abandoned salt mine in the Austrian Alps, which was the primary warehouse for a future mega-museum Hitler envisioned in his boyhood home of Linz, Austria. This edifice was to be the home for every masterpiece in the world. Among the great works were paintings by Michelangelo, Raphael, Rembrandt, and Da Vinci.[17]

The reclamation project became even more imperative when the commission learned about Hitler's special decree issued on March 19, 1945, entitled "Destructive Measures on Reich Territory." This order, referred to as the Scorched Earth Decree or Nero Decree (named for the Roman Emperor Nero [AD 54–68 AD]), was a final command to destroy the totality of German infrastructure including its artistic treasures and monuments if the Third Reich were to fall (which by 1945 was inevitable).

*The nightmare is over.* Fortunately, the Nero Decree was never activated; or if it was, it was never followed through. There were few left to do so and no heart to do it. The German army was a vanquished shadow of its former might, with young boys called up in a desperate last defense of Berlin and a beaten-down populace starving and living in the filth and rubble of war. On April 30, 1945, at 2:10 p.m., advancing American forces took possession of the vault, the Imperial Regalia, and the looted spear. A little more than an hour later, Adolph Hitler died by his own hand in a Berlin bunker. After the war, the Allies returned the stolen treasure to the Hofburg museum.

*The Shroud returned to Turin.* Under the direction of the king, the Shroud was returned from the Montevergine Abbey to Turin on October 26, 1946. It had been hidden away for seven years and kept safe from the bombs of war, the Ahnenerbe, and Hitler. Three decades later, the Shroud would become the subject of twentieth century scientific exploration, attaining the distinction as the most analyzed artifact in the world, a continuing mystery available for all to see.

# PART 3

Supporting Evidence Found in Scripture, Liturgy, Theology, and Prophecy

# INTRODUCTION

I have long been intrigued by the philosophy of the 13th century monk, Saint Thomas Aquinas, considered one of the greatest of all Christian theologians. Born in 1225, he was inspired by the writings of Aristotle, the founder of the scientific method. Attempting to create a synthesis between Christianity and the naturalism of Aristotle, Aquinas made rational arguments for the existence of God. He believed truth enters through two doors, the first coming through rational thought, and the second through faith built on revelation derived from the teachings of the prophets and the apostles. Integrating the two would lead to the understanding of God and the truth of his existence.

Theologians of old understood these truths as two sides of the same coin. Pope John Paul II compared faith and reason as two wings of a bird. Both are required for flight. Unfortunately, the past several hundred years have witnessed an unrelenting drive to separate the two. The Age of Reason, which took root in the eighteenth century, completely discarded the nonmaterial, beginning society's downward path toward secularism. This movement greatly accelerated after the publication of Darwin's *On the Origin of Species* in 1859, which offered the world a creation story without God.

Yet there was a time when scientists such as Newton, Galileo, Copernicus, and Kepler, openly acknowledged their faith in God. Their faith didn't prevent them from being good scientists. In fact, they believed they could use scientific discovery to more fully understand what they observed in nature, the greatness of the Creator. For Aquinas, a theologian, philosopher, and scientist, these disciplines were not mutually exclusive; and until the Age of Reason, they worked naturally together in a symbiotic relationship.

Therefore, following the tradition of Saint Thomas Aquinas, part 3 will investigate both sides of the coin for our closing exploration of the Shroud. One side will delve into observable aspects of the Shroud that are reflected in and supported by areas of theology, scripture, ancient liturgy, and prophecy. There is a wealth of material that contains concepts and direct written references that will clarify our understanding of the Shroud's recognized place within the vast world of Christianity. On the other side, we will conclude with a topic that is a true blending of faith and reason that would undoubtedly excite Aquinas. A phenomenon not easily explained, but there in plain sight, with a possible explanation for the faint image on the Shroud. It will encourage us to see both sides of the Aquinas coin, the unseen alongside the scientific.

## CHAPTER 16

# Revelations on the Shroud's Early History through Scripture and Liturgy

Jesus often spoke in enigmatic parables which contained riddles designed to instruct, but that also veiled certain truths from those who sought Him, not with pure intent, but to have Him arrested. I have developed over the years an intense interest in delving into these concealed messages locked in Scripture. The Bible suggests that God designed the search for truth to be a treasure hunt.

> It is the glory of God to conceal a matter;
> But the glory of kings is to search out a matter.
> (Proverbs 25:2)

> Therefore, seek and you will find. (Matthew 7:7 NKJV)

*Calvin's important question.* Two hundred years after the Shroud was first displayed in Lirey, France, the Protestant reformer John Calvin saw the Shroud at an exhibit in Nice, France. In his 1543 book *A Treatise on Relics,* Calvin wrote about a quandary he was having:

> How is it possible that those sacred historians, who carefully related all the miracles that

took place at Christ's death, should have omitted to mention one so remarkable as the likeness of the body of our Lord remaining on its wrapping sheet? This fact undoubtedly deserved to be recorded.

Calvin was dismissive of all relics, however, he brought up a legitimate question that is still debated, and cited by skeptics. Why are the Gospels silent regarding an image on the Shroud? There are two prominent theories that apply. One is the latent image theory, suggesting it was not immediately visible. Depending on the methodology used, experiments have shown that an image created by radiation may appear gradually over several years.

The second and more dominant theory among Shroud scholars requires consideration of the volatile anti-Christian era of the first century—when anything related to Christianity was in serious danger. The Jews viewed the Shroud as unclean and, even worse, something that wrapped a blasphemous criminal who was luring away Jews to be his followers. The Romans had little concern for Jewish antipathy against Jesus and His disciples, but as time progressed, they also wished to crush the underground movement of Christianity as a threat to the state.

It was during this tumultuous era that the early Christians retreated into the shadows, particularly through the second and third centuries, due to the reality of persecution and simply the need for self-preservation. With twelve periods of severe persecution from the first century until the Edict of Milan in AD 313, when Constantine announced official toleration of the Christian religion, it is no wonder veneration of sacred artifacts and writings were kept secret. William Ramsey, a renowned archaeologist who specialized in the early Christian Church, wrote, "It was the recognized duty of a Christian to use carefully veiled language."[1]

The necessity for secrecy had already begun when the Gospel writers were completing their respective narratives twenty to thirty years after the death and resurrection of Jesus. James, the half brother of Jesus, was killed in Jerusalem in the year 42. That same year, Peter was thrown in prison with the intent of killing him, but an angelic intervention thwarted those plans. It wouldn't be until after the fifth century, when Christianity was firmly ensconced, that concern over personal risk was no longer an issue. Islam would, of course, become an adversary in later centuries.

It was during those earliest times that the church developed a code of secrecy that eventually became known as "the discipline of the secret." The practice originated in the first century, yet persecution was also common during the time of the early reformers.[2]

Through the epochs of world history, secrecy was often a necessity. In our modern world, we might look at the navy posters of WWII with the words "Loose lips sink ships"; and when a navy ship went down due to a casual conversation overheard by an undercover friend/enemy, hundreds of men went down with it.

*Revered items.* Although the Shroud is not mentioned in the Bible after the resurrection, there are reports of items linked to the living apostles that were clearly revered. Scripture records that aprons and handkerchiefs associated with Paul circulated among the people for healing:

> So that from his body were brought unto the sick handkerchiefs or aprons, and the diseases departed from them, and the evil spirits went out of them. (Acts 19:12)

If Paul's handkerchiefs were considered sacred and instruments of healing, one can only imagine what kind of power believers would associate with the linen wrappings of Christ. For those who argue the burial wrapping was devoid of any image, as John Calvin did, would not the cloth stained with the atoning blood of Christ be worthy of mention? Yet there is complete silence. There must be a larger reason, the *discipline of the secret* provides an answer.

*To summarize*: The apostles simply could not reveal the continuing existence of the Shroud, fearing its destruction by either the Romans or the Jews. Persecution of the ancient church was fierce, and enemies of this new religion would confiscate and burn anything associated with Jesus. As an example, the Romans collected and even burned the bones of the martyrs to prevent them from becoming treasured relics offering strength for believers to stay true to their faith and endure hardships to come, which was a common practice for the persecuted faithful. Consideration of all these real dangers offers the most credible reason why the Bible is silent on the Shroud, following its discovery in the tomb.[3] The wise caution exercised by the early believers may be the only reason the Shroud remains to this day.[4]

*Exploring early liturgical evidence of the Shroud*

*The early second-century Gospel of the Hebrews.* This Gospel, noted by Eusebius as being apocryphal, describes a post-resurrection appearance of Jesus mentioned by Origen of Alexandria, who often referenced portions of the text. Although in fragments today, a segment reads, "When the Lord had given the linen cloth to the servant of the priest, he went and appeared to James."

Some scholars suggest that the person receiving the cloth may have been Peter, though opinion differs.[5] What is important here is that in the first decades of the second century, there was a reference to Jesus's Shroud being passed on as an important artifact for safekeeping. For this to be written in the early second century, it seems reasonable to assume knowledge of the Shroud was part of the secretive dialogue in the midst of that perilous era. Although, this was an apocryphal source it is difficult to deny that the reference of a linen cloth being handed off by Jesus to "the servant of the priest," whoever that may have been, is a significant piece of information in the larger landscape.

*A fourth century reference—covering the altar with linen.* As early as AD 325, during a council at the Baths of Trajan in Rome at the very beginning of the organized church, Pope Sylvester established by papal decree that the church should celebrate the holy sacrifice of the Mass, representing the body and blood of Christ, on a linen cloth consecrated by the bishop *as if it were the clean Shroud of Christ* (Dreisbach).

The dimensions necessary for a cloth to cover a rectangular altar table with a suitable drape at either end would support a knowledge of Jesus's long narrow burial linen. The AD 325 papal decree should help to negate a persistent misconception that Jesus's body was wrapped in strips of cloth like a mummy.

*More fourth-century liturgical practices—the Shroud's double image.* Bishop Theodore of Mopsuestia of Antioch (AD 350–428), a Syrian Christian theologian, was considered the greatest biblical interpreter of his time and one of the prominent spiritual heads of Christianity who wrote commentaries on such matters as theological and practical problems, the Lord's Prayer, and the Nicene Creed. Bishop Theodore's works became widely adaptive through their translation into Syriac at Edessa.[6]

A towering figure in the early Christian Church, he developed a catechism that has a profound relationship with the Shroud. His instructions stated that before the celebration of the Mass

> when they bring up the oblation at the offertory [the communion elements] they place it on the altar for the completed representation of the passion so that we may think of Him on the altar as if He were placed in the sepulchre after having received the passion. This is why *the deacons who spread the linens on the altar represent the figure on the linen cloths at the burial.* (Dreisbach; emphasis added)

The catechism adds to Pope Sylvester's papal decree with even more detail by directly describing images on the linen. Not only is the Shroud seen as a long, narrow linen cloth, but the two deacons represent the double image and are ceremonially incorporated into the most significant sacrament of the church—the celebration of the Eucharist or Holy Communion.

Kim Dreisbach in his *Liturgical Clues to the Shroud's History*, from which other references in this chapter have been drawn, offers a final perspective:

> Not only do we have mention of a *figure* on *linen*; but that *figure* is specifically identified as a *post*-passion image of Jesus on the linen burial cloths in the sepulchre.

This unique historical evidence strongly suggests the Shroud was not destroyed but survived the tomb, was important within the life of the church, and was symbolically incorporated into its principal sacrament (the Mass) and the institution of Holy Communion.[7]

*Sixth-century Mozarabic Rite.* Dreisbach highlights a stunning liturgical clue to the Shroud's existence incorporated into the Mozarabic Rite of Holy Week, sacred liturgy brought to Spain in the sixth century by Arab Catholics. This liturgical rite translates John 20:5–6 in the following manner:

> Peter ran with John to the tomb and *saw the recent imprints* of the dead and risen man on the linens.

This is an important early clue. In altering this verse to read, "And saw the recent imprints…," referring to Jesus on his burial linen, it implies knowledge of the Shroud's existence within the first few hundred years of the church.

*The Gospel narratives and brilliant lights*

All four Gospel accounts agree that the women were the first to arrive at the tomb on Sunday morning; however, this is where the agreement ends. Their descriptions of the angel(s) who appeared to them reveal several significant variations.

Mark states, "Entering into the tomb, they saw a young man sitting on the right side, *dressed in a white robe*, and they were amazed" (Mark 16:5 WEB; emphasis added).

Matthew wrote that an angel of the Lord had "rolled away the stone from the door and sat on it. His appearance was like *lightning*, and his clothing white as snow" (Matthew 28:2–3; emphasis added).

These two passages agree on the presence of one angel and the description of white clothing, one brilliant like lightening associated with the event.

Luke and John, however, speak of two angels. Luke writes, "While they were greatly perplexed about this, behold, *two men* stood by them in *dazzling clothing*" (Luke 24:4; emphasis added).

John's account describes Mary seeing "*two angels* in white sitting, *one at the head, and one at the feet*, where the body of Jesus had lain" (John 20:12; emphasis added).

These passages agree in essence, if not in exact detail. Any competent detective would expect eyewitness accounts to slightly differ. If they were in exact agreement, collusion might be expected, familiar circumstance found in many true-crime police accounts. The Scriptures, unlike any other religious writings, are unique in that the eyewitness discrepancies were not sanitized or made to conform to each other, adding credibility to the accounts as a result.

How and why these accounts differ may offer important insight. John's version is especially fascinating. Could the two angels in white at either end of the stone slab be a veiled reference to the double image on the Shroud? It was John who entered the tomb after Peter and "saw the linen cloth lying there and believed" (John 20:1–9).

To me, a common burial Shroud would not be foremost in John's mind at that time, let alone be the driving force that suddenly demanded his belief. To be recorded in Scripture in this manner indicates he had seen something extraordinary. The question is, What did John see that was so compelling? Could it have been the imprint of the image? If it had appeared by then, it could well have been the reason for his instant conversion.

There are not many things that could create that type of reaction; but the Shroud, as we know it today, would certainly be one of them. Could references to angels appearing like lightning be an allusion as to how the image was formed? Perhaps a burst of light followed by an empty cloth collapsed flat on the stone sepulcher? Collectively the four individual stories of angels in the tomb, robed in white, dazzling, like lightening—could prove to have meaning beyond allegorical embellishments.

CHAPTER 17

## Prophecy Fulfilled
## (Isaiah—Zechariah—David)

*What is prophecy?* Prophecy is defined as "a statement that something will happen in the future."

Within the biblical context, the great prophets of Israel included Moses, David, Elijah, Elisha, Isaiah, Ezekiel, Jeremiah, and Daniel, among others. Over a span of eight hundred years, they appeared at crucial times in Old Testament history to deliver their messages. This period is known as the prophetic age, which ended with the Babylonian captivity and dispersal in 586 BC. I have chosen a few significant prophecies that are integral with Christian theology.

*Isaiah, the prince of prophets.* We will begin this prophetic exploration by looking at Isaiah, the greatest of all the prophets. His name means "the Lord saves" and he was a contemporary of Amos, Hosea, and Micah, beginning his ministry in 740 BC, the year King Uzziah died. Isaiah unveils the full range of God's judgment and salvation upon his people. He declares God as "the Holy One of Israel" who must punish a rebellious nation but will later redeem them. It is the latter that makes Isaiah the most famous of all the prophets. He foretold of a coming Messiah seven hundred years in the future who would take the sufferings of His people and the world upon Himself as revealed in chapters 50 through 54. Since Isaiah had a clear view of what the "Messiah" would endure, and if the Shroud is, as declared by Pope John Paul II, a mirror of the Gospel, we should find prophetic reflections and perhaps a permanent record of the events that changed the world. The following verses show the depth and importance of Isaiah's prophecies.[1]

*The suffering Savior (Isaiah 53)*

> He is despised and rejected of men; a man of sorrows and acquainted with grief: and we hid as it were our faces from him; he was despised, and we esteemed him not. Surely he hath borne our griefs, and carried our sorrows: yet we did esteem him stricken, smitten of God, and afflicted. But he was *wounded for our transgressions*, he was *bruised for our iniquities*: the chastisement of our peace was upon him; and *with his stripes we are healed*. All we like sheep have gone astray; we have turned everyone to his own way; and *the* LORD *hath laid on him the iniquity of us all.* (Isaiah 53:3–6 KJV; emphasis added)

Isaiah paints a gripping story of Jesus rejected by His own people. He describes the suffering from wounds and bruising, by the brutality of scourging (stripes), and with that sacrifice the people are healed. It is all captured like a photograph in perfect detail on the Shroud.

> And he *made his grave with the wicked, and with the rich in his death*; because he had done no violence, neither was any deceit in his mouth. (Isaiah 53:9 KJV; emphasis added)

Verse 9 speaks of His grave with the wicked and death with the rich. How is this fulfilled? He died by crucifixion—a criminal's death—in between two thieves, yet He was buried in a rich man's tomb and wrapped in a rich man's Shroud. As an extremely fine linen cloth only someone with wealth could afford, the Shroud is a direct fulfillment of this prophecy.

In Isaiah 52, it speaks of Him being beaten more than any other man.

> As many were astonished at thee; *his visage was so marred more than any man*, and his form more than the sons of men. (Emphasis added)

The verse speaks to the brutality He would receive, especially regarding His "visage" or His face. The crown of thorns with deep lacerations all around His scalp produced streams of blood that dripped down all sides of His face and head. Combined with the massive scourging, He indeed suffered mightily, all clearly reflected on the Shroud.

Isaiah 50:6 also speaks of His back being smitten and His beard being plucked.

> I gave my back to the smiters, and my cheeks to them that plucked off the hair: I hid not my face from shame and spitting.

Clearly the Shroud shows a man whose back has been severely traumatized from the extensive scourging. While it is hard to say if the cheeks have been plucked, the Shroud shows a very evident cleft beard at the chin, as if someone had yanked out his facial hair.

There are no words that can adequately describe Jesus's ordeal, either in Isaiah's prophecy or the actual event of two thousand years ago. It was perhaps the most brutal crucifixion ever recorded until the gruesome practice was abolished by Constantine in the fourth century.

*A stunning description.* Addressing the nation of Israel, the prophet paints a vivid picture describing the sins of the people as if Israel were a beaten and severely wounded man—a description that can just as easily be applied to the evidence on the Shroud.

> From the sole of your foot—to the top of your head—there is no soundness, only wounds

and welts and open sores—not cleansed or bandaged or soothed with oil. (Isaiah 1:6 NIV)

Compare this description with the dorsal image, scanning from the feet to the head, we can see the nail wounds in the feet, over 120 scourge or whip marks from the ankles to the neck, blood pooling across the lower back from the side wound, and the head circled with puncture wounds from the crown of thorns. The Shroud image perfectly matches the description from Isaiah.

The Apostle Paul shows how Christ perfectly fulfilled this prophecy.

> For he hath *made him to be sin for us,* who knew no sin; that we might be made the righteousness of God in him. (2 Corinthians 5:21 KJV; emphasis added)

What would it look like for Jesus to become sin? We find the answer in Isaiah 1:6, and it is exactly what is seen on the Shroud.

*King David as prophet.* David was born in Bethlehem in the year 907 BC, during the era of the prophets. He was

Diagram depicting all the wounds seen on the dorsal image of the man on the Shroud and described in Isaiah 1:6 (© Vernon Miller, 1978)

the youngest of seven sons and a descendant of Ruth, the famous Moabite convert. He was described as a handsome young man who tended to the sheep of his father, Jesse. The people had recently anointed Saul as the first king of Israel, but he soon fell from divine grace. It was the prophet Samuel, the last of the judges of Israel, who anointed David as the next king. The young shepherd's victory over the Philistine Goliath and the demise of Saul brought on his ascension to the throne and the love of his people.

Most of the psalms are attributed to David, many with distinct prophetic implications. Psalm 22 is seen as a clear messianic prophecy for what the future Savior would endure. The psalm begins with the haunting words echoed by Jesus on the cross, "My God, my God, why have you forsaken me?" (Psalm 22:1). A few verses later, David sees specific details and recounts them in the first person, as if Jesus is speaking through him, yet it would be centuries before crucifixion was even invented as a method of execution.

> For dogs have surrounded me.
> A company of evildoers have enclosed me.
> *They have pierced my hands and feet.*
> I can count all of my bones.
> They look and stare at me.
> They divide my garments among them.
> *They cast lots for my clothing.* (Psalm 22:16–18 WEB)

As a mirror of this prophecy, the Shroud clearly depicts the piercing wounds in the wrists and feet; and more profoundly, despite artistic tradition that would forbid such a depiction, Jesus is portrayed naked on the Shroud, which is clearly implied in the psalm by the removal of His clothes to be gambled away by His oppressors. It is difficult to imagine any more profound grouping of fulfilled prophecies about the ordeal Jesus would face many centuries later.

*Zechariah speaks to wayward Israel.* Zechariah is considered one of the "minor" prophets from around 520 BC. He sees into the future and writes of the restoration of Israel and eventual acceptance of the Messiah they initially rejected when they called out for the crucifixion of Jesus. This prophecy, which has yet to be completely fulfilled, indicates a time in the future when the Jews will one day "look" upon the one they executed and will mourn what took place on that cross so long ago.

> I will pour on David's house, and on the inhabitants of Jerusalem, the spirit of grace and of supplication; and *they will look to me whom they have pierced*; and they shall mourn for him, as one mourns for his only son, and will grieve bitterly for him, as one grieves for his firstborn. (Zechariah 12:10 WEB; emphasis added)

Some biblical scholars hold to the prophetic principle of double reference or double fulfillment, which describes a near-term fulfillment and another in the distant future. This can be seen in Zechariah's prophecy where some Jews in the first century may have regretted their participation in the crucifixion. Yet this also appears to apply to a time in the future when Jesus returns to complete His mission of redemption and makes Himself known to Israel and Jews around the world. But this is also partially fulfilled through the Shroud as one can look today upon His pierced body and be moved to mourning. A beautiful exhibit on the Shroud, including a full-size replica, is open to the public at Notre Dame Center in Jerusalem and is maintained by the Pontifical Institute of the Catholic Church offering visitors that opportunity for reflection.

*Commentary.* This chapter started off with Isaiah, the prince of prophets, and his dramatic descriptions of a future Messiah who would receive all the wounds seen on the Shroud and even His death among the wicked and burial with the rich. No clearer example of fulfilled prophecy is found in all of scripture.

David described the Messiah as naked and in agony with pierced hands and feet. Zechariah also mentions Jesus's "piercing," a plausible reference to Jesus's side wound, along with references to the mournful who realized their guilt following the horrific execution of an innocent man, perhaps even the Son of God.

Recalling the view that the Shroud is a "mirror of the Gospel," it can be persuasively said that it also mirrors fulfilled prophecy, as we have seen so eloquently illustrated throughout the passages in this chapter.

# CHAPTER 18

## Signs from the New Testament

Along with biblical prophecy that foretold of the coming Messiah and the depictions of suffering seen on the Shroud, there are signs from the New Testament that add nuance to the portrait. Here are a few elements that provide more context for understanding the significance of this mysterious linen cloth.

*The face of God.* It is not an overstatement that one of the most haunting yet serene images, now well known around the world, is the negative image of the face on the Shroud, an image that went unrecognized for centuries until its unveiling in 1898 in Secondo Pia's studio.

The profound significance of God's face is a fundamental theme found throughout the Bible. No one in the Old Testament was ever allowed to see the face of God, not even Moses. When Moses requested of God, "Please show me your glory!" God's response was blunt, "You cannot see my face, for man may not see me and live... You will see my back; but my face shall not be seen" (Exodus 33:18–23 WEB). The meaning was

Negative image of the man on the Shroud (image courtesy of Barrie M. Schwortz collection, STERA Inc.)

clear—the glory of God is revealed in His face, a countenance so brilliant Moses would not have survived the encounter.

The Old Testament adds more about the face of God. In Numbers 6, Moses's brother, Aaron, is told to bless the children of Israel in the following manner, a scriptural reference that is also embedded in Christian orthodoxy and liturgy.

> The Lord bless you and keep you… The Lord make his *face* shine upon you and be gracious to you… The Lord turn his *face* toward you and give you peace. (Numbers 6:24–27 NIV; emphasis added)

This short blessing mentions the face of God twice. The message from biblical theology is that it is both blessing and favor when God turns His face toward you.

Many other references to God's face are found in such places as Leviticus (26:14–17), where God warns He will "set his face against them" if they turn to witchcraft or consort with the dead through mediums. Similarly, in Deuteronomy (31:17) God says, "I will hide my face" if they start following false gods—death is imminent. Similar verses are found in Psalm 22:9 and Isaiah 59:2. One of the most famous verses in the Old Testament is from 2 Chronicles 7:14, where God asks the people to humble themselves, turn from their wicked ways, and "seek my face."

Something changed dramatically between the Old and New Testaments when "the Word became flesh" in the person of Jesus. As mentioned, in the Old Testament, no one ever saw the face of God; but in the New Testament, multitudes were able to look upon Jesus during his three-year ministry with the apostles. Paul describes the profoundness and goodness of God's glory being revealed in the face of Jesus.

> Seeing it is God, that said, Light shall shine out of darkness who shined in our hearts, to give the light of the knowledge of the glory of God in

the *face* of Jesus Christ. (2 Corinthians 4:6 ASV; emphasis added)

What an experience it must have been to live near Jerusalem during the ministry of Jesus; a time of social upheaval but also the promise of hope and grace. For those who came to believe he was the Messiah, they were able to see his face and witness him as a man. But was seeing the face of Jesus only a first-century opportunity? Or was his face preserved on a linen cloth, offering that same opportunity to millions? In the early centuries, there were images etched on the catacomb walls of Rome. Beginning in the sixth century, icons of the True Likeness imprinted a stylized image of Jesus that still dominates the collective psyche. With the advent of photography and video in the high-tech era of the twenty-first century, the face of Jesus based on the Shroud has become a global phenomenon. Curiously, today we communicate more with images than we do with words. Websites such as Facebook, Snapchat, Instagram, X (Twitter), Google, and many others allow almost everyone on the planet with electricity and a computer or mobile device to see the image of Jesus as it appears on the Shroud.

When contemplating the widespread prominence of the face image today, a further question could be asked: Has the Shroud, as a result of science and technology, been brought to worldwide recognition for this particular time in human history? A time when faith is waning amid growing secularism? The answer is unknown, but we can at least appreciate the irony that science, so often at odds with "religion," has revealed countless discoveries that compel us to delve more deeply into the Shroud's mysteries.

❖

*The Shroud as a sign*

The first miracle, or sign, performed by Jesus was the turning of water into wine, as recorded in the second chapter of John: "This beginning of his signs did Jesus in Cana of Galilee, and manifested his glory" (John 2:11 ASV). Toward the end of the Gospel of John, we read, "Many other signs therefore did Jesus in the presence of the disciples, which are not written in this book: but these are written, *that ye may believe that Jesus is the Christ, the Son of God; and that believing ye may have life in his name*" (John 20:30–31 ASV; emphasis added). The purpose of signs in the New Testament was clearly stated.

The Shroud can easily be understood as another sign, a physical manifestation that can be seen and is accessible to anyone who looks. It brings to mind the story of doubting Thomas, the disciple who refused to believe that Jesus had risen until they were standing face to face. The result, of course, was Thomas's dramatic acceptance and undying conviction of the reality of Jesus. The Shroud can serve that same purpose today.

❖

*The sign of the prophet Jonah.* The Sadducees and Pharisees at the time of Jesus were the religious power brokers of the day. Collectively they believed that Jesus was a fraud, and their appointment was to catch him in a trap that would prove it. After all, the Pharisees believed the real Messiah would come from more noble circumstances, would live in a palace, and would have no association with the common people they deemed "sinners." They could believe that King David rose to prominence from a humble shepherd boy a thousand years earlier but refused to believe it could happen again. So these Jewish leaders, not only skeptical but also feeling threatened, addressed Jesus, "Teacher, we want to see a sign from you" (Matthew 12:38 WEB).

In essence, they were daring him to perform some sort of circus trick, like transforming a dog into a donkey. Only then might they believe. If he failed, they could ensnare him as a charlatan. But Jesus gave a mysterious response, at once a condemnation, as well as a foreshadowing of His own fate.

> An evil and adulterous generation seeks after a sign, but no sign will be given to it but the sign of Jonah the prophet... For as Jonah

> was three days and three nights in the belly of the huge fish [whale], so will the Son of Man be three days and three nights in the heart of the earth. (Matthew 12:38–40)

Jesus was telling the Pharisees that the only sign they would receive, as members of "an evil and adulterous generation," was His death, burial, and resurrection. If that were not enough, nothing would suffice.

The sign of the prophet Jonah, well known to these leaders, made Jesus's prophecy clear. Jonah's ordeal symbolized death, entombment, and release, as it would for Jesus. When the fulfillment of the prophecy occurred, it was the ultimate sign, validating everything Jesus had preached. And the physical evidence left behind was a deserted burial Shroud, as a witness to every generation.

The Shroud was also clear evidence of the demarcation point between the Old and New Testaments, the new covenant, and a sign, the purpose of which was to call people to believe their eyes, accept the truth, and enjoy the gift of everlasting life, as written in the Gospel of John.

> For my Father's will is that everyone who *looks* to the Son and believes in him shall have eternal life, and I will raise them up at the last day. (John 6:40 NIV; emphasis added)

❖

*A record of the transaction.* Let's consider something else about the deserted burial Shroud. We have examined the Shroud of Turin and the abundance of evidence it shows of a crucified man, all of which parallel the crucifixion of Jesus. The words of the prophet Isaiah are striking in the detailed descriptions of what would befall the Messiah in his death, and these, too, show a remarkable agreement with what we see on the Shroud. Throughout this book, there are many layers of evidence—from science, art, and history—that make a compelling case of the possibility of the Shroud's authenticity. At the same time, as we made clear in the beginning, without DNA from Jesus, we cannot make that determination with certainty.

Yet should there come a time when the cloth is reliably dated to the first century, which I believe is a strong possibility, then a whole range of topics for further study and interpretation will arise. In light of that, I have often felt that there are more parallels to be gleaned as to what the Shroud can symbolize, and one of them is the idea of a record of transaction. As a lifelong lecturer, I realized there are four words commonly used to describe the Shroud. It is often called a *relic*, an *artifact*, a *mystery*, and a *symbol*. There is nothing wrong with these words, but they fail to convey much meaning. Feeling like there must be another idea, another concept, I searched the Bible for all the words that describe what Jesus accomplished for us on the cross and realized there are four of them that all relate to a divine transaction.

The first word is *bought*: "You are not your own, for you were *bought* with a price" (1 Corinthians 6:19–20 WEB; emphasis added)

Next, in the same vein, the Scriptures use the word *purchased*: "Take heed, therefore, to yourselves and to all the flock...which he *purchased* with his own blood" (Acts 20:28 WEB).

The concept of *redeemed* follows third in our sequence, meaning "to buy, pay off or clear by payment." In today's world, if a person pawns a watch and receives a loan, he/she can redeem the item by paying off the loan. The apostle Peter emphasizes again how believers are redeemed, as in a transaction with the blood of Christ as the medium of exchange.

> Knowing that you were *redeemed*, not with corruptible things, like silver or gold...but with the precious blood, as of a lamb without blemish or spot, the blood of Christ (1 Peter 1:18–19 WEB; emphasis added).

The last word, *ransom*, is the most powerful of the four, defined by *Merriam-Webster* as "to free from captivity or punishment by paying a price." Here Jesus uses the word to describe his mission of sacrifice:

> For the Son of Man also came not to be served, but to serve, and to give his life as a *ransom* for many (Mark 10:45 WEB; emphasis added)

These four words intertwine to illustrate a transaction. Once that is complete, there is only one last component needed—that of the receipt.

*The receipt.* In a typical financial transaction, after the money is exchanged, the evidence of the transaction is given in the form of a receipt—a proof of purchase and a permanent record that documents the price paid.

The final thing Jesus said before his death was "It is finished" (John 19:30 WEB). The Greek word is *tetelestai*, which also translates to "paid in full."

When Peter and John ran to the tomb and *saw the linen cloth lying there*, conceivably, what they were looking at was in effect a receipt—proof of a purchase paid in full. Again, we have the persuasive elements coinciding with the Shroud: the record of blood from the crown of thorns, the scourge marks, the wound in the side, the nail wounds in the wrists and feet, the bruises on the face, and the abrasions on the knees and shoulders. Could the Shroud be an itemized receipt documenting everything that was paid to purchase salvation for humanity and for all who believe?

Without absolute proof of the Shroud's authenticity, this will always be a matter of faith. However, this important concept takes us beyond the linen cloth lying in the tomb as the first evidence for the resurrection causing John to believe. It leads to a vital theological concept that we have been bought, purchased, redeemed, and ransomed. Clearly these are words of transaction. There must be a record of it. The questions are, What is it, and where is it? There is only one possibility and is preserved in Turin, Italy, awaiting the next public exhibition when the whole world can once again behold the extreme price that was paid.

CHAPTER 19

## When Is a Scorch Not a Scorch? The Mystery of Holy Fire

A great deal of study from many sources worldwide have attempted to explain the image-formation process. Paints, dyes, pigments, and other known artistic methods have all been ruled out. We introduced some of the theories of image formation in an earlier chapter and discussed the shortfalls they presented. In this chapter we return to the scientific, the discipline of testing and measurements, to use Dr. Adler's characterization. Two analytical tools scientists have used for their investigations are *spectroscopy* and *UV florescence*. Both reveal important clues that may help unlock the mystery of how the image was formed.

To better understand these two fields, here is a brief summary to describe what each process entails and how it relates to the image.

*Spectroscopy* involves the interaction between light and matter and measures how light is absorbed, emitted, or scattered when analyzing different substances. Each type of atom or molecule reflects, absorbs, and emits electromagnetic radiation in its own characteristic way. These processes have been instrumental in detecting, determining, and quantifying the molecular and/or structural composition of the image, blood, and other substances found on the Shroud.

*UV fluorescence* is a technique in which ultraviolet radiation is used to excite chemicals within an object that causes them to release light in the visible spectrum. It is particularly useful to determine radiation emitted by various substances due to heat. To detect the influence of a thermal event, scientists will often use shorter wavelength radiation such as x-ray or ultraviolet light.

A serious fire damaged the Shroud in 1532. As a result, there is a pattern of burns and scorch marks on the cloth that, in places, have a similar visual colorization to the image on the Shroud yet with one major difference. When spectroscopy is used to analyze the burns and the image, the corresponding graphs are nearly identical, suggesting the image is a scorch created by a heat-causing event; however, when the Shroud image was analyzed with UV fluorescence, it did *not* fluoresce, indicating an absence of heat.

What does this mean? Even though the image looks like a scorch using spectroscopy, it isn't. As a result, the mystery of the image increases exponentially. These studies conclusively debunk the *hot statue* theory, which alleges that a medieval artist/forger crafted a sculpture and applied heat as a way of scorching the image onto the cloth. The image is not the result of heat.

*Mysterious fire found in the Bible?* Are there any clues in history or in the Bible narratives that deal with the subject of fires that did not give off heat? In fact, there are, one being a well-noted description on the day of Pentecost after the resurrection of Jesus.

> Now when the day of Pentecost had come, they were all with one accord in one place. Suddenly there came from the sky a sound like the rushing of a mighty wind, and it filled all the house where they were sitting. *Tongues like fire appeared* and were distributed to them, and one sat on each of them. (Acts 2:1–3 WEB; emphasis added)

On the day of Pentecost, Scripture describes the infilling of the Holy Spirit among the 120 believers waiting in the Upper Room. There were flames of fire that settled on each person's shoulder, yet nothing burned.

We have a similar example from the book of Exodus (3:2) in the Old Testament. When God called upon Moses, he saw a nearby burning bush and went to investigate. There was a fire in the bush, but it was not consumed, suggesting a similar manifestation as the Pentecost phenomenon.

These are extraordinary examples that offer major clues of a type of fire that produced no heat. What can be concluded is that the image on the Shroud may have been produced from a source of fire without heat. It is almost unimaginable, not only in the context of history but even today, nevertheless, it is well-documented in Scripture.

*Alternate light theory.* In 2011, researchers with the ENEA, an Italian agency for new technologies, published the result of their experiments using UV radiation in a peer-reviewed journal. As discussed in the chapter on theories of image formation, they determined that a short microsecond burst from a high-energy ultraviolet laser applied to a control sample of linen achieves the same depth and coloration as seen on the Shroud. And most important for this discussion is that the amount of heat generated was minimal. This is an astonishing piece of evidence.

Given all the possible methodologies of image formation, the micro-second burst is clearly one of the most compelling. Regardless of one's belief of what may have happened in the tomb, we are looking here at serious scientific experimentation which only now may be catching up to the Bible narratives.

> Listen, I tell you a mystery: We will not all sleep, but we will all be changed—in a flash, in the twinkling of an eye, at the last trumpet. For the trumpet will sound, the dead will be raised imperishable, and we will be changed. (1 Corinthians 15:51–52 NIV)

*Historical perspective.* Following on that theme, if you were to go back in time to the turn of the previous century, circa 1900, people walked almost everywhere. One might take a streetcar if you lived in a city because automobiles were only at the one-cylinder buggy level and were essentially only play toys of the rich. Marconi had just invented the concept of a radio (1896), but it took until 1920 for the first broadcast. Commercial aviation was not even conceived of; and neither were microwave ovens, a man on the moon, heart transplants, and computers, let alone a smartphone in every pocket. What were once deemed impossible for man are now commonplace.

The scientific discoveries and technical innovations over the last one hundred years were also once inconceivable. We must remind ourselves that "with God all things are possible," and our own human experience of seeing the first airplane becoming a space shuttle should remind us to refrain from putting limits on what he can or cannot do.

*The mystery of Holy Fire*

With the UV laser technology tests done on the Shroud, we see a mechanism that might get us closer to understanding the cause of the scorch not caused by heat. But there is another wondrous possibility to consider that may be beyond our capacity to comprehend, not unlike the Shroud itself.

A phenomenon known as Holy Fire or Holy Light occurs once a year on Orthodox Holy Saturday at two in the afternoon. It takes place in the edicule of the Church of the Holy Sepulchre in Jerusalem. The edicule is a small chapel-like structure within the larger church and encloses the tomb venerated since at least the fourth century as the burial place of Jesus. It only occurs one day out of the year and only from this tomb. The Orthodox have always believed it to be a sign of the resurrection. Orthodox Easter is not calculated the way Catholics and Protestants determine the date. Rather, it is the first Sunday after both the Jewish Passover and the spring equinox.[1]

Remarkably, there is a spontaneous appearance of light like a flame that burns without heat. Let's examine this recurring event that seems to be a stunning example of "fire that does not burn."

Sources show this mystical celebration has been going on for over 1,500 years and is the oldest recurring Christian ceremony in the world. One of the earliest documented accounts is from AD 385, when Etheria, a noblewoman from Spain, traveled to Palestine and wrote of witnessing the light that came forth from the small chapel covering the tomb which seemed to illuminate the entire church.[2]

Interior view from the dome of the Church of the Holy Sepulchre in Jerusalem during the ceremony of the Holy Fire (*Georgian Journal*)

In a current account, Haris Skarlakidis, a Greek architect by trade and an avid historian, traveled to Jerusalem many times and witnessed fifteen of these ceremonies. Captivated by the event, he wrote a book published in 2015, *Holy Fire*. He documents seventy historical accounts dating back to the year 330. Trekking to libraries all over the world, he searched through twenty-one obscure manuscripts and discovered numerous never-published firsthand accounts. Despite the span of over a millennium, there is a stunning similarity between all the descriptions.

From 867, a monk named Bernhard described an angel igniting the lamps that hung over the burial slab of Christ. No human assistance was involved. In 940, an important Muslim historian named Al-Mas'udi described a similar event:

> Helena built…the church known today as the Church of the Resurrection and since then

the fire appears there on Holy Saturday, the eve of Easter.

This was an important acknowledgment from someone other than a Christian.[3]

Joyous pilgrims with candles miraculously lit by Holy Fire (*Georgian Journal*)

Joyous pilgrims demonstrating the Holy Fire that doesn't burn (*Georgian Journal*)

(*Georgian Journal*)

From 920, a letter written by Arethas from the diocese of Caesarea to the emir of Damascus reads:

> Every year until now, on the day before His holy Resurrection, His holy and precious tomb

> works miracles…with the door being sealed…and the Christians standing outside it in the nave… there being a sudden flash the lamp alights, and again all the inhabitants [of] Jerusalem take from this light and light [their] flame.[4]

In 1172, a Russian abbot named Daniel documents how, on the evening of the Miracle of the Holy Light, they cleaned the church and filled the lamps in the edicule with fresh oil but did not light them. The tomb was closed with a wax seal. The following day, the bishop and deacons opened it again only to find the lamps lit and burning. They carried the lamps out of the tomb and passed the flame to all those holding candles outside waiting for the Holy Fire.[5]

Perhaps the most stunning eyewitness account occurred in 1192. The greatest Muslim leader of the Middle Ages was, without doubt, Saladin. He was the sultan of Egypt and Syria who famously defeated a large army of Crusaders in the Battle of Hattin that led to the capture of Jerusalem in 1187. At the height of his power, he ruled a kingdom that stretched from Egypt to Arabia. Saladin was celebrated by Muslims and respected by those in the West not only for his political and military skills but also for his generosity and chivalry. The following is an account of how Saladin experienced the phenomenon of Holy Fire firsthand over eight hundred years ago.

> On easter Eve [April 4, 1192], Saladin, surrounded by his retinue, went to the venerable Lord's sepulchre in Jerusalem. He went in order to discover the truth about the heavenly fire which customarily comes down by divine power on that day each year and lights a lamp. For some time Saladin and other Turks attentively watched the devotion of many Christian captives in shackles, as they beseeched God's mercy with tears. Suddenly, before their very eyes, the divine fire came and lit the lamp! At once it began to burn brightly. When they all saw this the people

were immensely moved. The Christians rejoiced and praised the greatness of God in loud voices, while the Saracens [Arabs or Turks that adhere to Islam] were stunned by such an obvious miracle, denying what they had seen and claiming that the fire was a crafty illusion contrived to fool them. Wishing to be certain on the matter, Saladin ordered the lamp which had been divinely lit to be put out. When it was put out, it was relit at once by divine action. The infidel ordered it to be out a second time: again, a second time it was relit; a third time put out, a third time relighted…The Sultan was astonished and painfully moved by the sight of the miracle and the faith and devotion of the Christians.[6]

Despite the Great Schism of 1054 that divided East from West, the Roman Catholic Church took part in the ceremony; in fact, until 1238, the entire Christian world celebrated the miraculous event and accepted its validity. However, later in the thirteenth century, Pope Gregory IX, with no known explanation, issued a decree denouncing the miracle and prohibited Latin clergy from participating. Since then, only churches aligned with the Eastern Orthodox Church have maintained the ceremony. This perhaps goes a long way to explaining why few in the West today have any awareness of Holy Fire. Not knowing what Gregory's motivation was, we can only speculate that the conflict and inevitable politics between East and West played a part.[7]

The following is an astonishing modern-day account of what happens during the ceremony. This comes from Diodorus, the Orthodox patriarch from 1981 to 2000:

> I enter the tomb and kneel in holy fear in front of the place where Christ lay after His death and where He rose again from the dead. I find my way through the darkness towards the inner

chamber in which I fall on my knees. I say certain prayers that have been handed down to us through the centuries and, having said them, I wait. Sometimes I may wait a few minutes, but normally the miracle happens immediately after I have said the prayers.

From the core of the very stone on which Jesus lay an indefinable light pours forth. It usually has a blue tint, but the color may change and take many different hues. It cannot be described in human terms. The light rises out of the stone as mist may rise out of a lake—it almost looks as if the stone is covered by a moist cloud, but it is light. This light each year behaves differently. Sometimes it covers just the stone, while other times it gives light to the whole sepulchre, so that people who stand outside the tomb and look into it will see it filled with light. The light does not burn—I have never had my beard burnt in all the sixteen years I have been Patriarch in Jerusalem and have received the Holy Fire. The light is of a different consistency than normal fire that burns in an oil lamp.

At a certain point, the light rises and forms a column in which the fire is of a different nature, so that I am able to light my candles from it. When I thus have received the flame on my candles, I go out and give the fire first to the Armenian Patriarch and then to the Coptic. Hereafter I give the flame to all people present in the Church.[8]

As the other patriarchs pass the flame among the people, there is great jubilation. The manifestation of fire and light is not limited to what happens inside the tomb, where the patriarch is reciting the prayers invoked for centuries. The blue light is active outside the tomb as well. Believers claim this miraculous light spontaneously ignites candles held in their hands. Everyone in the church waits with unlit candles in hopes theirs will ignite on its own from the light. Unlit oil lamps also catch fire by themselves and are witnessed by all the pilgrims. The blue flame moves rapidly to different places in the church with flashes described as a kind of lightning. Over the years, pilgrims attest to the validity of these events and have signed numerous testimonies verifying their experience.[9]

On Orthodox Holy Saturday, beginning around 11:00 a.m., Arab Christians gather around the church to sing songs that date back to the Turkish occupation of Jerusalem in the thirteenth century. At 1:00 p.m., a delegation of local authorities, many not Christian, pushes through the crowd to stand next to the church door. They represent the Romans during the time of Christ. The Israeli authorities go inside the tomb and certify there is no hidden source of fire. Just as the Romans did, they seal the tomb with wax, preventing any unauthorized entry. The local authorities certify no trickery is involved with the lighting of the candles.

At 1:45 p.m., the patriarch enters the church and removes his liturgical vestments to wear only a plain white robe as a sign of humility. They blow out all candles and lamps prior to the ceremony. Holding two large bundles of thirty-three unlit candles representing each year of Christ's life on earth, he breaks the seal and enters the chapel covering the tomb. The only light to be seen from henceforth will be the Holy Light and Holy Fire as he exits the tomb chapel, passing the miraculously lit candles to the other two patriarchs as described above.[10]

As phenomenal as this seems already, there is another attribute to this special fire that is of particular interest for those attempting to find a link to the source of the Shroud image. As mentioned in the testimony of Orthodox patriarch Diodorus, the flame does not burn the skin or the beard. It is warm but not hot. However, after about twenty minutes, the flame gradually takes on the thermal qualities of a normal candle.[11]

*The skeptical viewpoint.* There are always skeptical opinions toward anything that suggests a miraculous origin. Adamantios

Korais is a fellow Greek who derides the whole thing as the "machinations of fraudulent priests." In 2005, he conducted a demonstration on Greek television of how candles dipped in white phosphorus spontaneously ignited about twenty minutes after being exposed to the open air. Other skeptics have followed suit with similar accusations.[12]

However, these skeptics fail to answer some basic questions: where does the blue light come from? Where do the flashes of lightning inside the church come from? How do common candles brought in by pilgrims spontaneously ignite as the light passes by them? And lastly, there is the fact that Holy Fire is barely warm and only gradually takes on the quality of normal fire. Phosphorus, on the other hand, is very unstable, burns exceedingly hot, and emits toxic gases. No beards would be spared if the fire were from phosphorus. Nor would noxious, unbreathable air go unnoticed. It is easy to make accusations of fraud; however, there is no proof to support the allegations. (See end notes for further discussion)

*The experiments of Giulio Fanti.* Professor Fanti, whose various scientific studies we have described earlier, is an associate professor in the Department of Mechanical Engineering at Padua University in Italy. In 2019, he witnessed the Holy Fire ceremony firsthand, arriving in Jerusalem with enough equipment to perform basic experiments and measurements. He experienced all the phenomena for himself and put the Holy Flame up to his own beard, and it did not burn. Fanti made two key observations relevant to the Shroud. The first was comparing the spectral characteristics of a candle lit with normal fire versus a candle lit with Holy Fire; they appear identical. Just by observing the flame, you cannot discern that one has a lower temperature than the other.[13]

The second observation is even more significant. Fanti held a control sample of linen up to the two flames at a distance of three centimeters and performed multiple experiments over different durations of time. In every case, the normal candle fire burned the fabric while the candle lit with Holy Fire only created a light singe or a surface browning, demonstrating a clear difference in heat.[14]

Just like the burning bush or the tongues of fire at Pentecost, Holy Fire has the same nonburning quality. Then perhaps it should be given consideration as a possible cause for the Shroud image.

However, it might not be the fire but the phenomena leading up to the manifestation of fire that may provide an answer.

Fanti writes that Russian scientist Andrey Volkov, a plasma specialist, observed in 2008 how "the appearance of Holy Fire is accompanied by the appearance of plasma."[15] Volkov received a PhD in physics and mathematics from the Moscow Engineering and Physics Institute in 1987. In 2012, he served as the head of the ionization and plasma laboratory, and today he is a professor of mechanics and materials at the National Research Nuclear University of Russia.

Plasma is a particularly fascinating and unique form of matter. The Massachusetts Institute of Technology (MIT) describes it as follows:

> Plasma is super-heated matter—so hot that the electrons are ripped away from the atoms forming an ionized gas. It comprises over 99% of the visible universe. In the night sky, plasma glows in the form of stars, nebulas, and even the auroras that sometimes ripple above the north and south poles. That branch of lightning that cracks the sky is plasma, so are the neon signs along our city streets. And so is our sun, the star that makes life on earth possible.
>
> Scientists call plasma "the fourth state of matter," along with solid, liquid and gas. Just as a liquid will boil, changing into a gas when energy is added, heating a gas will form a plasma–a soup of positively charged particles (ions) and negatively charged particles (electrons).[16]

Plasma behaves differently from a gas and has a "collective behavior" that allows the plasma to flow like a liquid, while sometimes the atoms stick together to form clumps. This characteristic may relate to the Holy Fire as described earlier by Patriarch Diodorus:

> The light rises out of the stone as mist may rise out of a lake—it almost looks as if the

> stone is covered by a moist cloud [plasma], but it is light... At a certain point, the light rises and forms a column [changing shape as with plasma].

What is immensely curious is how plasma is associated with intense heat, yet the Holy Fire is not hot. It does not burn to touch it. According to Volkov, there is a low-heat form of plasma that can occur in the air but only with extremely high humidity, which acts as an electrical conductor. Curiously, the climate of Jerusalem at Easter is relatively dry with an average humidity of 51 percent (weather-atlas.com). Therefore, it appears to be low-temperature plasma in defiance of conditions that would allow it to occur.[17]

Skarlakidis described what Volkov observed and measured in 2008:

> The plasma phenomenon, which is believed to take place in the interior of the church, is entirely inexplicable and without justification from a scientific standpoint. The high point for his measurements came when the Holy Fire appeared while the patriarch was enclosed in the sepulchre interior. The unexpected measurement was recorded at 14:04 Jerusalem time. Approximately two minutes later, the patriarch came out with the Holy Fire.[18]

The fluctuation that occurred with his measurements was the electrical load. In an interview, Volkov stated the following:

> Prior to the appearance of the fire there was an electrical discharge...which is apparent even without the equipment—many feel that during the coming of the Holy Fire, the hairs on their arms stand up.[19]

To summarize, prior to the manifestation of Holy Fire, (1) there is the unexplained presence of plasma, (2) the air becomes electrically charged, and (3) an electrical discharge occurs the moment Holy Fire appears.[20]

In 2012, an article was published in the Russian journal *Science and Religion,* with four scientists contributing, including Volkov. Adding to what has already been discussed, they offered the following observations:

> At the descent of the Holy Fire, flashes of light diffuse across the walls of the church. These flashes may "descend" from the ceiling to the floor, simultaneously lighting candles... The appearance of the flashes on the church walls, as well as its chaotic movements, could be explained as a glow of low-temperature plasma. We can conclude that at the moment of the descent of the Holy Fire, one or many rather strong electrical discharges took place, which are apparently the reason the candles were lit.[21]

Volkov clearly observed that before the Holy Fire manifested, an electrical discharge occurred. Fanti, a longtime proponent of coronal discharge as a cause of the image, documents how the formation of plasma is always associated with coronal discharge. A coronal discharge is the plasma curtain that is created when air around a conductor gets ionized.[22] As a reminder, plasma is a cloud of atomic particles where all the electrons have broken free from their respective molecules.

*Comprehending the phenomena.* Is it possible to apply these observations to the image on the Shroud? Based on the work of physicist John Jackson, perhaps the body became "mechanically transparent" as it instantly converted to a "volume of light." The body could have disappeared in a flash, resulting in an immediate discharge of electrical energy, forming a field of low-temperature plasma highly charged with electrons occupying the exact same space where the body had just been—somehow mildly singeing the burial cloth. The assumed conversion to light preceding the electrical discharge may also have had an impact on image formation, as demonstrated by the UV laser experiments. This theory, first described in chapter 6, incorporates many elements depicted in these pages and joins other proposals in this ongoing conversation.

*Commentary.* The sequence of observable events that lead up to the manifestation of Holy Fire may be the answer we have been looking for to explain the faint image left behind as an echo or ripple from a transformational phenomenon without the use of heat. Perhaps it is another example of the mysterious fire that does not burn, as referenced in the Bible.

The wonder of Holy Fire occurs only one day in the year and in only one place on earth. It was first recorded almost 1,700 years ago and continues to this day. When looking for an explanation, science can only take us so far. Perhaps it is time to consider the miraculous.

# THE CLOSING ARGUMENT

At the beginning of this book, I proposed an either-or proposition: either the evidence points to the Shroud of Turin as the authentic burial shroud of Jesus, or it must be the product of human effort. In the final analysis, the reader must judge for him or herself whether the case for authenticity has been made; you are a member of the jury. So having presented the case, I would like to offer a closing argument in favor.

It has been a long voyage of fact-finding and a reasonable interpretation of evidence. We have heard numerous experts testify in the areas of science, history, artistic creation, and theology. Forensically we have compared the catalogue of wounds suffered by the man of the Shroud with those known to have been endured by Jesus and have seen a nearly identical match. Carbon 14 dating results from 1988 have been shown to be inconclusive at best, from abandoning the original protocols to the selective presentation of findings. At the same time, we have described new dating methods that are pointing toward the first century. We have also analyzed the inexplicable image and considered several theories including the stunning phenomenon of Holy Fire for clues as to how the image formed.

Those on the opposing side have failed to show how the image was created by an artist either in the Middle Ages or any other time. In fact, no technique for duplicating the image on the Shroud has come close. In that regard, I reiterate comprehensive statement by the STURP team in 1981:

> No pigments, paints, dyes, or stains have been found on the fibrils. X-ray, fluorescence, and microchemistry on the fibrils preclude the

possibility of paint being used as a method for creating the image.

Just as a juror in a trial, you have to assess the evidence, keeping in mind the following questions: What is reasonable? What is probable? What makes sense? Do the facts presented in this book rise to the standard of a "preponderance of evidence," a measure widely accepted in our legal system? For my part, the Shroud, with the documentation presented here, easily rises to that level of proof required for a successful verdict. Now, I leave the decision in your hands.

Through your deliberation, my sincere hope is that you have been persuaded to the side of authenticity or at least toward a desire to continue delving deeper. As I described in my introduction, this journey was like embarking on an archeological dig, and the Shroud of Turin has provided a most abundant site for exploration, one which I trust you have enjoyed and found valuable. May this *Shroud Encounter* continue to be a source of inspiration with more truths still waiting to be unearthed.

# NOTES

*Foreword*

1. John Walsh, *The Shroud* (New York: Random House, 1963), 9.
2. Mike Shotwell, *Immersed in Red, My Formative Years in a Marxist Household* (Illumify Media Global, 2020).

*Introduction*

1. "Summary of STURP's Conclusions," Shroud.com, www.shroud.com/78conclu.htm.

*Chapter 1: The World of Art—Modern Attempts to Replicate the Shroud*

1. Ian Wilson, *The Blood and the Shroud* (New York: The Free Press, 1998), 98.
2. Author's conversation with Isabel Piczek, Shroud researcher, artist/physicist.
3. John Heller and Alan Adler, "A Chemical Investigation of the Shroud of Turin," *Canadian Society of Forensic Sciences Journal* 14, no. 3 (1981): 99.
4. Isabel Piczek, "Is the Shroud of Turin a Painting?" Shroud.com, 1995, www.shroud.com/piczek.htm.
5. "A Letter from Secondo Pia," *Shroud Spectrum International*, no. 18, pt. 4 (March 1986): 6–12, www.shroud.com/pdfs/ssi18part4.pdf.
6. Thomas De Wesselow, *The Sign: The Shroud of Turin and the Secret of the Resurrection* (New York: Penguin Books, 2012), 23.
7. Charles Freeman, "The Origins of the Shroud of Turin," *History Today* 64, issue 11 (November 2014): 6, www.historytoday.com/archive/origins-shroud-turin.
8. Charles Freeman, dialogue with author on ShroudStory.com, c. 2015.
9. Erich Junger and Andrew Dalton, "The Shroud, Geology and the Rock of Ages," *Science and Faith Institute* (2019): 19, https://www.academia.edu/71986450/The_Shroud_Geology_and_the_Rock_of_Ages_002_?email_work_card=title

10. Thibault Heimburger, "Comments about the Recent Experiment of Professor Luigi Garlaschelli," *Shroud.com*, 2009, 1–3, www.shroud.com/pdfs/thibault-lg.pdf.
11. Barrie Schwortz, "Is the Shroud of Turin a Medieval Photograph?" Shroud.com, 2000, 2, www.shroud.com/pdfs/orvieto.pdf.
12. Ibid., 1.
13. "Aftermath: Stages of Human Decomposition," Aftermath: Specialists in Trauma Cleaning and Biohazard Removal, www.aftermath.com/content/human-decomposition.
14. Quote from description of documentary *Did Leonardo Da Vinci Create The Mysterious Shroud Of Turin?*, YouTube channel "Wisdom Land," August 21, 2017.
15. Isabel Piczek, "Alice in Wonderland and the Shroud of Turin" Leonardo da Vinci references, 1996 shroud.com/piczek2.htm
16. Walter McCrone, *Judgement Day for the Shroud of Turin* (Amherst, New York: Prometheus Books, 1999), 88.
17. Ibid., 75.
18. John H. Heller, MD, *Report on the Shroud of Turin* (Boston: Houghton Mifflin Company, 1983), 177.
19. McCrone, *Judgement Day for the Shroud*, 104.
20. Ibid., 104, 142.
21. Ibid., 142.
22. Dr. Gilbert Lavoie, who debated McCrone on Chicago radio show, 1998, in discussion with author.
23. Raymond Rogers, "Frequently Asked Questions," *Shroud.com*, 2004, 1, www.shroud.com/pdfs/rogers5faqs.pdf.
24. Raymond Rogers and Barrie Schwortz, *A Chemist's Perspective on the Shroud of Turin* (Morrisville, North Carolina: Lulu Press, 2008), 38.
25. McCrone, *Judgement Day for the Shroud*, 161.
26. Ibid., 106.

*Chapter 2: Science Tackles the World's Greatest Unsolved Mystery*

1. Tom Minnery, "The Shroud of Turin: Scientists Conclude It's Not a Forgery," *Christianity Today*, February 20, 1981, 44–45, www.christianitytoday.com/ct/1981/february-20/shroud-of-truin-scientists-conclude-its-not-forgery.html.
2. Kenneth Weaver, "The Mystery of the Shroud," *National Geographic Society*, June 1980, 750.
3. Ibid.
4. Beth Spring, "A Shroud of Turin Scientist Speaks Out: Evidence That Nearly Demands a Verdict," *Christianity Today*, October 7, 1983, 58, www.christianitytoday.com/ct/1983/october-7/shroud-of-turin-scientist-speaks-out-evidence-that-nearly.html.

5   John Heller, *Report on the Shroud of Turin* (Boston: Houghton Mifflin Co., 1983), 218.
6   Heller, *Report on the Shroud of Turin*, 1.
7   Spring, "Shroud of Turin Scientist Speaks Out," 58.
8   Minn Minnery, "Scientists Conclude It's Not a Forgery," 44–45.
9   Heller, *Report on the Shroud of Turin*, 221.
10  "Summary of STURP's Conclusions."

*Chapter 3: Forensic Analysis of the Body*

1   Tzaferis, Vassilo, "Crucifixion – the Archeological Evidence," *Biblical Archaeology Review* (Jan/Feb 1985): 44–53, https://www.baslibrary.org/biblical-archaeology-review/11/1/6.
2   "How Long Was Men's Hair during the Time of Christ?" Frequently Asked Questions (FAQ), Shroud.com, www.shroud.com/faq.htm#7.
3   Frederick Zugibe, *The Crucifixion of Jesus: A Forensic Inquiry* (New York: M Evans and Company, 2005), 34.
4   Wilson, *Blood and Shroud*, 23.
5   Gilbert Lavoie, *Unlocking the Secrets of the Shroud* (Allen, Texas: Thomas More, 1998), 79–86.
6   Pierre Barbet, *A Doctor at Calvary* (New York: Image Books, 1963), 109, 116.
7   Tzaferis, "Crucifixion – the Archeological Evidence," 44–53.
8   Robert Bucklin, MD, JD, "Autopsy on the Man of the Shroud" (1997), https://www.shroud.com/bucklin.htm.

*Chapter 4: Analysis of the Blood*

1   Thibault Heimburger, "A Detailed Critical Review of the Chemical Studies on the Turin Shroud," Shroud.com (2008): 24, www.shroud.com/pdfs/thibault%20final%2001.pdf.
2   Kelly Kearse, "Blood on the Shroud of Turin: An Immunological Review," Shroud.com (2012): 14, www.shroud.com/pdfs /earse.pdf.
3   Ibid., 16.
4   Adler, "Nature of the Body Images," 2.
5   Lavoie, *Unlocking the Secrets*, 94–95.
6   Alan Adler, "Nature of the Body Images," 2.
7   Kori Shivpoojan, "Time since Death from Rigor Mortis—Forensic Prospective," *Journal of Forensic Sciences and Criminal Investigation* 9, no. 5 (July 2018): 1, www.juniperpublishers.com/jfsci/pdf/JFSCI.MS.ID.555771.pdf.

8. "Were the Three Days and Three Nights That Jesus Was in the Grave a Full 72 Hours?" Bible.org, www.bible.org/question/were-three-days-and-three-nights-jesus-was-grave-full-72-hours.
9. Mark Antonacci, "An Unrealistic Approach and Analysis of the Blood Flows on the Shroud of Turin," TesttheShroud.org, 2018, 1–4, www.testtheshroud.org/_files/ugd/97f3f2_fca512686df44b4987098da7d8a6f20f.pdf.
10. Alan Adler, *The Orphaned Manuscript, A gathering of Publications on the Shroud of Turin,* (Turin, Italy: Effata Editrice, 2002), 61–62.
11. Ibid., 105.
12. Heimburger, "A Detailed Critical Review," 24.

*Chapter 5: Understanding the Image*

1. Alan Adler, "Chemical and Physical Aspects of the Sindonic Images," *The Orphaned Manuscript* (Turin, Italy: Shroud Spectrum, 2002), 22.
2. Ibid., 15.
3. Giulio Fanti and Roberto Maggolio, "The Double Superficiality of the Frontal Image of the Turin Shroud," *Journal of Optics A: Pure and Applied Optics*, no. 6 (June 2004): 491–503, www.sindonology.org/reviews/doubleSuperficiality.shtml.
4. Adler, Alan. "Chemical and Physical Aspects," 15.
5. Ibid., 13–15.
6. Ibid., 13–15.
7. Ibid., 18.
8. Ibid., 13–15.
9. Thierry Castex, email to author, August 4, 2021.
10. Lavoie, *Unlocking the Secrets*, 104–111.

*Chapter 6: Theories of Image Formation*

1. John Jackson, PhD, *The Shroud of Turin: A Critical Summary of Observations, Data, and Hypotheses* (The Turin Shroud Center of Colorado, 2017), 79.
2. Raymond Rogers and Anna Arnoldi, "The Shroud of Turin: An Amino-Carbonyl Reaction (Maillard Reaction) May Explain the Image Formation," Shroud.com (2003): 3, www.shroud.com/pdfs/rogers7.pdf.
3. Andrew Silverman, *A Burst of Conscious Light* (Rochester, Vermont: Park Street Press, 2020), 27.
4. 4. John Jackson, *The Shroud of Turin: A Critical Summary of Observations, Data and Hypothesis* (Colorado Springs: Turin Shroud Center, 2017), 83.
5. Mark Antonacci, *Test the Shroud* (St. Louis: LE Press, 2015), 111–127.
6. Giulio Fanti, "Body Image Formation Hypotheses Based on Corona Discharge," International Conference on the Shroud of Turin,

Columbus, Ohio, August 2008, http://citeseerx.ist.psu.edu/viewdoc/download?doi=10.1.1.153.8776&rep=rep1&type=pdf.
7 Sergio Prostak, "Scientists Suggest Turin Shroud Authentic," *Science News*, December 21, 2011, www.sci-news.com/physics/scientists-suggest-turin-shroud-authentic.html.

*Chapter 7: The Linen Cloth—First Century Textile?*

1 John Tyrer, "Looking at the Turin Shroud as a Textile," *Textile Horizons*, December 1981, 39-40.
2 Ada Grossi, *Jewish Shrouds and Funerary Customs: A Comparison with the Shroud of Turin* (2012), 39-40, www.independent.academia.edu/AdaGrossi.
3 Tyrer, "Looking at the Turin Shroud," 37.
4 Diana Fulbright, "Akeldama Repudiation of the Turin Shroud Omits Evidence from the Judean Desert," *Proceedings* (Frascati, Italy: ENEA, 2010) 4.
5 Ibid.
6 Ibid.
7 Ibid.
8 Mechthild Flury-Lemberg, "The Linen Cloth of the Turin Shroud: Some Observations on Its Technical Aspects," *Sindon*, December 2001, 56.
9 Diana Fulbright, "A Clean Cloth: What Greek Word Usage Tells us about the Burial Wrappings of Jesus." 2005. 7-10. https://shroud.com/pdfs/n62part7.pdf.
10 Victor Tunkel, "A Jewish View of the Shroud of Turin." *BSTS Newsletter*, no. 6, pt. 5 (May 12, 1983): 1, www.shroud.com/pdfs/n06part5.pdf.
11 Tyrer, "Looking at the Turin Shroud," 39.
12 Ibid., 39–40.
13 Grossi, *Jewish Shrouds*, 2.
14 Ibid., 6.
15 Flury-Lemberg, "Linen Cloth of the Turin Shroud," 60.

*Chapter 8: The Carbon-Dating Fiasco*

1 Joseph Marino, *The 1988 C-14 Dating of the Shroud of Turin: A Stunning Exposé* (Columbus, Ohio: self-pub., 2020), 2–3.
2 Emanuella Marinelli, "The setting for the radiocarbon dating of the Shroud" (2012), 4, shroud.com – pdfs – marinellivppt.pdf.
3 Marino, *The 1988 C-14 Dating*, 14, 16.
4 Ibid, 126–134.
5 Antonacci, *Test the Shroud*, 308.
6 Giorgio Bracaglia, *Uncovering the Paradox within the Holy Shroud Guild* (Honeoye Falls, New York: Holy Shroud Guild, 2019), 227.

7. William Meacham, *The Rape of the Turin Shroud* (Raleigh, North Carolina: Lulu Press, 2005), 84.
8. Harry Gove, *Relic, Icon or Hoax: Carbon Dating the Turin Shroud* (Bristol, United Kingdom: Institute of Physics Publishing, 1996), 218–219.
9. Marino, *1988 C-14 Dating*, 111.
10. P. E. Damon et al. "Radiocarbon Dating of the Shroud of Turin," *Nature* 337, no. 6208 (February 16, 1989): 611–615, www.shroud.com/nature.htm.
11. Meacham, *Rape of the Turin Shroud*, 94–95.
12. Ian Wilson, *The Shroud: The 2000-Year-Old Mystery Solved* (London: Bantam Press, 2010), 264.
13. Meacham, *Rape of the Turin Shroud*, 102.
14. Susan Benford and Joseph Marino, "Textile Evidence Supports Skewed Radiocarbon Date of Shroud of Turin," Shroud.com, 2002, 8, www.shroud.com/pdfs/textevid.pdf.
15. Marino, *1988 C-14 Dating*, 340, 346.
16. Ibid., 14-15.
17. Gove, *Relic, Icon or Hoax*, 220–221.
18. John Klotz, *The Coming of the Quantum Christ* (Riverdale, New York: self-pub., 2014), 116.
19. "John Cornwell Interviews Edward Hall," *The Tablet*, 14 January 1989, 38.
20. Marino, *1988 C-14 Dating*, 494–495.
21. Michael Tite, interview by Chantal Dupont, *Radio Courtoisie*, 1989. https://www.shroud.com/pdfs/n25part1.pdf.
22. Boyce, David, quoted in D.J. McDonnell, *The Great Holy Shroud Dating Fraud of 1988*, EWTN.com.
23. Michael Tite, interview by BBC, *Witness*, March 14, 2016.
24. Alan Adler et al. "Further Spectroscopic Investigations of Samples of the Shroud of Turin," in *The Orphaned Manuscript* (Turin, Italy: Shroud Spectrum, 2002), 98, www.shroud.com/pdfs/ssi43part9.pdf.
25. Benford and Marino, "Textile Evidence," 4.
26. Ibid., 5.
27. Ibid., 2.
28. Riggi, di Numana, Giovanni, "Rapporto Sindone," Milano 3M Edizioni, English translation by John D'Arcy (unpublished) (1988).
29. Benford and Marino, "Textile Evidence," 1.
30. T. W. Case, *The Shroud of Turin And The C-14 Dating Fiasco: A Scientific Detective Story* (Cincinnati: White Horse Press, 1996), 73.
31. Rogers, "Studies on the Radiocarbon Sample," 192.
32. Ibid., 191.
33. William Meacham, "The 'Restoration' of the Turin Shroud: A Conservation and Scientific Disaster." *E-conservation*, February, 2010. https://hub.hku.hk/bitstream/10722/208511/1/Content.pdf.

34 Giulio Fanti and Pierandrea Malfi, *The Shroud of Turin: First Century after Christ!* (Boca Raton, Florida: CRC Press, 2016), 222.
35 Casabianca, "Radiocarbon Dating of the Turin Shroud," 8.
36 Tristan Casabianca et al., "Radiocarbon Dating of the Turin Shroud: New Evidence from Raw Data," *Archaeometry* (March 22, 2019), https://doi.org/10.1111/arcm.12467.
37 K. V. Turley, "A Holy Week Interview with a Shroud Researcher, Now a Catholic Convert." *National Catholic Register*, April 11, 2020, www.ncregister.com/news/a-holy-week-interview-with-a-shroud-researcher-now-a-catholic-convert.
38 Edward Pentin, "Interview with Liberato de Caro: New Scientific Technique Dates Shroud of Turin to around the Time of Christ's Death and Resurrection," *National Catholic Register*, April 19, 2022, www.ncregister.com/interview/new-scientific-technique-dates-shroud-of-turin-to-around-the-time-of-christ-s-death-and-resurrection.
39 L. De Caro, T. Sibillano, R. Lassandro, C. Giannini, and G. Fanti, "X-ray Dating of a Turin Shroud's Linen Sample," *Heritage* 5, 860–870 (2022): 6, https://doi.org/10.3390/heritage5020047.

*Chapter 9: The Challenge of Art History*

1 Thomas De Wesselow, *The Sign: The Shroud of Turin and the Secret of the Resurrection* (New York: Penguin Group, 2012), 22.
2 Ibid., 99.
3 Ibid., 131.
4 Ibid., 121.
5 Ibid., 123.
6 Ibid., 122.
7 Ibid., 131.
8 Ibid., 131–132.
9 Balsiger and Minor, *Case for Christ's Resurrection*, (Orlando, Florida: Bridge-Logos, 2007), 113–114.
10 Ibid., 113–114.
11 Gary Vikan, *The Holy Shroud: A Brilliant Hoax in the Time of the Black Death* (New York: Pegasus Books Ltd., 2020), 77.
12 Ibid, 84.
13 Luigi Fossati, "The Face of Christ in the Copies of the Holy Shroud." *Shroud Spectrum International*, no. 26, pt. 3 (1986): 4, www.shroud.com/pdfs/ssi26part3.pdf.
14 Ibid.
15 Ibid.
16 Daniel Scavone, "The Shroud of Turin in Constantinople," *Daidalikon* (Wauconda, Illinois: Bolchazy-Carducci Publishers, 1988), 314, 316.
17 Ibid.

*Chapter 10: Clues from the Early Centuries: Piecing Together the Historical Trail*

1. Eusebius Pamphilus, *Eusebius' Ecclesiastical History: The Ten Books of Christian Church History—Complete and Unabridged*, trans. Arthur Cushman McGiffert (Andansonia Publishing, 2018), 35.
2. Ibid., 65–70.
3. Ibid., 35.
4. Ibid., 35.
5. J. B. Segal, *Edessa: The Blessed City* (Oxford: Oxford University Press, 1970), 62–64.
6. Liz Trotta, *Jude: A Pilgrimage to the Saint of Last Resort* (New York: Harper Collins, 1998), 112–113.
7. Wilson, *Blood and Shroud*, 164.
8. Ida Toth, "The Epigraphy of the Abgar Story," *Inscribing Texts in Byzantium* (Oxfordshire, United Kingdom: Routledge Publishing, 2020), 77.
9. Wilson, *Blood and Shroud*, 161–175.
10. Trotta, *Jude: A Pilgrimage*, 99.
11. Drews, *In Search of the Shroud*, 53.
12. Wilson, *Blood and Shroud*, 152.
13. Philip Dayvault, *The Keramion: Lost and Found* (New York: Morgan James Publishing, 2016), 60.
14. Note: In 2002, Phil Dayvault, a Shroud scholar and investigator since 1973, traveled to Şanlıurfa, Turkey in search of ancient oil lamps which depicted the Shroud face or image. While in the depths of the Şanlıurfa Archaeological Museum, Dayvault discovered the mosaic, which he immediately recognized and captured in a photograph. After years of subsequent research and forensic comparisons, Dayvault concluded that the ISA Tile, or the Keramion, had served as "the prototypic model of numerous ancient classical depictions of Jesus Christ." Most importantly, the mosaic bore many unique, individual characteristics for comparison purposes derived from the Shroud image.
15. Dayvault, *The Keramion*, 233–239.
16. Ibid., 61.
17. Ibid., 67.
18. Drews, *In Search of the Shroud*, 58.
19. Wilson, *Shroud: 2000-Year-Old Mystery*, 136.
20. Emanuella Marinelli and Marco Fasol, *Light from the Sepulcher* (Fort Collins, Colorado: Gandolin Press, 2015), 95.
21. Giulio Ricci, *The Holy Shroud* (Rome: Centro Romano di Sindonologia, 1981).
22. Ibid., 34.

*Chapter 11: The Trail of Ancient Icons*

1. Mark Antonacci, *Resurrection of the Shroud* (New York: M Evans Co., 2000), 124.
2. Wilson, *Shroud: 2000-Year-Old Mystery*, 135–136.
3. Wilcox, *Truth about the Shroud*, 102.
4. Fanti and Malfi, *Shroud of Turin: First Century after Christ*, 63.
5. Ibid., 107.
6. Ibid., 86.
7. Thaddeus Trenn, "The Shroud of Turin: A Parable for Modern Times," *Journal of Interdisciplinary Studies* 9, no. 1/2 (1997): 5, www.shroud.com/trenn.htm.
8. *Codex Vossianus Latinus*. Vatican Library, Codex 5696, fol.35. www.newworldencyclopedia.org/entry/Image_of_Edessa.
9. Drews, *In Search of the Shroud*, 49.
10. Ibid., 46.
11. Ibid., 47
12. Ibid., 48.
13. Wilson, *Shroud: 2000-Year-Old Mystery*, 159.
14. Toth, "Epigraphy of the Abgar Story," 86.

*Chapter 12: The Intrigues of Medieval History*

1. Wilson, *Shroud: 2000-Year-Old Mystery*, 156–159.
2. Segal, *Edessa*, 216.
3. Mark Guscin, "Sermon of Gregory Referendarius," Shroud.com, 2004, 12, www.shroud.com/pdfs/guscin3.pdf.
4. Fanti and Malfi, *Shroud of Turin: First Century after Christ*, 54–55.
5. Wilson, *Shroud: 2000-Year-Old Mystery*, 185.
6. Ibid., 108.
7. https://shroud.com/pdfs/ohioscavone.pdf
8. John Jackson, "Foldmarks as a Historical Record of the Turin Shroud," *Shroud Spectrum*, no. 11, pt. 4 (June 1984): 9, www.shroud.com/pdfs/ssi11part4.pdf.
9. Thomas Madden, *The New Concise History of the Crusades* (New York: Barnes and Noble, 2006), 101.
10. Ibid., 103.
11. Bob Atchison, "Passion Relics and the Pharos Church in Constantinople," My World of Byzantium, www.pallasweb.com/deesis/church-virgin-pharos-relics+-constantinople.html.
12. Ibid.
13. Madden, *New Concise History of the Crusades*, 116.
14. Ibid.
15. David Perry, *Sacred Plunder: Venice and the Aftermath of the Fourth Crusade* (University Park: Pennsylvania State University Press, 2015), 15.

[16] Wilson, *Shroud: 2000-Year-Old Mystery*, 214.
[17] Perry, *Sacred Plunder*, 14.
[18] Ibid., 2–5.
[19] Ibid., 130.
[20] Markwardt, *Hidden History of the Shroud of Turin*, 194.
[21] Perry, *Sacred Plunder*, 13–14.
[22] "Fourth Lateran Council (1215) Regarding Saint's Relics (canon 62)," Papal Encyclicals Online, translation taken from decrees of the ecumenical councils, ed. Norman P. Tanner, www.papalencyclicals.net/councils/ecum12-2.htm#62.
[23] Perry, *Sacred Plunder*, 180.
[24] Carlos Evaristo, *The Untold Story of the Holy Shroud* (Fatima, Portugal: Regina Mundi Press, 2011), 53.
[25] Wilson, *Shroud: 2000-Year-Old Mystery*, 214.
[26] Scavone, "Documenting the Shroud's Missing Years," *Proceedings of the International Workshop on the Scientific Approach to the Acheiropoietos Images* (Frascati, Italy: ENEA, 2010), 2, https://shroud.com/pdfs/ohioscavone.pdf.
[27] Wilson, *Shroud: 2000-Year-Old Mystery*, 210–211.
[28] Evaristo, *Untold Story*, 54.
[29] Ibid., 53.
[30] Scavone, *Documenting the Shroud's Missing Years*, 5.
[31] Evaristo, *Untold Story*, 54.
[32] Wilson, *Shroud: 2000-Year-Old Mystery*, 217.
[33] Ibid., 214.
[34] Markwardt, *Hidden History*, 196–197.
[35] Ibid., 198–199.
[36] Nathan Dorn, "Templar Secrets at the Law Library of Congress?" *Library of Congress Blog*, September 12, 2011, https://blogs.loc.gov/law/2011/09/templar-secrets-at-the-law-library-of-congress.
[37] Wilson, *Shroud: 2000-Year-Old Mystery*, 197.
[38] Piana, Alessandro, "The Holy Shroud and Othon de La Roche: Notes for a Working Hypothesis on the 'Missing Years,'" Pasco, Washington, Shroud Conference, July 20, 2017, 5, www.academia.edu/35676898/The_Shroud_and_Othon_de_La_Roche_N11.
[39] Emmanuel Poulle, "The Holy Shroud and the Dating of the Codex Pray," *Cielt*, April 2003, 7.
[40] Ibid., 17–18.
[41] Wilson, *Blood and Shroud*, 285.
[42] Ibid., 289.
[43] Andrew Casper, *An Artful Relic—the Shroud of Turin in Baroque Italy* (University Park, Pennsylvania: Penn State University Press, 2021), 10.
[44] Wilson, *Blood and Shroud*, 289.
[45] Ibid., 292.
[46] Casper, *Artful Relic*, 26.

47 Ibid., 5–6.
48 Evaristo, *Untold Story*, 92.
49 Wilson, *Blood and Shroud*, 282–296.
50 Casper, *Artful Relic*, 5.
51 Wilson, *Shroud: 2000-Year-Old Mystery*, 241, 276.

*Chapter 13: The d'Arcis Memorandum*

1 Wilson, *Shroud: 2000-Year-Old Mystery*, 102.
2 Vikan, *Holy Shroud*, 234.
3 Ibid., 229.
4 Vikan, *Holy Shroud*, 144.
5 Herbert Thurston, "The Holy Shroud (of Turin)," *The Catholic Encyclopedia*, vol. 13 (New York: Robert Appleton Company, 1912), www.newadvent.org/cathen/13762a.htm.
6 "Shroud of Turin: Proof of the Resurrection or a Fourteenth Century Hoax," *Ministry: International Journal for Pastors*, July 1979, www.ministrymagazine.org/archive/1979/07/the-shroud-of-turin. www.ministrymagazine.org/archive/1979/07/the-shroud-of-turin.
7 "Letter of His Holiness Pope Francis to Mark the Extraordinary Exposition of the Holy Shroud," La Santa Sede, April 11, 2020, www.vatican.va/content/francesco/en/letters/2020/documents/papa-francesco_20200409_lettera-ostensione-sindone.html.
8 Nick Squires, "Pope Benedict Says Shroud of Turin Authentic Burial Robe of Jesus," *The Christian Science Monitor*, May 3, 2010, www.csmonitor.com/World/Europe/2010/0503/Pope-Benedict-says-Shroud-of-Turin-authentic-burial-robe-of-Jesus.
9 Shroud of Turin to Make Rare Live TV Appearance at Easter," Union of Catholic Asian News, March 11, 2013, www.ucanews.com/news/shroud-of-turin-to-make-rare-live-tv-appearance-at-easter/67672#.
10 "The Popes and the Holy Shroud," *La Stampa*, April 19, 2015, www.lastampa.it/vatican-insider/en/2015/04/19/news/the-popes-and-the-holy-shroud-1.35274250.
11 The Shroud of Turin: Proof of the Resurrection or a Fourteenth-Century Hoax?" *Ministry: International Journal for Pastors*, 1979, www.ministrymagazine.org/archive/1979/07/the-shroud-of-turin.
12 "What Is the Shroud of Turin?" Catholic Straight Answers, https://catholicstraightanswers.com/what-is-the-shroud-of-turin.
13 "The Popes," *La Stampa*.
14 Ibid.

# RUSS BREAULT

*Chapter 14: Confirming the Historical Trail Through Pollens-Minerals-DNA*

1. Antonacci, *Resurrection of the Shroud*, 109–114.
2. Avinoam Danin, *The Origin of the Shroud of Turin from the Near East as Evidenced by Plant Images and by Pollen Grains* (1998), www.shroud.com/danin2.htm.
3. Avinoam Danin, *Botany of the Shroud: The Story of Floral Images on the Shroud of Turin* (Jerusalem: Danin Publishing, 2010), 40.
4. Avinoam Danin, Alan Whanger, Mary Whanger, and Uri Baruch, *Flora of the Shroud of Turin* (St. Louis: Missouri Botanical Garden Press, 1999), 12.
5. Danin, *Botany of the Shroud*, 54.
6. Ibid.
7. Mary and Alan Whanger, *The Shroud of Turin. An Adventure of Discovery*, (Franklin, TN. Providence House Publishers, 1998)77-78
8. Cynthia Crewe, *Plant Motifs on Jewish Ossuaries and Sarcophagi in Palestine in the Late Second Temple Period*, (England: University of Manchester, 2005), http://static1.1.sqspcdn.com/static/f/784513/21627387/1358095491917/1.pdf?token=3UwkxlzNSCjIk9V8CnJHGQuhi44%3D.
9. Wilson, *Blood and Shroud*, 104.
10. Ibid., 105.
11. Dalton and Junger, "Rock of Ages," 17.
12. G. Barcaccia et al., "Uncovering the Sources of DNA Found on the Turin Shroud," *Scientific Reports* 5, (2015), www.nature.com/articles/srep14484.
13. Tia Ghose, "Is It a Fake? DNA Testing Deepens Mystery of Shroud of Turin," Live Science, October 23, 2015, www.livescience.com/52567-shroud-of-turin-dna.html.
14. Aldo Guerreschi and Michele Salcito, "Further Studies on the Scorches and the Watermarks," Shroud.com, 2005. www.shroud.com/pdfs/aldo4.pdf.

*Chapter 15: Hitler's Quest for the Shroud*

1. Ann Wise, "Italian Monks Reportedly Hid the Holy Shroud from Hitler," ABC News, April 8, 2010, www.abcnews.go.com/International/italian-monks-reportedly-hid-holy-shroud-hitler/story?id=10320593.
2. Antonio Parisi, "The Day the Shroud Mocked Hitler," *Diva E Donna*, April 13, 2010.
3. Evaristo, *Untold Story*, 109.
4. August Kubizek, *The Young Hitler I Knew* (New York: Arcade Publishing, 2011), ch. 17, 20.
5. Ibid.
6. Alex Ross, "The Unforgiven," The New Yorker, August 10, 1998, re: interview with Gottfried Wagner

7. Albert Spear, *Inside the Third Reich* (New York: Simon and Schuster, 1997), 96.
8. Dagmar Paulus, "From Charlemagne to Hitler: The Imperial Crown of the Holy Roman Empire and Its Symbolism" (University College London, 2017): 2, https://cpb-eu-w2.wpmucdn.com/blogs.bristol.ac.uk/dist/c/332/files/2016/01/Paulus-2017-From-Charlemagne-to-Hitler.pdf.
9. Britannica, T. Editors of Encyclopedia, "Heinrich Himmler," *Encyclopedia Britannica*, October 3, 2021, www.britannica.com/biography/Heinrich-Himmler.
10. Nicholas Goodrick-Clarke, *Black Sun: Aryan Cults, Esoteric Nazism, and the Politics of Identity* (New York: New York University Press, 2003), 166–169.
11. Nigel Gradden, *Otto Rahn and the Quest for the Holy Grail* (Kempton, Illinois: Adventures Unlimited Press, 2008), 106.
12. Ibid., 146.
13. Jeff Matthews, "Raiders of the Lost Shroud," Naples: Life, Death, & Miracles, July 2010, www.naplesldm.com/shroud.php.
14. Wise, "Italian Monks."
15. Ella Rozett, "List of Black Madonnas—Montevergine," Interfaith Mary, www.interfaithmary.net/blog/montevergine.
16. Wise, "Italian Monks."
17. Noah Charney, "Hitler's Hunt for the Holy Grail and Ghent Altarpiece," The Daily Beast, December 21, 2013, www.thedailybeast.com/hitlers-hunt-for-the-holy-grail-and-the-ghent-altarpiece.

*Chapter 16: Revelations on the Shroud's Early History through Scripture and Liturgy*

1. Larry Stalley, "Four Veiled References to the Shroud of Turin in the New Testament," Academia.edu, 2021, 3, www.academia.edu/45127440/Four_Veiled_References_to_the_ Shroud_of_Turin_in_the_New_Testament.
2. Arthur Barnes, "Discipline of the Secret," *The Catholic Encyclopedia*, vol. 5 (New York: Robert Appleton Company, 1909), www.newadvent.org/cathen/05032a.htm.
3. John Evangelist Walsh, *The Bones of St. Peter* (Manchester, New Hampshire: Sophia Institute Press, 1982), 170.
4. Barnes, "Discipline."
5. Diana Fulbright, Proceedings of the International Workshop on the Scientific approach to the Acheiropoietos Images, ENEA Frascati, Italy, May 4–6, 2010.
6. Dom Gregory Dix, *The Shape of the Liturgy* (London: Dacre, 1960), 282.
7. Father Albert Dreisbach, "Liturgical Clues to the Shroud's History," Shroud.com, 1995, www.shroud.com /dreisbch.htm.

*Chapter 17: Prophecy Fulfilled: (Isaiah—Zechariah—David)*

1. "Intro to Isaiah," International Bible Society, www.biblica.com/resources/scholar-notes/niv-study-bible/intro-to-isaiah/.

*Chapter 19: When Is a Scorch Not a Scorch? The Mystery of Holy Fire*

1. Bishop Auxentios of Photiki. "The Paschal Fire in Jerusalem: A Study of the Rite of the Holy Fire in the Church of the Holy Sepulchre," HolyFire.org, Berkeley, California, 1999, www.holyfire.org/eng/doc_PaschalFireJ2.htm.
2. Niels Christian Hvidt, "Miracle of the Holy Fire," True Life in God, www.Davidtlig.org.uk/miracle.html.
3. Haris Skarlakidis, *Holy Fire: The Miracle of the Light of the Resurrection at the Tomb of Jesus* (Athens, Greece: Elea Publishing, 2015), 55, 59.
4. Auxentios, "The Paschal Fire."
5. Ibid.
6. Skarlakidis, *Holy Fire*, 155.
7. Ibid., 15.
8. "Jerusalem's Annual Paschal Miracle: The Holy Fire," Monastery Icons, www.monasteryicons.com/product/Jerusalems-Annual-Paschal-Miracle-The-Holy-Fire/did-you-know.
9. Ibid.
10. Hvidt, "Miracle of the Holy Fire."
11. Giulio Fanti, "Is the Holy Fire Related to the Turin Shroud?" *Global Journal of Archaeology and Anthropology* 10, issue 2 (2019): 2.
12. "Holy Fire Ceremony at the Church of the Holy Sepulchre," Facts and Details, www.factsanddetails.com/world/cat55/sub352/entry-5772.html.
13. Fanti, "Is the Holy Fire Related?" 4.
14. Ibid., 5.
15. Ibid., 2.
16. "What Is Plasma?" Plasma Science and Fusion Center, www.psfc.mit.edu/vision/what_is_plasma.
17. Skarlakidis, *Holy Fire*, 133.
18. Ibid., 133.
19. Ibid.
20. Ibid., 134.
21. Ibid., 135–136.
22. "Corona Discharge," Thierry Corp, www.thierry-corp.com/plasma-knowledgebase/corona-discharge.

Note: The subject of Holy Fire is not without controversy. Statements made by various members of Orthodox clergy suggest the fire that emanates from the Holy Sepulchre is lit from a lamp that is kept inside the Edicule and not from a miraculous source. This clearly contradicts the testimony of Diodorus, the Orthodox Patriarch from 1981 to 2000. However, even if such allegations are true, Giulio Fanti is adamant that the fire has qualities that are unique and distinct from ordinary fire which he tested and measured in 2019. The observations made by Russian physicist Volkov further validate that unusual observable phenomena occur inside the church during the ceremony which seems to correlate with cold plasma. He also measured strong electrical activity within minutes of the patriarch emerging from the Edicule with his candles lit. It indicates that even if the fire originates from a "natural" source, it still manifests attributes that correlate with biblical similarities seen in the burning bush of Moses and the tongues of fire at Pentecost. Haris Skarlakidis unearthed dozens of historical references dating back over a thousand years, some of which were from non-Christian sources. In searching for clues as to how the image on the Shroud came to be, we are looking for a phenomenon that appears like a scorch visually and spectrographically yet is not the result of heat. Regardless of questions related to its source, the measurable attributes of Holy Fire offer a compelling clue with biblical counterparts as support.

# ABOUT THE AUTHOR

Russ Breault is a lifelong lecturer and researcher on the Shroud of Turin, believed by millions to be the burial cloth that covered Jesus in the tomb. Russ attended the original United States scientific symposium in 1981 and has taken part in many conferences since as a moderator or keynote speaker. He is a member of the Shroud Science Group, a global consortium of scientists and scholars dedicated to further research. He is also a board member of the Shroud of Turin Education and Research Association Inc. (STERA), founded by Barrie Schwortz, the official documenting photographer for the famous 1978 Shroud of Turin Research Project Inc. (STURP). He was an advisor to Museum of the Bible in Washington, DC, for the development of a world-class exhibit that opened in February of 2022 and was a primary speaker for the opening session. Russ Breault is a founding board member and senior advisor to SignFromGod.org, an education ministry about the Shroud of Turin.

Russ has lectured at hundreds of colleges, universities, and churches of all denominations and appeared in several documentaries seen on CBS, History Channel, Discovery, and EWTN. He was an advisor for the CNN series *Finding Jesus,* along with interviews on *Good Morning America* and ABC's *World News Tonight*. He has carefully observed and considered the Shroud up close on several occasions. Along with his expansive knowledge of the Shroud, he has developed a deep knowledge of Scripture with expertise in many other areas of Christian apologetics.

Russ is president and founder of the Shroud of Turin Education Project Inc. with a simple mission statement: "To advance the knowledge of the Shroud to a new generation." He hosts two websites, www.ShroudEncounter.com and www.ShroudUniversity.com, along with a YouTube Channel, Facebook page, and Instagram page all under the "Shroud Encounter" moniker.

In addition to his lifelong involvement with the Shroud of Turin, Russ has had a long career in Christian television.

After seven years of higher education, he earned a bachelor's and master's degree, both with high honors. Married for over forty years, he is the father of three daughters with six grandchildren.

> *It is the glory of God to conceal a thing: but the honor of kings is to search out a matter.*
> —Proverbs 25:2 KJV

> *Seek and ye shall find.*
> —Matthew 7:7

For information on sponsoring a Shroud Encounter event for your church, school, or community. Contact Russ Breault through his website at www.ShroudEncounter.com